Dear Heather,

with thanks for u -
wonderful attitude! ♡

and Love,

[signature]

Oct '19
Dublin

Love is Green

Compassion as responsibility in the ecological emergency

by
Lucy Weir

Series on Climate Change and Society
VERNON PRESS

Copyright © 2020 Vernon Press, an imprint of Vernon Art and Science Inc, on behalf of the author.

All rights reserved. No part of this publication may be reproduced, stored in a retrieval system, or transmitted in any form or by any means, electronic, mechanical, photocopying, recording, or otherwise, without the prior permission of Vernon Art and Science Inc.

www.vernonpress.com

In the Americas:	*In the rest of the world:*
Vernon Press	Vernon Press
1000 N West Street,	C/ Sancti Espiritu 17,
Suite 1200, Wilmington,	Malaga, 29006
Delaware 19801	Spain
United States	

Series on Climate Change and Society

Library of Congress Control Number: 2019942263

ISBN: 978-1-62273-372-9

Product and company names mentioned in this work are the trademarks of their respective owners. While every care has been taken in preparing this work, neither the authors nor Vernon Art and Science Inc. may be held responsible for any loss or damage caused or alleged to be caused directly or indirectly by the information contained in it.

Every effort has been made to trace all copyright holders, but if any have been inadvertently overlooked the publisher will be pleased to include any necessary credits in any subsequent reprint or edition.

Cover design by Vernon Press.
Cover image by Matilda Moreton, www.matildamoreton.com.
Cover background image designed by Freepik.

Table of Contents

Acknowledgements

What I mean by love being green, as well as the obvious connection I make in this book between ourselves as enmeshed in ecological, green (and blue) systems, is that it is innocent, in the sense of wide-eyed and curious, like a child. I am well aware that the word used in that sense can be disparaging. But while compassion might seem on the surface to be anti-rational, and as Erasmus has it, a fool's game, most recent research is finding empirical support for the idea that love is inherent to our capacity to survive. It is also fresh, like new growth, and tough, in the sense that it is resilient, and demanding. All these come to mind when I think of being 'green', and I owe my own incipient investigations, and discussions, in this area, to my upbringing, with all its inherent contradictions. Thanks, then, to my family and to the Highlands of Scotland for the pageantry and the pain.

I started my PhD as a student of the late Dr Thomas Duddy, a poet and philosopher who worked at the National University of Ireland in Galway. I hope this book will spur an interest in his beautiful poetry. Tom introduced me to the work of Professor Paul W. Taylor who I contacted without any real expectation of response. He replied with generosity and brilliance in handwritten, insightful letters that were a joy to receive and that helped enormously in my attempts to understand, and re-imagine, biocentrism in the light of a systems-based approach. Professor Taylor died in 2015 and I hope that this book will in some small measure draw attention to the valuable work he undertook, and bring him more readers. I also owe a debt of gratitude to Professor Graham Parkes of University College, Cork, an acutely sensitive and brilliant scholar of both Nietzsche and Dōgen. Professor Jason M. Wirth of the University of Seattle turned me towards Zen and I am deeply grateful: Gassho.

I contacted a large number of philosophers and academics during the course of my research. I am humbled by their kindness. During the preparation of this manuscript, I have been in situations more desperate than I could previously ever have imagined, and yet I have felt supported and illuminated by my relations and relationships, so thank you to all who connected with intelligence and imagination. Thank you to the publisher,

Vernon Press, who has taken a leap of faith, and especially thanks to Argiris Legatos, and to Carolina Sanchez, who have been professionality incarnate in their dealings with me.

Finally, thanks, my Noel, for understanding compassion intimately. And to Joseph, Harry and Ella, the deepest bow, for you have given what should never have been asked, and yet you grow.

Introduction

This book links two apparently distinct issues: moral agency, and the ecological emergency. It does this through exploring three themes: free will, the "good" of systems (and the practice implications of these), and compassionate attunement, with all that results from such attention. Put simply, and in the context of the ecological emergency, I propose that we revise our understanding of what we are, and are not, free to do. I argue that it is only by incorporating the fullest possible understanding, scientific and rational, of all that we are, that we can elicit the sufficient conditions to respond to the ecological emergency (a phrase I unpack briefly below, and in much more detail throughout the book).

I argue that, notwithstanding my own optimism about the resilience of our species, and my acceptance of the unpredictability of the future, the ecological emergency is the fundamental threat of our time. To respond requires a fundamental shift in perspective. If enough of us make this critical shift in how we understand ourselves, and if, as a consequence, we elicit compassion in response, rather than our current reaction to the emergency, we will shift the trajectory enough to mitigate some of the inevitable mass human suffering and systems collapse. The longer we continue to treat the ecological emergency as an external problem, the deeper the suffering and collapse will be. Ultimately, we will be left in a much more fragile state as a species, with less capacity to retain the key elements that make humanity humane. The emergency is in us, and we are in it, as Timothy Morton points out.[1]

Our agency is the sense in which we are free to choose what to do, and our moral agency is the sense in which we are free to choose to do good, or evil (that is, to mitigate or to inflict suffering, deliberate harm or destruction). By taking what we know of evolutionary biology to its logical

---

[1] See Timothy Morton, *The Ecological Thought,* Harvard University Press, (2010); in relation to explaining more complex features in terms of more basic features, see Edward Slingerland and Mark Collard, *Creating Consilience: Integrating the Sciences and the Humanities,* New York: Oxford University Press, (2011).

conclusion, that is, by taking a rational, scientific approach, we must accept that our current general understanding of both our freedom to act, and our separability from all else, is an illusion.

Therefore, I explore in detail what remains, if anything, of our agency, and in particular, what replaces our moral agency. I go on to explore the nature of systems of energy dissipation, which is one way of looking at ourselves in context. In the narrow corner of existence, here in the ecosphere, within which we live, have come into being, and are sustained, it makes sense to talk of "the good" of systems, including our own. Therefore the fact/ value distinction is an illusion, and there are right, and wrong, ways to act. However, I attempt to describe how different this approach is from conventional ethics. We only become agents by paying attention, because it is only through attention, or realisation, that we elicit the attitude - compassion - that allows options that are good for us to emerge, or become real.

"The ecological emergency" is a phrase that encompasses both the environmental crises of pollution, deforestation, desertification, mass species extinction, and climate change, and also the human attempts to conceptualise this impact. The phrase is controversial. Among those who deny that an emergency of any kind exists are fatalists who, arguing from "naturalistic" reasons, believe there is nothing to be done:

> Humans' actions, regardless of their effect on other organisms, are natural and perfectly acceptable ... we should be allowed to live out our "evolutionary potential to [our own destruction] because this is "nature's way".[2]

At the other end of the spectrum are those who believe there is no crisis to concern ourselves with, and that any attempt to articulate what is happening as an emergency is overblown hysteria. The most recent, and perhaps most widely disseminated, articulation of this position is laid out in Steven Pinker's recent book, *Enlightenment Now* which dismisses the fears that climate change and other environmental threats are "existential".[3] He cites a litany of examples that illustrate the human capacity for ingenuity in the face of resource depletion, and the slowing of exponentially harmful processes, like habitat destruction, when societies

---

[2] Richard A. Watson, "A Critique of Anti-Anthropocentric Biocentrism", Environmental Ethics, 5 (1983): 245–56.

[3] Steven Pinker, *Enlightenment Now: The Case for Reason, Science, Humanism and Progress*, New York: Penguin Books (2018).

meet a certain level of prosperity for their citizens. His position fails adequately to acknowledge that the emergence of anthropogenic climate change continues despite attempts by governments to agree on globally applicable legislation. It does acknowledge, however, that Garrett Hardin's analogy of "the tragedy of the commons" has shaped these negotiations to date.[4] As a result, globally, we face more extreme weather events resulting in mass forced migration with all the geopolitical and social instability that creates, and threats to agriculture and water supplies leading to food, and water shortages. These are in addition to the collapse of natural systems, from populations of insect pollinators like bees, to complex carbon capture systems like tundra and forests, on which human health and well-being depend.

There are, of course, also those who deny that any problem at all exists, or that we have any level of responsibility to protect and conserve other species or habitats, reduce pollutants, value biodiversity, or even see the threats to humanity as something we owe it to ourselves to address. This group remains averse to the notion that humans have any responsibility for the fates of other species. It depends on ideologies that have supernatural deities and magical thinking at heart. I will address the problems with ideological thinking separately. Here, I will echo the Scottish ecologist and pioneer of the conservation movement in The United States, in remarking, "the world, we are told, was made especially for man – a presumption not supported by all the facts."[5]

As governments and legislators begin to acknowledge the emergency, based on the vast consensus of scientific evidence, and work to formulate a response, conflicting approaches emerge. One approach demands that the nations that built empires during the industrial revolution be held accountable for their historical emissions, while others consider that only the contemporary situation matters.[6] Meanwhile, among the populace, attitudes are becoming more divergent, and views on how, and whether or

---

[4] Garrett Hardin, "The Tragedy of the Commons", Science, 162 (1968): 1243-1248.

[5] John Muir quoted in Lori Gruen, Dale Jamieson and Christopher Schlottmann, *Reflecting on Nature: Readings in Environmental Ethics and Philosophy*, New York: Oxford University Press, (2012): 23.

[6] https://www.theguardian.com/environment/2011/apr/21/countries-responsible-climate-change.

not, to respond depend on people's underlying beliefs and ideologies, some of which are flagrantly anti-enlightenment.[7]

Attitude is the basis of action. Our propensities for valuing one set of responses over another (for instance those which prioritise equality over those that prioritise loyalty to a group) are largely intuitive, as Jonathan Haidt shows in his collated research. However, we are also capable of reflecting on the influence of intuitions, as well as that of vested interests.[8] The pressure to contract the moral compass is huge, and again, we can look to Hardin for the analogy of a limited, or "lifeboat", ethic.[9] This book will argue that adopting such an ethic creates less resilience, not more, among human communities in situations of crises, and that the non-dualist understanding of agency makes a persuasive case for the survival benefits of "the golden rule", and an extending of compassion, even in extremis. An attitude of compassion is, to put it simply, a better survival strategy than fear, both individually, and collectively. Love can be tough, as well as gentle. Elinor Ostrom's refutal of Hardin's "tragedy of the commons" does much to support this argument.[10] Of course there are limits to the amount that any individual or society can give, but the non-dualist elicitation of compassion, tempered by continuous research and application of the science related to compassion in action, and applied equally to the self and to the other, provides an innovative basis from which to respond to the current emergency. We must balance the needs of the individual, the society and the broader systems within which both the former are couched, and we must recognise that the internal and the external worlds are far more intertwined than a technological, dualistic approach implies. This applies to our freedom to act as much as it does to what impact our actions will have: realisation as response, rather than reaction, is the only way we can shift the paradigm, and therefore the trajectory on which we are, collectively, headed.

This book is based largely on my PhD thesis, which was initially an examination of the theory of respect for nature laid out in the book of that

---

[7] Leiserowitz, A., Maibach, E., Roser-Renouf, C., Feinberg, G., & Rosenthal, S. "Climate change in the American mind: October, 2015". *Yale Program on Climate Change Communication.* Yale University and George Mason University. New Haven, CT (2015).

[8] Jonathan Haidt, *The Righteous Mind*, New York: Penguin, (2012).

[9] Garrett Hardin, "Lifeboat Ethics: The Case Against Helping the Poor", *Psychology Today*, (1974), 800–812.

[10] Elinor Ostrom, *Governing the Commons: The Evolution of Institutions for Collective Action*, New York: Cambridge University Press, (1990).

name by the American philosopher, Paul Taylor.[11] Taylor took the Enlightenment ideas of Immanuel Kant, particularly the reasoned notion that we treat individuals as "ends in themselves" and extended the argument to include anything that could be said to have conditions that are "good" for it. Since all living organisms have conditions that are "good" for them, this led him to develop the theory of respect for nature, a rational basis on which to understand our obligations to other creatures.[12]

I began by critically examining, and revising, Taylor's thesis, and this led me to a broader, more relational, systems-based approach. I found myself having to revise what it means to be a moral agent. I went on to explore what "good" might mean in the context of systems, and the relationship between individual agency, or free will, and the notion of being entirely embedded in, or enmeshed, in, and as, systems.

For reasons entirely beyond my control, including the untimely death of my original supervisor, the second half of my thesis broadened my exploration of realisation as agency. It came to include a phenomenological understanding of enlightenment, based on the Zen tradition of Dōgen Zenji, the thirteenth century Japanese Zen Master who turned the traditional idea of working towards this Buddhist notion on its head. His understanding of how to live an enlightened life, or even a life worth living, is outlined in the *Shōbōgenzō: Treasury of the True Dharma Eye*, and it was to this text that I turned to unpack a deeper understanding of what it might mean to be an agent, if that meant paying attention first.[13]

Therefore, to a large degree, and mainly because of events that happened to me, rather than anything I was free to choose, my thesis, and therefore this book, became an exploration of the paradox of agency. My research began to bridge the apparently irreconcilable approaches of analytical, and phenomenological, philosophy. We have been led to believe, based on the hangover of Judeo-Christian and Cartesian worldviews, in certain dualisms (mind/ body; this world and the next; the spirit and the flesh). We can and should use reason, science, and the moral insights that an analytical approach allow to reconsider these dualisms.

---

[11] Paul W Taylor, *Respect for Nature: A Theory of Environment Ethics,* Princeton, N.J.; Woodstock: Princeton University Press, (1986).

[12] I have chosen not to capitalise the word "nature" when referring to ecological systems and species, and to the natural world, because in doing so I follow the convention adopted by Paul Taylor.

[13] Dōgen, *Shōbōgenzō: Treasury of the True Dharma Eye,* trans. Kazuaki Tanahashi. Boston: Shambhala, (2010).

When we do, we come to realise that the interaction between the internal and the external worlds is far more enmeshed that dualistic thinking can account for. This phenomenological, Zen-inspired insight shifts how we then interact. Such a shift requires a considerable effort of attention, particularly given the almost impenetrable dominance of the cultural paradigms of dualistic thinking.

Yet, we have the capacity to pay attention to our enmeshment and when we do, we can experience compassion arising from this attention. Compassion, or love as I call it in the title, allows options to emerge, to come into our awareness. In a sense, by paying attention, we become conduits through which compassion allows the good of systems to be realised.

The idea that allowing ourselves to attune to compassion is the central work in responding to the ecological emergency appears paradoxically ineffectual. Paying attention to the situation does not seem to offer us much in the way of action. Yet it is only through this realisation, along with a recognition of our non-dual nature, that we elicit the attitude which allows options to emerge that allow us to become resilient enough to mitigate the suffering we have caused. What is emerging, in this emergence, and emergency, is a challenge to develop an understanding of what compassion, or love, really means.

Summary of Chapters

I fear that by the time this book comes to publication, my defence of the phrase "ecological emergency" will be obsolete. There will no longer be a case to answer, because we will have incontrovertible evidence that climate change, pollution, habitat loss and species extinction constitute, by all measures, an emergency for our species, as well as for the majority of our co-evolved species, particularly vertebrates that require similar conditions for survival to ourselves. In the first chapter, I explore the various perspectives on the emergency. I give a brief exposure to the perspective of those who maintain that the whole notion is an invention by those who resent progress, and that the so-called emergency has been exaggerated, hyped up or even invented.[14] I touch on the other end of the spectrum: that we are doomed no matter what we do.[15] I spend more time

---

[14] Andrew Chitty, "Ideology and Climate Change Convictions", *Climate Change and Humanities* conference, Sussex University, (Nov 2013).

[15] Decca Aitkenhead, "Enjoy Life While You Can", Interview with James Lovelock, *The Guardian*, 1 March 2008, Environment Section, (March 1, 2008).

unpacking what the emergency actually consists in, and from here, I go on to explain why our current approaches to this burgeoning crisis are, and can only be, ineffectual. This contrasts with the view taken by Pinker, and therefore, it is that argument that I begin addressing in this chapter. The emergency is just that, and a technological approach will not and cannot fix it. I will discuss why in chapter two.

The first chapter is therefore an overview and exploration of the belief systems that underlie the different perspectives on the ecological emergency. I explore the narratives implicit in the different approaches and pay particular attention to what these say about our understanding of what (human) moral agency can do. In particular, in preparation for a specific focus on Taylor's theory of "respect for nature", I consider how a broad range of perspectives views the relationship between moral agency, moral considerability, and biophysical systems.

Some perspectives consider humans to be distinct, while others expand the circle of ethical consideration to all sentient beings.[16] Further perspectives reason that the phenomenon of life itself is distinctive and therefore deserves this special kind of considerability. Moving further still from the human centre is the view that all biophysical systems, including the non-living systems that underpin and interact with living systems, are ethically considerable.

Beyond these is an alternative approach that sees no essential difference, because of no separation, between nature, background, existence or environment, on the one hand, and humanity on the other. In Morton's terms, we are "enmeshed". This is an extension of the very old debate about whether or not humans are a part of, or radically distinct from, other kinds of existence on the planet. I take the approach that humans are biologically consistent with, and that therefore it is reasonable to consider them a part of, other evolved systems.

---

[16] There is no hard and fast distinction between "moral" and "ethical" but a useful rough dividing line for the purpose of this book is to think of "moral" as referring to the personal value system one uses to decide on what is the right thing to do. "Ethical" acts are therefore more broadly social. For example, I am a "moral" agent, in this sense, because I, personally, can decide to act respectfully towards others. An ethical system, like the theory of "respect for nature", is a broader social norm that might put me under a less personal, more communal obligation to adhere to its principles (although I can only do so because I am a "moral" agent: hence the difficulty with making a hard and fast distinction).

I then extend Timothy Morton's approach in contending that the ecological emergency is not composed of isolated problems, and therefore cannot be solved by the kinds of belief systems that emphasise our distinctiveness. This is a narrative we have been heavily dependent on for four hundred years or so.[17] It is time to review the context with the recognition that we are inside the results of interactions (climate change, biodiversity loss, habitat destruction, for instance) and they (pollution, radiation, modified food) are inside us.

We are distinct enough to be able to perceive these interactions, but we must also acknowledge that we are so implicitly involved and included in them. This perception is inseparably a part of the interaction. How to conceive of this relationship becomes a framing problem, but it also offers an opportunity to re-examine our understanding of our moral agency. By reviewing what we mean by both "moral" and "agent", we shift our understanding of responsibility, which is both our ability to respond, and our ability to be accountable. We are looking out at, but also from within, the issues to be considered, but it is precisely this capacity we have to understand, or realise, this explicit implicitness that allows us to develop a clearer idea of our role in the ecological emergency.

Bringing the conceptual frameworks into focus is also key to understanding how differently the problems (or fabulations) of the ecological emergency are viewed, differences that become irreconcilable and that lead to attitude polarisation. On the one hand, there are those who conclude the problems have been ignored or played down; on the other, those who believe they have been exaggerated, hyped up or even invented. Even where there is agreement that the problems need addressing, views on what sort of response is viable are strongly divergent, often aggressively so.

My second aim is to reflect on the implications for philosophical practice arising from this revised idea of what responses are available to us in the context of this tendency to divergence. If we are enmeshed within an

---

[17] "The analysis of nature into its individual parts ... this method of work has also left us as a legacy the habit of observing natural objects and processes in isolation, apart from their connection with the vast whole; of observing them in repose, not in motion; as constraints, not as essentially variables; in their death, not in their life." Engels, Friedrich, *Socialism: Utopian and Scientific*, trans. Barrie Selman, from *Marx & Engels: Collected Works, Volume 24* (1874-1883). (International Publishers. New York, NY: 1989): 299. Quoted in Ross Wolfe, "Man and Nature" in *Thinking Nature*, Timothy Morton and Ben Woodward, (eds), (2011).

ecological emergency and responding with increasingly disparate reactions, I ask what prospects are there for mitigating this tendency since attitudinal divergence, or polarisation, is a major obstacle to any prospects for finding convergence in response.

In researching attempts to reframe our response, I focus on Paul Taylor's biocentric ethic, since this is one route to broadening the locus of value. Outlined in his book, *Respect for Nature*, it moves the locus of value from humanity to every organism, since each can be considered an "end in itself", and thus provides a universalisable basis for response to our impact on other systems.

In the second chapter, in order to look in more detail at what we mean by moral agency, at how this overlaps with our understanding of how we can respond, and what we have responsibility for, I explore in detail Taylor's argument for a biocentric ethic. Because I want to consider us in the context of the ecological emergency, I focus on how Paul Taylor has characterised our relationship with other entities. Taylor takes the rationale of Kant, to treat individuals as "ends in themselves" (rather than instruments, or utilities, that are only worth protecting if they benefit someone or something else), and extends it to the "more than human world".

Taylor's reasoning crystallises around the idea that (most) humans consider ourselves as agents, in the sense of self-directed individuals, and moral, in the sense that we can be held accountable for duties and responsibilities imposed by human cultural systems. For this to be the case, we need to have some sort of freedom to act on the basis of our rational understanding.

He proposes that since all individual living organisms have conditions that are "good" for them, because they allow them to maintain themselves, or survive, and reproduce, therefore all living organisms are ends in themselves. What we do to these organisms matters, morally, because we, being free, have the capacity to benefit or harm them.

This gives me a starting point from which to unpack what, if any, agency and moral agency we have, if we investigate what science tells us about our evolutionary history and relationship within that context to other organisms and systems. On this basis, I find that our freedom to act, and therefore our agency, in the traditional, dualistic sense, is an illusion. We cannot be moral agents in the way Taylor has described. We are firmly enmeshed along with all other evolving, and indeed, all other material systems. We, and all else, are here as a result of an almost infinite series of reactions, none of which we have control over.

I consider in detail arguments that humans are free to act in a way that is distinct from any other organism in the rest of existence. I conclude that there is no basis for this claim. This turns our ideas of right and wrong, good and evil, upside down. There is no essential difference, because of no separation, between nature, background, existence or environment, on the one hand, and humanity on the other. From enlightenment, that is, a scientific, rational perspective, the debate is over: humans are biologically consistent with, and therefore part of, natural systems.

This leaves me wondering what kind of agency we might still have. We are the context for a set of interactions (climate change, biodiversity loss, habitat destruction, for instance) that have emerged precisely because we have deluded ourselves into believing that we are in control, that we are free to act, or not to act. I wonder what would happen if we shifted perspective and considered what we might actually be free to do if we let the illusion of control over action and reaction go.

Part of our evolutionary inheritance is that we have consciousness. I argue that this is no more than a happy accident: we were not "designed" as conscious beings. It became part of our evolutionary heritage, a survival advantage. We developed the conditional, the "what if?" imaginary.

We are part of a vast interlinked network of reactions that run from the beginning of time through to our, and on a much vaster scale, the universe's, demise. It is precisely our capacity to realise this, to use our capacity for conscious awareness, reasoning, and the scientific method, to use, in other words, the tools of the enlightenment, that gives us the only kind of agency, and therefore the only kind of moral agency, we can reasonably claim to have.

If this seismic shift in understanding our agency could be brought about, we could begin to pay attention to our context. It is this, paying of attention, that allows a latent set of options to emerge. It is how we pay attention that counts.

Taking a non-anthropocentric, non-dualist understanding of our agency on board is a position I have come to as a result of the close study of other "environmental ethics" and most closely of all, of Paul Taylor's "respect for nature". This idea of respect is linked in interesting ways to John Rawls' idea of self-respect, as outlined in *A Theory of Justice*. Self-respect, in the sense of how we see ourselves and our potential, and permission, to participate, is a key element in how we engage in, and contribute to, the democratic process. We are as involved as we think we have a right to be, given how much value ourselves. This echoes our ability to engage in responding to the ecological emergency: we are only likely to respond if we deem ourselves to have a right, a role, to be at home in the ecological context, to be a participant in the unfolding universe, through how we interact.

The theory I propose in this book moves beyond Rawls and Taylor, although it owes them much. Respect keeps things at a distance. I argue in Chapter Three that the knowledge we now have of evolutionary theory, and recent research on neural science, makes it clear that we can no longer maintain this objective stance. We are not atomistic elements, but systems flowing within systems within which we have co-evolved. The climate and ecological emergency is in us and we are in it. They have arisen precisely because we conceive of ourselves, mistakenly, as separate. We are not separate. We are not just catalysts of the emergency, but interactive features in it, as Morton has pointed out.[18] The interaction over which we have the only measure of freedom is in how we pay attention, our attitude, and even that is not something over which we exercise control. Rather, we elicit an attitude, a "spirit" to use Daniel Dennett's brilliant co-opting of the word ("that's the spirit!"), through reflection, or realisation. Realisation gives us an important insight into our responsibility. I now move to show how this insight interacts with a revised understanding of "good". If the attitude that comes into being when we pay attention to our circumstances is compassion, as I argue that it is, since compassion is the most obvious human response to an acknowledgment that we are enmeshed in chains of interaction, entrapped in cause and effect, the next phase is to consider where this might lead.

Taylor's proposal of a "life-centred" ethic is a useful starting point: treating individual organisms as "ends in themselves" is justifiable, or would be, if individual organisms could be uniquely identified. The problem is that organisms are in a state of flux, interactive, and sometimes very short-lived. The boundaries between organism and system become more difficult to define the closer we look.

Taylor also identifies the idea that all organisms are teleological beings with "goods" that they pursue, and that, therefore, conditions can be "good for" other organisms in a parallel sense to the way that conditions can be "good for" humans. Again, I consider this in the light that it is the relationships within systems, rather than atomistic individuals themselves, that are relevant foci for understanding "goods".

---

[18] Timothy Morton, *The Ecological Thought* (op. cit.).

This leads me to consider what is elicited when we do pay attention, or realise, in this way. I conclude that compassion, or love, is the most substantially evident, instinctive, rational and effective attitude that emerges when we reflect in detail on our own and indeed, on the universal situation that all systems are in. It is through allowing a compassionate attitude to be elicited by paying attention, or realisation, that options for action emerge. The act of realising what is happening right now creates just enough of a pause, a space, for compassionate attunement to occur, and this allows options to arise, or become evident, that would otherwise remain latent.

Compassion, I conclude, is the human manifestation of a set of values, of what is "good for" systems and entities, that exists within the universe. It is "the good" of our enmeshment, and it is through this realisation that our agency emerges.

This allows me to contrast the difference between "external" or "technological" approaches to the ecological emergency, to the lifeboat ethic, with its limitation on inclusiveness, and my own proposals for how we can see ourselves in context, and what kind of response this gives us access to. I show that only the latter gives us sufficient effectiveness as respondents, given the nature of our enmeshment.

Chapter Four reflects on the issue of practice. So far, I have shown how seeing ourselves as systems flowing within systems within which we have co-evolved can elicit a deep compassion for ourselves. This extends to both our human relationships, and to all systems unfolding through time, cause, and effect.

Having shown that particular conditions are "good" for the systems that create and sustain us, even though we are never free of our enmeshment, when we become aware of a compassionate attitude arising, this shifts how we engage. Here, I want to consider what the practical implications are of this dual realisation: that we can elicit compassion, and that this gives us a right way to respond to "the good" of systems. I want to explore both how this dual realisation interacts, and also to look at the problems that emerge as a result of taking this approach to our agency.

Biodiversity loss, the production of plastics, the loss of habitats through desertification and deforestation, are all "bad for" systems by this analysis since systems can no longer graduate the flow of energy. There is a very rational and scientific basis to "the good", therefore. This interruption of the graduated flow is either because energy is blocked, or else because it cannot be filtered through systems and is lost. To realise our agency in the context of the ecological emergency, then, is to turn our attention to discriminating between activities that block, and ones that graduate this dissipating flow.

There are a number of ways in which this theory elicits a set of practices, including reviewing and altering how we talk about our relationships, and revising how we act in discussions on the emergency. When we alter where we focus our attention, we shift how we relate, in particular to the more violent relationships of our enmeshment.

We can practice through mindful commentary and observation on, and drawing back to attention, those relationships in the societies and political communities we inhabit that block the dissipation of energy or that are, in other ways, "bad for" systems.[19] I explore the idea that what realisation offers is a way, in the sense of a manner, of engagement with relationships. Rather than a goal-oriented focus on any interaction, these approaches allow human participants in discussion to step back from ideological commitments. They can do this by realising both that their agency is tied up with how they are viewing the conditions they find themselves in, and so with their attitude, and also that an unreflective commitment to an ideology is at the heart of attitude divergence. I consider Ostrom's principles for cooperation, along with other work on compassionate, or cooperative, achievement in social and community situations, and look at the application of this approach more globally. Finally, I consider the idea of practice. It is a practice, both in the sense of a way of doing, and in the sense of repetitive action in order to improve, to elicit a compassionate attitude, one that also automatically includes humility. Non-violent communication, compassionate achievement and understanding what it is to have a compassionate mind all facilitate interactions, and will help us to develop the level of resilience we need to deal with the ecological emergency as it unfolds.

Mitigation and adaptation are recognised, vital elements of our response to the emergency, but these are also internal processes. Mitigating our own sense of anger, loneliness and grief, and adapting to the kind of world

---

[19] Timothy Morton has written extensively about how a reasonable view of life is to see it as striving towards its own ending. Nevertheless, picturing the graduated dissipation of energy is useful as a way of understanding how systems work, when "capturing" as much energy as possible to dissipate. When we understand ourselves in this context, we can see that our good and the good of functioning systems that graduate the flow of energy by capturing it (as biodiverse communities of living organisms and ecosystems, for instance) then we can understand why it is in our interests to allow those systems to maintain themselves, given that our capacity to dissipate (eat, breathe, and so on) depends entirely on theirs.

and world view that results from increasing extremes and fragmentation will allow us to remain resilient, cooperative and flexible.

We need also to recognise that section of the human population that (often as a result of a genetic glitch) is unwilling to participate in a cooperative, non-violent response. Here I will discuss both ideology, and "free riders" (as described in Samuel Harris' _The Moral Landscape_).[20] Harris has some useful ideas on what to do in practical terms with "free riders", something I come to explore in the context of how to implement a practice that both recognises the illusion of free will, and yet allows societies, groups and organisations to manage exploitation, free riding and non-cooperation in the context of response to the ecological emergency.

In the final chapter, I anticipate some of the main criticisms of the approach I have outlined in the book so far. I acknowledge the difficulties with talking about being enmeshed, but also imagining that we can "step back" and that this gives us access to a response that frees us, in a sense, from the inevitability of our reactions. We can never achieve a "view from nowhere". I argue that this approach allows us to get a view from now, here, a complete acknowledgement of our conditionality, the conditionality of our commitments (however firmly held) and the condition of the planet, on which we depend. I reiterate the effort required to step back in this sense, and deal with the criticism that this effort requires too much of us, or is insufficiently proactive.

I address the difficulty with envisaging a non-competitive "anti-meme", one that defies reproduction, and the problem that there can be no general theoretical framework to the activity of "agency as realisation". I go on to address criticisms relating to the experiential nature of this approach: if agency as realisation is an experience, is it paradoxical to propose this as a theory?

I argue against the potential criticisms of passivity, fatalism, quietude and impracticality or ineffectiveness. I discuss the idea that the attitudes of humility and compassion can be viewed as ethically neutral, despite our tendency to view these attitudes as ethical virtues. I defend the notion that we can in fact approach our experience with ethical neutrality because we have the capacity to step back from ideology and ideals. Finally, I address the criticism that this approach is simply a shallow version of Zen Buddhism.

---

[20] Samuel Harris, _The Moral Landscape_, New York, Free Press, (2010).

In considering the implications and areas for further research, I observe that there have been limited attempts to bridge the gap between the fields of neurological studies into free will, and responses to climate change and other ecological emergencies. I suggest that much more research would be warranted in this area. We need multidisciplinary work to understand agency, attitudes, response and responsibility, contextualised in the ecological emergency and its implications. This could involve fieldwork in a number of areas, including studies on the impact of specific forms of meditation and yoga which take an underlying integrated approach, on attitudes and practice, particularly in the context of ecological awareness. This echoes Harris' approach to ethics as "natural philosophy", or science, rather than as an abstract element of the humanities. Scientific understanding could, in turn, be strengthened if there was a clearer understanding of the manner in which conceptual frameworks and narratives play a role in how evidence is presented, and that bringing this to light can help to avoid the kind of attitude divergence and entrenchment that currently haunts this area of discussion.

Understanding ourselves as systems within systems requires the revision of how we describe our relations and use language. The arts, crafts, literature, and other creative explorations could all help us to re-imagine how we relate, as could our work choices and options. I suggest that extensive scope exists for a philosophical approach to the ecological emergency in facilitating the discussions and negotiations between parties with different ideological priorities. By bringing these priorities to light, and seeing them as part of the perceiver's context, it is possible to take a view from "now, here", in approach to these issues.

We are in a precarious and dangerous situation. We both need to, and can, respond by realising the agency we have. Nevertheless, we cannot simply impose or enforce this as a systematic approach. Instead, we must find ways of communicating through becoming aware of, understanding, and developing a creative relationship with, our context. This relationship is necessarily experiential, non-competitive, and effortful. Yet the practice itself has the consolation of creating a deeply enriching experience, and through practice, of course, we become more skillful. We realise our interrelatedness, and our agency becomes a response that is both creative and compassionate. One momentary shift of perspective changes how we approach all our relationships.

In some ways, this is a book in the old philosophical style, since it asks, among other things, how to live. It addresses the question of free will, through asking what kind of agency, if any we have. It puts this into a contemporary context, framing us in an ecological emergency, but it sees this as non-dualistic, not an external issue but an issue of perception. Many see our situation as biologically determined: our evolutionary (genetic) inheritance has not kept pace with our species' ecological (environmental) impact.[21] I see it as a philosophical one: our responses rely at least as heavily on how we understand and respond to the narratives we inherit as they do on our physiology. My research establishes that there are grounds for sobering pessimism: our species has the capacity for responsibility, but it requires an effort to take an objective view of the narratives that frame our response. It is easier to distract ourselves than it is to pay close attention. However, there are two reasons why such pessimism might not be entirely warranted. Firstly, the effort of paying attention by a single person has exponentially cumulative effects, given the systematic character of our involvement. Secondly, exercising the close attention that agency as realisation implies is its own reward: the consolation for this effort is enriched appreciation, and a more compassionate experience of oneself and one's relationships.

Realising the kind of agency we have, and exercising this, offers a coherent response to the ecological emergency. It allows us to accept and acknowledge the limits of our own action, but fully to open to, and respond with, compassionate attunement. It therefore mitigates the harm, as well as the suffering, that is caused by attempts to avoid or escape the current context, both to humans but also to other species and systems. Compassion, humility and forgiveness create their own responses to the recognition of our interrelatedness. The main motivation for wanting to respond to the ecological emergency is to avoid, or at least mitigate, the catastrophic effects it will have on human affairs. However, the paradoxical conclusion of this dissertation is that we can only change the trajectory of the human narrative by coming to an understanding that our capacity for action lies in the effort we make to be completely aware of our current context. Given the perilous condition we are in, we certainly have an incentive to respond in this way.

---

[21] We could see this as analogous to how we consume: "We love sweets and fats, of which in Pleistocene times humans could seldom get enough. But now we overeat and grow fat." Holmes Rolston III, "The Future of Environmental Ethics", in David Keller (ed.), *Environmental Ethics: The Big Questions*, Chichester: Wiley-Blackwell, (2010): 566.

Chapter One

Context

What is "the ecological emergency"?

There are many ways to look at "the ecological emergency", a phrase coined by Morton, whose concern with the intimacy of our involvement leads him to conclude, "We can't spit out the disgusting real of ecological enmeshment. It's just too close and too painful for comfort".[1] "Disgusting", like "delicious", is a label of taste, the implicitly human "we" arriving at a conclusion too close to call: we cannot get enough space to consider our relationship with what is going on, because it is part of our going on. Yet it is this intimacy that is chewing us up because we have no point at which to stand, Archimedes-like, to turn things around. The problem lies primarily in the illusion that the emergency, if it exists, is outside us. That is the crux of this investigation.

Pinker in *Enlightenment Now* maintains that humankind is making progress on every measure, including in the context of the environment. I examine his argument and conclude that in this facet at least, he has failed to recognise the degree to which energy sequestered from other systems erodes their effectiveness. This, in turn, undermines the context within which human systems operate. His approach suggests that problems in the environment are external, and technological. However, given that we are contextualised, and must recognise ourselves as being inseparably enmeshed, his argument fails in its own terms, since it fails to recognise this scientific truth. Seeing the problems as being "outside" us assumes that a technological approach will and can fix them. It can not. He makes some extremely cogent and valuable points about the kind of societies that develop which allow for human flourishing, including making the

---

[1] Timothy Morton, *The Ecological Thought* (op. cit.): 124; again in Lisa Klarr, Ryan Vu and Gerry Canavan, *Ecology and Ideology*, Durham, N.C.: Duke University, (2010): 56.

specific point that compassion, as a form of altruism, is inherent in at least some humans (he cites women as embodying this attitude), and I take up the discussion at this point, as well as discussing the dangers of autocratic, tyrannical regimes to the progress made since The Enlightenment.

I follow this with an analysis of the ideological spectrum of approaches to nature, environment, or what I will term, the ecological context. I show that, as Jonathan Haidt in *The Righteous Mind* has argued, we are variously primed to sit at some point on a morally intuited spectrum.[2] Until we realise this, we will be bound to an ideological position and unable to recognise the limitations of our intuited responses, and unable to successfully discuss, or help shift the perspective, of those whose intuitions put them on a different part of the spectrum. Ideological thinking, therefore, cannot solve the problems we face as a result of the ecological emergency. We cannot avoid the fact that our intuitions shape our responses, but we can step back from these, and see ourselves in the context of intuitive drives. This can help others also subject to these forces to step back, and this can allow us to take a discussion of responses forward in a more productive, potentially more effective way.

Beyond the view illustrated by Pinker's position are those that acknowledge the emergency and call for a response.[3] This implies that "the Anthropocene", a term that recognises the deep impact of the human species on other evolved systems, is something over which we have some level of control, or influence.[4] Before beginning to talk about the multiple perspectives on "the ecological emergency", it is worth spending a moment considering what Morton meant by that phrase. Evidently, there is something particular about the use of the word "ecological", rather than the more commonly used word "environmental", that needs attention. *Oikos*, the Greek for home, family or household, provides us with the prefix, *eco*, that we use in both the words economy and ecology.

In referring to an "ecological" emergency, Morton is asking us to acknowledge that we are in, and a part of, it. It is where we live, what we are at home in. It includes what Morton has termed "hyperobjects", the vast intangible (and much debated) fluctuations in global temperature patterns that are variously termed "climate change" or "DAGW"

---

[3] William Moyers, "Wendell Berry: Poet & Prophet", <http://billmoyers.com/episode/full-show-wendell-berry-poet-prophet/>.

[4] The proposal that the Earth has entered a new geological era in which a key driver of the planet's systems is human activity.

(Dangerous Anthropogenic Global Warming).[5] It also includes the subtle chemical alterations that take place under the skin as a result of the presence of synthesised pollutants and other by-products of industrialised living.

This is a shift from the idea of "environment", a word that captures a relationship between atomistic organisms, on the one hand, and what surrounds them, their neighbourhood, on the other. We do not need to be at home in our neighbourhood. We can inhabit it, and yet live in relative isolation from all else in it, if we choose to. The shift, in Morton's phrase, is therefore from something about which we can concern ourselves as citizens or members of a community, to something about which we are concerned because it is the place where we eat, it is what we consume, and it is also what consumes us, how our bodies metabolise, what is preserved when we consume preservatives, and how we return to dust, or ashes. We cannot exist outside the ecological emergency because it includes what is happening within us. While Judeo-Christian, and Cartesian dualism taught us to consider heaven and earth, soul and flesh, mind and body, and by extension, human and nature, as occupying two different and separable realms, we must revise this illusion as a result, both of our scientific understanding, and of the degree of anthropogenic impact such dualisms have created.

The second part of the phrase, the idea of an emergency, is equally important. Morton exploits its ambiguity: it is urgent and threatening, but it is also the dynamic and transient context that is emerging into our awareness, bringing with it new forms of engagement, new relationships. In order for us to consider how to respond to species and habitat loss, erosion, pollution, climate change and the associated issues of human impact, we have to shift not just how we understand human responsibility but also how we decide to frame the conditions within which any response takes place. In summary, "the ecological emergency" is a dynamic, on-going set of conditions that involves us, not just as catalysts, but as interactive features. We need to acknowledge that what we are involved in is bringing us into an unfamiliar relationship with the reference points we have traditionally used to guide our activity. We need to investigate the whole in-here, out-there relationship as a matter of urgency.

---

[5] Timothy Morton, *Hyperobjects: Philosophy and Ecology after the End of the World*, University of Minnesota Press, (2013).

Scaremongering

From some perspectives, there is no emergency whatsoever to view: the so-called emergency has been exaggerated, hyped up or even invented.[6] From others, we are doomed no matter what we do.[7] I referred to Richard Watson's observation in the introduction: perhaps we are an evolutionary cul-de-sac, destined to be burned up in our own rapacious hunger for energy. We have failed to learn to live within the limits of exploiting other systems for energy, reducing the sources and resources to fragmented, depleted systems that then no longer maintain themselves but burn or block, stagnate or flood out, suffocating other systems, creating more fragility, less resilience. There is a price for our lack of appreciation of the basic rules of evolution. Cooperation within systems is a necessary corollary to survival. There is aggression and competition, certainly, but symbiosis is the strategy adopted by all systems that maintain themselves for sustained periods of time. A certain give and take must develop in order for complexity, and therefore longevity, of systems to succeed. Our failure to recognise and respect this is leading to the weakening of our chances of species longevity. This is a pity, because we have a lot to offer: the development of languages, arts, sciences, and a deep appreciation of beauty. Developing consciousness has been a masterclass in awareness, and we simply do not know of another creature that has our capacity for self-reflection.

Stephen Pinker in *Enlightenment Now* would most likely say that pessimism about our prospects is largely informed by "progress deniers" and their "romantic declinism". He argues robustly that the world we now live in is quantifiably better in every measure than the world our ancestors, or even our grandparents, lived in.

In some sense, of course, this is true. He is right to point out that life expectancy, calories consumed, gross world product and incomes are all on the rise, while infant and maternal mortality, death from famine, starvation and extreme poverty are on the decline.[8] Yet while Pinker is concerned to emphasise that the human species has always managed to deal with apparently overwhelming problems before they become existential threats, even he has had to admit that the ecological emergency (or those aspects of it that he recognises, predominantly climate change) is so globally threatening, and so overwhelmingly all-pervasive, that the

---

[6] Andrew Chitty, "Ideology and Climate Change Convictions" (op. cit.).

[7] Decca Aitkenhead, "Enjoy Life While You Can" (op. cit.).

[8] Pinker, Steven. *Enlightenment Now* (op. cit.): Chapter 10: The Environment.

chances of coming up with viable solutions in the time available are rapidly diminishing. When he does present potential solutions, they are universally technological in nature and take no account of the scientifically based notion that we are a part of, and not apart from, the systems we evolved within. He makes no mention of the need to review our perspective on our relationship with these systems.

There is an unevenness in Pinker's optimism about our capacity to respond effectively to the ecological emergency (The Environment and Climate Change are the two measures he considers). For instance, he agrees that climate change is an issue, but says that he is optimistic that along with all the other existential crises of our time, we will deal with it, just as we have dealt with all the existential crises of previous times. However, then he enunciates in detail all the risks that climate change poses, and how little we are doing about it, and we are left wondering why he thinks we are suddenly going to turn around and focus on something that falls so neatly and precisely into what he sees as a "tragedy of the commons".

There are a number of indicators, including in Thomas Picketty's monumental account of inequality, that imply that social fragmentation leads to an exacerbation of the ecological emergency[9]. Yet Pinker himself brushes off inequality with a version of the rising tide lifting all boats argument. This demonstrates the polemic nature of Pinker's approach: he promotes a version of quantitative analysis that he maintains is incontrovertible, but his selective use of data is demonstrably as informed by ideology as any qualitative-based research.

Even given the increase in intra-societal inequalities, we in the industrialised global North have more stuff than we know what to do with, created from resources that are mined, dredged, bombed or filtered from countries in the global South at a fraction of the selling price. Pinker's optimism that we can go on with business as usual is pure pollyanna. He points out at various junctures that nature is recovering in line with the flourishing of human societies. However, when we dig down into the detail, there are two issues: first, statistics he uses are selective (tree cover has increased, according to one report, by seven percent since 1982, but this is contradicted by other satellite research which suggests both that deforestation continues apace, and that where reafforestation is taking place, it is doing so largely as a result of monoculture planting of non-

---

[9] Piketty, Thomas, and Arthur Goldhammer, *Capital in the Twenty-First Century*, Cambridge Massachusetts: The Belknap Press of Harvard University Press, (2014).

native species, and not through allowing complex forest ecosystems to recover).[10] Therefore, even if the statistics he uses are correct (which is controversial), the quality of the "return of nature" to regions now more intensely farmed, for instance, is often hugely diminished, much less diverse and less species-rich than what had originally been removed. More monocultural, less diverse, and therefore less resilient ecosystems provide far less protection against flooding, are less able to resist disease and fire, and fail to recreate the hugely complex and intricate systems that provide the kind of ecological context we require for our own human thriving.

Pinker has not considered the idea that human economy is nested in ecological and other (for instance, geological, climate, and so on) systems, let alone the idea I will explore in due course that ecological (and other) systems are nested in us, and we in them. Industrialisation has been good for humanity, and it is hard to argue with at least some of the benefits it has brought. Pinker argues that any costs in pollution and habitat loss have to be weighed against these gifts (lights for our homes, population increase, emancipation from hard or forced labour). He posits a hierarchy of needs that are met in order: first, we generate wealth, then we consider social emancipation, then we consider the environment. He does not appear to consider that progress is a complex of intertwined cycles. He is optimistic that we will not exploit any system to its total destruction, and yet that is exactly what human societies have done time and again.[11] If we lose the systems that allowed us to generate wealth in the first place, we are likely to undermine what supports and sustains the very economies and lifestyles that we have brought into existence. This is exactly what is happening now in China, for instance, where pollution costs around one percent of its annual GDP, and kills around 1 million people per year.[12] It is happening with the depletion of soils wherever agriculture is practiced as an industry, and the destruction of the vast and complex webs of

---

[10]https://www.independent.co.uk/environment/tree-cover-increase-world-deforestation-farming-rainforests; Weisse, Mikaela and Elizabeth Dow Goldman "Global Tree Cover Loss Rose 51 Percent in 2016". World Resources Institute Website. October 23, (2017). https://www.wri.org/blog/2017/10/global-tree-cover-loss-rose-51-percent-2016.

[11] See, for instance, Jared Diamond's comprehensive exposition of social breakdown in Diamond, Jared, *Collapse: How Societies Choose to Fail or Succeed*, New York: Viking, (2005).

[12] Ernest Kao, "Air Pollution is Killing One Million People and Costing Chinese Economy 267 Billion Yuan per Year, Research from CUHK Shows", South China Morning Post, (2 Oct 2018).

ecosystems in the tropics, cleared for agriculture, or mining, or logging. The quality of life of those whose livelihoods depend on these industries are hugely negatively affected by them and gains in wealth and education, often pale into insignificance by comparison.

Pinker differentiates between moral and practical concerns in a way that is, quite simply, puzzling. The fate of our children in 2525, or of the black rhinoceros are, he says, spiritual concerns. Perhaps he means that they are abstract concerns, because they do not relate directly to our survival. Certainly, there is a difference between the immediate demands of survival and the more diverse concerns we face when considering other species, or the distant future. Yet the concerns are not unrelated, and nor is the hierarchical approach either honest or accurate. We deal with immediate practical concerns, but we must also understand that the more distal and distant (the ozone layer, climate change) requires our attention, and these are also intimately tied to our own survival. Particularly when we understand what kinds of creatures we are, enmeshed in, and of, the systems that sustain and create us, we cannot simply consider the proximal and then the distal because to do so is to fail to appreciate that we are not built first from near, and then from further systems. We need a certain air quality, and a certain stability of climate, as well as food that is grown in reasonably healthy soil. We are related to, and nested in, both the immediate and the global, and the more we understand the kinds of systems we are, the more urgent it becomes to consider both long-term and distant, as well as short term and immediate, issues as being interrelated.

Pinker is a key example of a thinker who advocates a technological solution to environmental problems. He who maintains a staunch belief in the capacity of humanity to deal with issues like climate change from an engineering, and therefore essentially mechanistic, perspective.

James Hansen's *Storms of my Grandchildren* invites us to ponder a more sobering view of "progress".[13] Evidence of our failure to sense a relationship with other species is clear in the record of wildlife population changes between 1970 and 2012, as reported by the World Wildlife Fund. Decreases of approximately 38% in terrestrial wildlife, 36% in marine wildlife and an astounding 81% in freshwater wildlife are shocking statistics and the cause is incontrovertibly human activity. At the base of the food chain, the phytoplankton population had, by 2010, dropped 40% since 1950. Carbon emissions, caused by human industry, are now the

---

[13] Hansen, James, *Storms of my Grandchildren*, London: Bloomsbury, (2011).

highest they have been since the age of dinosaurs, 66 million years ago, and from physicist Geoffrey West's *Scale*:

> ... a modest 2° C change in ambient temperature leads to a 20 to 30 percent change in growth and mortality rates. This is huge and therein lies our problem.[14]

The ecological emergency that even Pinker, in his acknowledgment of climate change, admits we face in societies across the globe, arises from how we view the world, as much as from how we view one another. How we view the world, and us in it, affects how we understand our freedom and capacity to act. This implies that "the Anthropocene", a term that recognises the deep impact of the human species on other evolved systems, is something over which we have some level of control, or influence, not through technology, but through attitude.[15]

The emergency is in us

The problems we face as a result of our impact, as a species, on other systems have emerged out of deeply rooted ideas we have of our relationship to the rest of existence. One narrative considers that the space we occupy, as a species, is so minimal that the planet itself is virtually unaffected. This view is more difficult to maintain the more images that satellites and the space station make available: human impact is visible, and that which is invisible - pollution and climate change - is evident in other ways, including changing weather systems, and impacts on human, and non-human, systems and their fragmentation and collapse.

There are those who consider that the changes taking place as a result of the Anthropocene are somehow beneficial for the human species, that fewer large mammals are advantageous, or that if we want to, we could keep such mammals alive as would enhance human amusement or the advancement of human knowledge.[16] Pinker's arguments fit into a broader group, including these optimists and also those who regret recent

---

[14] Geoffrey B West, Scale: *The Universal Laws of Growth, Innovation, Sustainability, and the Pace of Life in Organisms, Cities, Economies, and Companies*, New York: Penguin Press, (2017).

[15] The proposal that the Earth has entered a new geological era in which a key driver of the planet's systems is human activity.

[16] Thomas Gale Moore, "Global Warming: A Boon to Humans and Other Animals", Hoover Institution Working Paper, Stanford, (1995); Bjørn Lomborg, *Cool It: The Skeptical Environmentalist's Guide to Global Warming*, New York: Alfred A. Knopf, (2007).

extinctions, but who reason that human ingenuity will at least ensure that human flourishing can and will continue. The survival of the human species is not only entirely separable, for people holding this view, from the flourishing of anything else. The changes humans are bringing about are seen as more exciting, offering more potential benefits, than anything natural selection without human impact would have managed:

> There were doubtless periods in the transition so picturesque that any change in the kaleidoscope seemed as if it must inevitably be a change for the worse. Yet changes came, and unsuspected beauties were revealed.[17]

Yet all the views described above excise humans from nature. Nature is used to describe the living world, or sometimes to describe the living world and all else besides (rock, water, air, the rest of the universe, ourselves in nature). Natural is contrasted with supernatural, or unnatural, where the latter means "against the order of nature" and the former means "above the laws of nature". For George Edward Moore, "natural" is contrasted with "intuitive", and this split is the basis of his idea that we must be wary of the "naturalistic fallacy", the claim that evaluations arise from natural states of affairs, an idea I will return to when discussing the problems with an ethical approach.[18]

What I am referring to here is the idea of "naturalism" depicted by Richard Watson: the idea that the human species has indeed engendered a dangerously destabilising situation, but that this has been an inevitable outcome of its own evolutionary trajectory. There is nothing to be done. We are doomed because, as natural beings, our every activity (including our responses and reactions), is subject to natural "laws" or probabilities. Nothing that the human species does can be considered immoral or even wrong. We are simply following a pre-ordained course and it is as inevitable that we follow it through to this wave of destruction as it is that night follows day.

According to James Lovelock, humanity will run its course and we, its members, must just accept that it will destroy countless other species, and

---

[17] Richard Rowe, "Tolerance", *The Philosopher:* VIII, (1930).

[18] I am interpreting Moore as an intuitionist, in the sense that he argues that "good" is intuited as an "object of thought", not inherent in objects themselves. G. E. Moore, *Principia Ethica* (Cambridge University Press, 1993). See also Oliver Curry, "Who's Afraid of the Naturalistic Fallacy?" Evolutionary Psychology (2006): 234–47.

cause vast suffering to its own, along the way.[19] Lovelock estimated that we could face the loss of seven out of the projected eight billion humans who will be in existence within the next twenty years.[20] This "extinction event", will, he says, also involve the loss of most of those species which are relatively close to us – a great proportion of the larger mammals (except those ones we use to feed ourselves), marsupials, fish, amphibia and birds - which depend on the same kind of environment that we do, and which will not, without direct human intervention, be able to protect themselves from the loss of that environment as a result of human impact.

Lovelock shrugs off the need for any ethical reaction, although he does seem disappointed at human intelligence.[21] We are past the tipping point and if there is any obligation to do anything, it is to enjoy ourselves while we can, because the future is bleak. It is possible to infer from Lovelock's vision that this apocalyptic series of events might, in the end, cause a kind of awakening.[22] If that were to happen, survivors might (naturally) experience a mass change of heart and spontaneously understand that their species was responsible and so, in some new sense, must they be, for how they relate to the ecological context. On the other hand, there is still the possibility that the human species will reject any sense of responsibility and continue to exploit and destroy other systems or even that evolution may take another turn and the human evolutionary experiment may fizzle out altogether, for this or unrelated reasons.

---

[19] James Lovelock, *The Revenge of Gaia: Earth's Climate in Crisis and the Fate of Humanity*, New York: Basic Books, (2006).

[20] Lovelock has admitted in interviews that this prediction may be premature (see, for instance https://www.theguardian.com/environment/2016/sep/30/james-lovelock-interview-by-end-of-century-robots-will-have-taken-over).

[21] Leo Hickman, "James Lovelock: Humans Are Too Stupid to Prevent Climate Change", *Guardian*, 29 March 2010, section Environment <http://www.theguardian.com/science/2010/mar/29/james-lovelock-climate-change>.

[22] Lovelock himself has used an extended metaphor to describe what humanity has done in terms of an adolescent, waking up with a smoking gun in her hand, surrounded by dead animals. This image implies that the adolescent was not knowingly responsible, just as the human species is not knowingly responsible, for what it did, since it was "asleep" when the carnage took place. To aim and shoot to kill now, however, would be a different thing altogether. This strongly echoes my argument that our agency is not what we think it is. We are agents when we realise what is happening, as it is happening, but this agency is a realisation of an attitude, so is not free will in the traditional sense.

The future is hard to predict, even with natural, probabilistic, laws to guide us. Lovelock, Watson, and others, effectively imply that, up to now, humans have, like all other naturally arising systems, been subject to conditions out of our control, whether those are to do with limitations to our own evolved intelligence and ability to make connections, or whether they are to do with the larger context of evolution itself. In this narrative, our activity is as natural and inevitable as gravity and just as the laws of probability shape gravitational activity, so they shape what we have done.

If denialists argue that we not in an emergency, and apocalyptics argue that we are natural, and therefore we are in an emergency, but there is nothing we can do about it, antagonists could be characterised as arguing that (whether we are natural or not) the rest of the natural world is hostile and alien, and requires suppression. During the nineteenth century, when European expansionism was at its height, as Bruno Latour put it, a "we shall overcome" attitude may have been thought an entirely appropriate response.[23] Even now, this reaction is evident among those who experience "natural disasters": Nature is the monstrous Other who will overwhelm us if we do not strike back, preferably pre-emptively.[24] The human response is based on the capacity to exercise a strong (mental) determination, translated into the (physical) action of overcoming adverse (physical) circumstances.

Extending the argument from antagonism to the enemy within, there is also the view that we now perceive pressure to lower current rates of

---

[23] Bruno Latour, "It's Development, Stupid!" or How to Modernize Modernization?, in Jim Proctor, ed., *Postenvironmentalism*, MIT Press, (2008), commenting upon T. Nordhaus, and M. Shellenberger, *BreakThrough: From the Death of Environmentalism to the Politics of Possibility*, New York, Houghton Mifflin Company, (2007).

[24] An exploration of nature as Other is a frequent theme in environmental ethics literature. One instance of such an exploration is the one undertaken by Steven Vogel: "this view of nature calls us to something like a *Gelassenheit*, a recognition that we are not the world and that its concrete reality and thereness, its Otherness from us, are irreducible and irremediable. The world resists us, and always has more to it than we think is there, and so to think and act in it is at the same time to call into being forces that go far beyond what we know and intend." Steven Vogel, "Nature as Origin and Difference: On Environmental Philosophy and Continental Thought", *Philosophy Today*, 42, (1999), 169-81: 173.

consumption as, in Guy Claxton's words, "loss, sacrifice and threat".[25] Claxton (quoted in King's essay) argues against the idea that we would willingly change our ways. It will take more than education to wean us from a consumer lifestyle that now intertwines with our beliefs. Even if we attempt to restrain ourselves, the rewards are less obvious, less tangible, than those immediate and somewhat addictive gratifications of consumption. As Claxton (quoted in King) puts it, "one wants, and one wants not to want. The problem is how to translate the wanting not to want into not wanting".[26] Here, our beliefs about responsibility within a dualistic framework become most evident. We can be in conflict with ourselves, having both a (mental) determination, and a (physical) capacity to respond differently, but insufficient (mental) strength to put that capacity into (physical) practice.

Ethics or pragmatism

Once we accept, on the basis of scientific data, that the ecological emergency is real, we next have to review the arguments around whether or not we have the capacity, and obligation, to respond effectively and mitigate its impact. I want to separate those that understand our responsibility as primarily ethically neutral and those that understand our responsibility as primarily ethical. Of the first set, many see an ethic arising out of other reasons and capacities for response but the ethic is not the primary motivation. Brown, Flavin and Postel in their "Vision of a Sustainable World" paint a scenario set in 2030 in which we have managed, with effort, to bring our societies and communities into line with what the rest of the biosphere can sustain.[27] The views set out below effectively describe the various paths by which we could come to such a scenario.

The prevailing political responses to the ecological emergency rest on the understanding that individuals, groups, communities or states only act in their own interests. In this scenario, it is taken as a given that whatever capacity to respond we have is governed by decisions we make, which in

---

[25] King, Roger J. H. "Playing with Boundaries: Critical Reflections on Strategies for an Environmental Culture and the Promise of Civic Environmentalism", *Ethics, Place and Environment*, 9 (2006), 173–186.

[26] King, (Ibid.).

[27] Lester R. Brown, Christopher Flavin and Sandra Postel, "Vision of a Sustainable World", in *The World watch reader on global environmental issues* (New York: Norton, 1998), 299–315.

turn are based on self-interested goals. Calculations are made to assess what "eco-system services" are "worth" economically and these are then weighed up against what are seen as competing interests of human populations: jobs, cultural traditions, and so on.

It is possible that, if those goals are reductionist enough and if we continue on the trajectory they inevitably imply, we risk facing a version of what Derek Parfit has described as "the repugnant conclusion", the species reduced to bare survival in a world stripped back to mechanistic functionality.[28] Dale Jamieson points this out in his assessment of the discussions on climate change that purported to take good will and a common purpose as starting points:

The problem with this approach is that it assumed good will and a common purpose on all sides. However, not everyone wanted global action on climate change. Most of the oil producing states were opposed, and so were many influential actors in the United States.[29]

Ideological, self-interested, short-term, and political concerns outweigh broader, more neutral considerations of scientific calculus, and the common good. The political and economic consequences of continuing impact are pitted against the potential mitigation of these effects: more tangible present benefits trump the uncertain future. In any case, we who are alive now will benefit not one whit from acts that aim to secure the future and there is no guarantee that any of our progeny, if we have any, will benefit either.

Still, self-interested is the view that rejects the economic or political tallying of interests and moves instead towards a focus on the preservation of species and ecosystems for their emotional or therapeutic benefits. John Muir described the sequoia forests of California as "living cathedrals" and argued that nowhere was it more possible to achieve a sense of peace than in the wild places.[30] Thoreau and Emerson argued similarly for the preservation of wild (or semi-wild) places because nature generates a

---

[28] Derek Parfit, *Reasons and Persons*, OUP, (1984).

[29] Dale Jamieson, "Climate Change, Consequentialism, and the Road Ahead", *Chicago Journal of International Law*, 13 (2015): 440–68.

[30] John Muir, "The Wild Parks and Forest Reservations of the West and Hetch Hetchy Valley", reprinted in David Keller, *Environmental Ethics: The Big Questions* (op. cit.): 96–97.

sense of reverence.[31] Humanity (or at least some of its more sensitised members) has the capacity to recognise and resonate with the inherent aesthetic, experience awe and humility at the magnificence and magnitude of unpeopled places, and understand its loss or destruction as short-sighted and tragic.

The balance of interests in arguments from these early advocates of wilderness or biodiversity preservation, the likes of Muir, Thoreau and later, Holmes Rolston III and others, imply that, while it is heart-breaking to lose the wild places, it is the human, transcendent soul that is mostly harmed by their loss. This is because humans alone have another dimension for understanding and responding to wild nature. Reduced to its crude base, this kind of approach could be characterised as one that views our responsibility as generated by, and serving, human self-interest first (and any other interests only by extension).

Rachel Carson moves the grounds for exercising our capacity to respond from the spiritual to the physiological. Her strongest appeal to halt the use of pesticides and stop the destruction of the complex interrelationships in biodiverse systems was that their continued use affected the physiological survival of human individuals. This was information we could respond to by changing our interventions in natural systems (primarily through banning certain pesticides). Carson's slant, like those of the other writers mentioned above, needs to be seen in the context of the concerns and pressures of particular historical and social conditions. After all, even Charles Darwin was reluctant to publicly express his religious beliefs (or lack of them) for fear of reprisal. It is possible, therefore, that the emphasis in these writers' works was skewed to reflect concerns that they felt their readers could most easily identify with and, given the context, these were, vastly predominately, human concerns.

Leopold, Muir, Carson, Thoreau and Emerson all gave ear to non-human voices.[32] They were part of a movement to take account of non-human

---

[31] Ralph Waldo Emerson, *Nature*, Boston: James Munroe and Company, (1836); Lawrence Buell, "Ecological Contemplation as Spiritual Practice: The Case of Henry David Thoreau" (*Buddhist Ecology and Environmental Studies* conference, Cambridge, MA: Center for the Study of World Religions, Harvard Divinity School, 2005); Holmes Rolston III, "The Pasqueflower", *Natural History*, Vol. 88 Issue 4, April (1979): 6.

[32] Thoreau, Henry David. *Walden: A Life in the Woods.* New York: Ticknor and Fields. Dover Thrift Editions. (1854); John Muir, *Travels in Alaska 1915*, Modern Library Inc, (2002); Aldo Leopold, *A Sand County Almanac With Essays on Conservation from*

interests and to act with consideration for those interests, and this extended from a narrative that followed the tracks of the changing human relationship to the wild. From the hunter-gatherer's placating, awe- (or fear-) inspired worship of the "spirit within" all things, the narrative told how the relationship metamorphosed into one of the alienated, industrialised, human subject thirsting, either for solace or inspiration, among the wild spaces, seeking to reconnect to the umbilicus to Mother Earth as the sustaining "source".[33]

In antithesis to Pinker, Leopold questioned the benefits of increased human comfort at the vast cost to the non-human, and particularly to "wild nature" and was, therefore, one of the first thinkers of the "global North" to place human interests firmly within, and connected to, ecological interests.[34] What we lose, when we gain material comfort, must be weighted differently against what we gain, if what we lose (the extinction of species) is irreplaceable, whereas what we gain depends on continuing, unsustainable loss. It is hard not to feel some empathy for Pinker's account: most of us would find a return to candlelight and travel by cart something of a retrograde step. On top of which, Leopold characterised the loss (of other species) as affecting humans, because humans alone notice the loss (consciously). In this sense at least, he still represents a self-interested approach.[35] Human responsibility, in these narratives, was primarily a question of (enlightened) self-interest, and only by extension, the interests of habitats, other species, and so on. Looked at like this, Pinker and Leopold meet one another around the back

---

Round River, New York: Ballantine Books, (1970); Rachel Carson, *Silent Spring,* Penguin, (1965); Ralph Waldo Emerson, *Nature,* Boston: James Munroe and Company, (1836).

[33] Another who I have not mentioned, but who was seminal, even if his views were ridiculed, in propounding an ethic centred on reverence for non-human life was Albert Schweitzer. See Mike W. Martin, *Albert Schweitzer's reverence for life: ethical idealism and self-realization.* (Aldershot, England: Ashgate, 2007).

[34] Aldo Leopold, A Sand County Almanac: (op. cit.); see also J. Baird Callicott, In Defense of the Land Ethic: Essays in Environmental Philosophy, SUNY Press, (1989).

[35] "Self-realisation" is the key concept in Leopold, and in Deep Ecology in general and it certainly implies that more than the individual self is "realised". Nevertheless it is still dependent on a kind of sleight of hand, where the first and most pertinent question to be answered is, what is it good for, to me? The picture I am more interested in exploring is the non-dualistic one, where the self becomes meaningless in a process of realisation that recognises an explicit awareness, but nevertheless sees this awareness as arising and dying away, moment by moment, and so having no particular form, or identity, or "self".

of the spectrum: both put human interests first, but come to opposite conclusions.

Reframing a response to anthropogenic impact for reasons that go beyond self-interest has been the work of the field of environmental ethics. Trying to translate a concern for the non-human world into ethical terms has proved elusive, to say the least. Concerns expressed in pragmatic, aesthetic, emotional and therapeutic terms are relatively easy to conceive of. We can even see a rationale for extending a kind of honorary person-hood to other animals who exhibit recognisable responses to the infliction of pain or suffering, but to talk of a moral duty beyond this becomes increasingly diluted, less convincing.[36]

Central to the field of environmental ethics are questions about how we can conceive of our relationship with the living and even with non-living, non-human individuals and communities. The nub of the argument is that our relationship to (variously) nature, the environment or the rest of existence involves duties or responsibilities that parallel those we owe to other people. To understand what these duties might be, we are back to the question of how humans fit into the rest of biophysical existence, and what this implies about our relationship with it.

Environmental ethics is predicated on the position that human impact has created a critical situation, but also that at least some humans have an ability to respond and are therefore under some sort of obligation to act to reverse, or mitigate, what is going on. Robin Attfield, in his Paris paper, defines four positions which emerged more or less chronologically as perspectives from which to develop an environmental ethic.[37] It must be said that each term describes a range of positions which more or less fall within each scope. The four are anthropocentrism, zoocentrism, (which could also be called sentientism or rationalism), biocentrism and ecocentrism. Without attempting to do justice to any, but merely in the

---

[36] Peter Singer, in *The Expanding Circle: Ethics, Evolution, and Moral Progress*, Princeton, NJ: Princeton University Press, (2011) is probably the best-known popular proponent of the view that there are good grounds for positing something that characterises a broader set than just humans (sentience, or a capacity for suffering) in deciding who or what is owed moral consideration. This is always going to give a hierarchical result: humans considered first, then, say, chimpanzees, and so on.

[37] Robin Attfield, "Reconciling Individualist and Deeper Environmentalist Theories? An Exploration", in *The Structural Links between Ecology, Evolution and Ethics*, ed. Donato Bergandi, *Boston Studies in the Philosophy and History of Science*, 296, Springer Netherlands, (2013): 127–39.

spirit of contextualising Paul Taylor's biocentrism, they can each be understood as advocating a particular perspective from which to approach our ethical response to the environment, and, more specifically, to the problematic relationship we have with it (manifested as biodiversity loss, and so on).

The arguments circle around what to include as qualifying characteristics for moral consideration. At each point on the spectrum, it is possible to identify a locus, whether that is the select set of human characteristics required to qualify for boarding Hardin's lifeboat, or the mirroring dewdrops in the net of Indra, where every point in the universe is a relevant centre of consideration, since all are interdependent.[38]

An emerging consensus on human responsibility

All these views (apart from the last one mentioned) depend on the narrative that Taylor spells out in detail, where a particular category of beings (humans) are moral agents, in the sense of being self-directed individuals who can be held accountable for duties and responsibilities imposed on them by a cultural system they recognise.[39] This category, moral agents, both can and ought to take responsibility for this emergency.

If this narrative is an accurate reflection of the relationship, humans and the non-human world really are different categories. Humans are the sole protagonists able to take responsibility for their impact. Interestingly, if we look at the kinds of justification that have been used for self-interested, exploitative human interventions, they are, in exact parallel, those that posit two categories of existence: humans, who are intrinsically valuable, and can value, on the one hand, and the rest of existence, which may be instrumentally valuable, and cannot value, on the other.[40]

---

[38] See, for instance, Francis Cook's analysis of Hua-yen Buddhist conceptions of the interdependence and identity in the relationship between humans and the natural world in J. Baird Callicott and Roger T. Ames, (eds), *Nature in Asian Traditions of Thought: Essays in Environmental Philosophy*, SUNY Press, (1989): 219. Parallel arguments are made in the field of general ethics supporting the notion that an ethic does not require an external, supernatural justification but can be inherent within the system it operates on. See, for instance, H. L. A. Hart, "Are There Any Natural Rights?", *Philosophical Review*, 64 (1955): 175–91.

[39] Paul W Taylor, *Respect for Nature* (op. cit.): 33.

[40] Lynn White, "The Historical Roots of Our Ecological Crisis", *Science*, 155 (1967).

This dichotomous vision arises partly a result of our evolved condition: an extravagant evolutionary process that has led, accidentally, to human self-conscious experience. The way we view ourselves is heavily influenced by our physical, biological condition: we live within our skins and our identity is bound up in this fact. However, at least as important in shaping how we see ourselves are the social and historical contexts that create our sense of identity and, most relevantly here, the narrative we almost universally accept of ourselves as self-directed, autonomous, beings, with the capacity to respond, in some sense consciously, to what we encounter.

Wendell Berry in *The Landscape of Harmony* characterises, or perhaps caricatures, two extreme attitudes taken by humans in the perception of their relationship to nature. The first group we can call the nature lovers "who sound as though they are entirely in favour of nature". Here, Berry equates "nature" with the biosphere:

> They believe, at least in principle, that the biosphere is an egalitarian system, in which all creatures, including humans, are equal in value and have an equal right to live and flourish.[41]

In this rendering, humans are one single point in a matrix that includes all living existence on the planet and that is, potentially, one harmonious whole. The idea that humans, and all else, can "flourish" in this matrix suggests that it is predominantly benign and it is this that Berry rightly takes the nature lovers to task for. However, Berry also points out that "nature conquerors":

> ... have no patience with an old-fashioned outdoor farm, let alone a wilderness. These people divide all reality into two parts: human good, which they define as profit, comfort and security; and everything else...[42]

"Everything else" is a "stockpile of natural resources" that will eventually be translated, through human requisitioning, into "human good". Berry is aware that the polarised attitudes he mentions are largely the result of certain processes of acculturation. Where there has been a cultural facilitation towards integrating the subjective and the objective, the

---

[41] Wendell Berry, *The Landscape of Harmony*, Five Seasons, (1987): 31.

[42] (Ibid.): 31.

relationships are treated as mirrors of one another.[43] On the other hand, in contexts where the segregation of perspective means that there is no inherent recognition of a connection between one set of relationships and another, the resulting fragmentation has caused dissonance: there is no longer an accord between sets of relationships, or a recognition that each affects the other.

In the context of contemporary understandings and explanations, an agnostic, physicalist view of how humans fit into the ecosphere is an appropriate starting point for reviewing the different perspectives outlined above.[44] Given this starting point, I have chosen to use Taylor's work as a catalyst for this attempt to separate out a view that best reflects our current understanding of the human/nature relationship, particularly as this relates to our responsibility.

Attitude divergence in the context of the ecological emergency

Attempts to disentangle the ethical and practical problems that beset responses to the ecological emergency, in particular, and environmental ethics more generally, consistently run into a key feature of the field: attitude divergence. The polarisation, and fragmentation, of views that become entrenched, and increasingly eagerly defended, makes it almost impossible to develop a strong, coherent, widely accepted response.

J. Baird Callicott's work on the triangulation of human, animal and environmental rights elicited an early instance of vigorous caricaturing when one respondent "exploited [Callicott's extreme, and somewhat inexperienced, reading of "the land ethic"] for polemical purposes."[45] Callicott was labelled an "eco-fascist", the first known instance of this epithet. He later recanted the extremism implied by his reading, but the stage was set for what was to become a regular feature of any discussion about responses to anthropogenic impact, both in the philosophical world and beyond, into the political.

---

[43] An analogy, referred to earlier, that is explored in depth in Francis Cook's essay (op. cit.).

[44] "In order to discover what sort of human life is valuable we must first consider what kind of thing a human being is." Andrew Brennan, *Thinking About Nature* University of Georgia Press, (1988): Preface, xii.

[45] J. Baird Callicott, "Introductory Palinode", <http://jbcallicott.weebly.com/introductory-palinode.html> ; "Animal Liberation: A Triangular Affair", *Environmental Ethics*, 2, Winter (1980): 311–38.

To question that human capacities are at the apex of the evolutionary ladder is seen by hierarchists as little less than heresy.[46] Attfield expresses his incomprehension that anyone could view the complex cognitive capacities of humans as anything but "higher" processes which are, therefore, intrinsically more valuable than processes like photosynthesis.[47] Policies and practices designed to rebalance human with non-human interests are sometimes called "human-hating".[48] On the other hand, those who resist calls for such a rebalancing are labelled, in their turn, "anti-human".[49]

The tendency towards increasing divergence is particularly evident throughout debates on social and conventional media, between "deniers" and "warmists", representing a more general sense of ideological divisiveness.[50] There is a parallel divergence in how we, in the global North, live (where and how material resources, from food to plastics are "produced", and where they go after we have finished with them), and the idea we have of how we live (shaped by the – largely unexamined – narratives that underpin our understanding of our condition).[51] There is

---

[46] Even Holmes Rolston III, an avowed hierarchist when it comes to human valuing, recognises the difficulties with using the word "higher" in reference to species in biology. See, Holmes III Rolston, "Caring for Nature: From Fact to Value, from Respect to Reverence", *Zygon*, 39 (2004): 277–302.

[47] Robin Attfield, "Biocentrism, Moral Standing, and Moral Significance", *Philosophica*, 39 (1987): 47–58.

[48] See, for instance, Eugene Hargrove's discussion of "The Monkeywrench Gang" in David Keller (ed.), *Environmental Ethics: The Big Questions*, (op. cit.): 327ff.

[49] http://ecosense.me/index.php/views-articles Patrick Moore's website and views are highly relevant in this respect.

[50] Corby Wind Farm Ex-Candidate: "I Won"", *BBC*, (1 November 2012), Section UK Politics http://www.bbc.co.uk/news/uk-politics-20168738 ; Mitch Parsell, "Pernicious Virtual Communities: Identity, Polarisation and the Web 2.", *Ethics and Information Technology*, 10 (2008): 41–56.

[51] This tendency to allow our attention to be distracted from what goes on "behind the scenes", from sewerage systems, to manufacturing, to food production, is referred to extensively by Timothy Morton (see, for instance, Timothy Morton, *Hyperobjects: Philosophy and Ecology after the End of the World* (op. cit.). For a recent detailed treatment of the idea that we have implicit, unexamined sets of narratives underpinning our belief and value systems, see Andrew Chitty, "Ideology and Climate Change Convictions" (op. cit.):"What I have in mind is not so much ideology in the sense of a more or less explicitly political set of factual and normative beliefs but in the sense of a more fundamental take on the human condition and human history - what we could call "human condition imaginaries"."

little convergence on how to frame the problem of anthropogenic impact, or even on whether or not a problem exists, but there is also little convergence on the narratives that underpin beliefs about what, if anything, should be done.

In the sense that I will use it in this work, ideological thinking is the tendency to base moral or ethical principles (in this chapter, I use the words virtually interchangeably) on a set of ideas that might have a political, or a religious, origin, and to use this as a framework for approaching and interpreting new evidence.[52] Just as liberal ideology could incline its adherent towards evidence that supports stronger government intervention for public goods and social justice, so a more conservative (or, in American parlance, Republican) stance will incline its proponent towards evidence that supports self-interest and the free market as forces that will lead to social benefits. In the context of the ecological emergency, it is easy to translate these narratives into those that underpin the embracing of evidence that more state intervention is necessary to control human impact, and those that consider relevant only evidence for less state intervention (and that, by extension, do not admit to the negative impact of human activity). The underpinning narratives play a key role in how evidence is assessed.

Divergence in negotiations: the law of diminishing returns

If the fundamental take we have on the human condition and human history is causing divergence in the theoretical field, the chances of any successful discussion and negotiation in practice are also bound to diminish. There is an increasing likelihood of fragmentation between groups adhering to different narratives, and it follows that this situation is likely to decrease opportunities for future convergence both on how to frame, and on how to respond to, the ecological emergency (if it is even conceived as such).

---

[52] There is a case to be made for defending a distinction between "moral" and "ethical" on, for instance, grounds of personal (moral) versus social (ethical) applicability and up to this point, I have respected that distinction However, since I am proposing that we question the usefulness of an ethical approach, and show that there is no centre to a "moral" agent, I will, from here on, largely follow the example of Hans-Georg Moeller in his usage in *The Moral Fool : A Comparative Case for Amorality*, New York: Columbia University Press, (2009). I therefore stick less rigidly to the personal/ social division, on the grounds that I am questioning the use of both terms.

We need to find a way to understand how human moral responsibility, and moral agency, operates in the context of the wider-than-human sphere, particularly when we perceive human impact as having created a crisis in that sphere. This requires us to reflect on whichever aspects of the narrative underpinning our beliefs about the human/nature relationship have remained unexamined. However, we also need to find a way to understand whether there is any way to overcome the divergence that arises in discussions of theories that posit grounds for an environmental ethic. Unless we do so, any finding will lack practical applicability.

Let us turn, therefore, to one voice that rationalised an extension of a traditional, Kantian, ethic: that if a thing has a "good" of its own, it should be treated as a centre of value, as something that deserves consideration, and respect. That is the basis of the theory of "respect for nature" put forward by the philosopher and ornithologist, the late Professor Paul Taylor.

Paul Taylor's moral agents, patients and considerability

Taylor advocated a three-stage process in his account of biocentrism, moving from a recognition of an organism's inherent worth to its moral considerability and on to what moral agents owe that organism. His book is an extended untangling of the concerns implicit in each step but he begins by demarcating clear boundaries between the entities and issues under consideration, and among these is the idea of where our responsibility lies: in our moral agency.[53]

The idea of moral agency has remained relatively unexamined in the field of environmental ethics compared, for instance, to ideas of where to locate value, who to include in (moral or ethical) consideration, and so on.[54] The idea that humans are moral agents with at least some level of responsibility to at least some set of "moral patients", is barely questioned and Taylor's account, while it is careful to delineate what is included by the

---

[53] Taylor, (Ibid.): 14-25.

[54] Robin Attfield, "Biocentric Consequentialism: Pluralism and the "Minimax Implication": A Reply to Alan Carter", *Utilitas*, 15 (2003), 76–91; Attfield, "Biocentric Consequentialism and Value-Pluralism: A Response to Alan Carter", *Utilitas*, 17 (2005): 85–92. This is part of an extended discussion between Attfield and Carter on biocentric consequentialism.

term, is no exception.[55] However, Taylor's account is persuasive for other reasons, and is therefore worth the effort of analysis. He clearly demonstrates the evolutionary relationship between the human species and all others, and hence, humanity's peripherality, at least from the perspective of biophysical evolution.[56] He gives a careful account of the relationship between the well-being or, more broadly "good", of an organism, and its teleological instinct to pursue this "good."[57]

When Taylor is laying this out, he implies a distinct correlation between the recognition and acknowledgement of "the good" of organisms and human agency. On the basis that organisms, like humans, pursue certain conditions that benefit them (their "goods"), then they, along with humans, are "ends in themselves", teleological centres with goals. None of these centres need be aware that they are pursuing the goal of their "good", as long as there are human moral agents on the scene to provide this recognition, and with the capacity to respond to the recognition. Importantly, none of these teleological centres is intrinsically more important than any other: all have evolved through the same process, and their similarity to, or difference from, humanity, is immaterial when it comes to their worth. All have inherent worth equally, and Taylor's theory is radically egalitarian as a result of this conclusion.

For Taylor, we are able to take responsibility for our disruptive and destructive impact on other living systems, both for our own sakes, but more fundamentally, because it is "the right thing to do". "Moral agents" are those kinds of beings (and only certain human beings fall into this category, as far as Taylor is concerned) that "can have duties and responsibilities" and that can "be held accountable" for what they do.[58] Moral agents exercise these duties and responsibilities both towards

---

[55] The notable exceptions, as I have already mentioned, are those who posit human "naturalness" as the basis of our destructive activity but who argue that we are, therefore, inevitably going to continue until our rampage of destructive impacts results in our own population crash. This, of course, strongly echoes the narrative of Thomas Robert Malthus in *An Essay on the Principle of Population,* (1789), http://www.gutenberg.org/ebooks/4239: "Necessity, that imperious all pervading law of nature, restrains them within the prescribed bounds. The race of plants and the race of animals shrink under this great restrictive law. And the race of man cannot, by any efforts of reason, escape from it." (Chapter One).

[56] Taylor, *Respect for Nature,* (op. cit.): 116ff.

[57] (Ibid.): 60ff.

[58] (Ibid.): 14.

themselves (other moral agents) and towards those they recognise as having inherent worth: moral patients.

Moral patients fall into two main groups. Some humans and perhaps some other living organisms sometimes pursue their own goods conscious of the fact, while much of the time all these organisms do not (while asleep, for instance) and yet, those goals do not go away, even when the moral patients are unconscious of them. Depressed people, impoverished people, animals in captivity, and so on are sometimes internally or externally restrained from pursuing their own goods; nevertheless at least some of these will know that they have goods, even if they cannot manage to pursue them, or even if they deliberately pursue their own destruction. The second category of moral patients are those that pursue their own goods instinctively, or, perhaps one could even say, inherently, just because this is the kind of thing they are (this includes, therefore, all organisms that instinctively direct themselves towards sources of light, heat or nutrition, and away from sources of pain, or threats of annihilation). This group never has any awareness that it is pursuing a "good", but it does so, nonetheless.

Moral considerability, in this context, is the exercise of deciding which set of patients to include in the moral realm. Taylor includes both. Others may decide to exclude one, or change the boundaries of both, based on a different set of foundational beliefs, or ideals, or a religious commitment.

Cartesian dualism is the obvious alternative approach and Descartes sought to demonstrate conclusively that as long as organisms in pursuit of goals are unaware of such a pursuit, they simply exist and that is all. Therefore if moral agents decide that it would benefit humanity to dissect such an organism, there is nothing, morally, wrong with that. Other traditions, secular and religious, have views on how we ought to behave towards the non-human world, advocating a hierarchical approach. Almost all posit a moral agent, on the one hand, and the rest of existence, on the other.

Traditional ethics has a clear boundary: humans alone are the subject of moral considerability. Where questions arise, these are around humans who fall into a grey area: embryos and foetuses, future people, people who are incapable of moral deliberation.[59] However, including all these kinds of people blurs the boundary: there is no relevant distinction between

---

[59] For a contextualised discussion of future humans, see Clark Wolf, "Environmental Justice and Intergenerational Debt", in David Keller (ed.) *Environmental Ethics: The Big Questions* (op. cit.): 545–550.

those who have nervous systems and are not human, and those who have less functional, or virtual, nervous systems, and are human, unless we revert to the claim that all humans, and only humans, are possessed of souls.[60]

We can legitimately reject that claim, coming at this from a scientist perspective, on the basis that it cannot be falsified, and cannot be examined. That allows us to turn to a third problem for ethicists in deciding who or what to include in moral consideration. Systems, communities, or other holons are diverse and complex, and have no single evolutionary drive, unlike individual organisms. While it may make sense to move the locus of consideration from an individual human to an individual of another species, the difficulty with shifting consideration to entire systems is that there is no teleological centre on which to focus attention.

Taylor's egalitarianism creates difficulties with the moral considerability of different and sometimes conflicting interests. An egalitarian ethic strives for the flourishing of all organisms equally, but this is in tension with the competitive nature of evolution, and even with human needs. The deliberate killing of individual organisms by humans is incompatible with Taylor's environmental ethic but living as part of the natural world implies that we ought at least to allow for the possibility of exercising our capacity, as human animals, to "fit in" with nature in this way.[61]

Taylor's narrative of the moral considerability of "wild places" could be interpreted from a conservative perspective as implying that privatisation of lands is the only way to guarantee the full moral consideration of the wild communities of organisms living there. However, it might also be possible to argue that only through state ownership can both human-to-human and human-to-non-human moral considerations be balanced.[62] Perhaps, however, only community ownership of land is consistent with

---

[60] A point made in detail by Joel Feinberg, "The Rights of Animals and Unborn Generations", in *Rights, Justice, and the Bounds of Liberty: essays in social philosophy,* Princeton University Press, (1980), Chapter 8.

[61] Claude Evans, J., *With Respect for Nature: Living as Part of the Natural World,* (State University of New York Press, 2005). Garrett Hardin, "Who Cares for Posterity?" in Louis P Pojman and Paul Pojman (eds), *Environmental Ethics: Readings in Theory and Application,* Boston, Mass.: Wadsworth, 2012).

[62] Peter Singer, "Famine, Affluence and Morality", *Philosophy and Public Affairs,* 1, 3, Blackwell, (Spring 1972): 229-243.

the full moral considerability of wild members of that community.[63] It is not clear, therefore, from Taylor's account, that a common strategy for environmental protection could easily be found. However, it is clear that he views human moral agency as unique and special, although the basis for such uniqueness is not explicitly established.

Moral egotism

These various interpretations of Taylor's moral considerability in the context of different ideological approaches illustrate how the issue of moral responsibility diverges, depending on the underlying narrative. In one respect, this turns on whether we believe that our most important basis for making decisions is self-interested or virtue-based, whether it requires an emotional engagement or can be entirely rational.[64] In this section, I set out the various perspectives in order to locate Taylor's position on the spectrum.

During the 1960s, Garrett Hardin developed perhaps the most radically conservative response yet to what he saw as increasing pressure on biological systems for human survival. He couched his argument in ethical terms but with the proviso that "ecology, a system-based view of the world, demands situational ethics".[65] For Hardin, the current situation was untenable: the focus on human rights-based ethics had favoured egalitarianism, but the short-term concerns of an egalitarian system would always ensure environmental degradation since it is based on the needs of those who are currently alive and the principle that they have a right to survival.

Hardin, therefore, proposed an unequal distribution of wealth or privilege, so that those agents with more interest in preservation – those with more wealth, and therefore more to "pass on" – will better protect what is theirs, even if this is at the expense of the majority who will very likely suffer and perhaps even die as a result. At this end of the ethical spectrum, then, the circle of moral considerability is contracted to include only a favoured few humans and nothing else, but the motivation for this

---

[63] Fiona Mackenzie, "A common claim: Community land ownership in the Outer Hebrides, Scotland," 1, (2010). Retrieved from
http://www.thecommonsjournal.org/index.php/ijc/article/view/151/120.

[64] Peter Singer and Michael Slote, Philosophy TV http://www.philostv.com/peter-singer-and-michael-slote/.

[65] Garrett Hardin quoted in David Keller (ed.), *Environmental Ethics: The Big Questions* (op. cit.): 438.

contraction is to protect not only the favoured human few but also, crucially (Hardin is a biologist, after all) the "whole world".[66]

Hardin's thesis, largely based on Malthusian population dynamics, was developed as a morally pragmatic response specifically to the problems of habitat and species loss, one strand of what has become the ecological emergency. His "lifeboat ethic" is a proposal that the only way human agents can meet our moral obligations towards ourselves, as a species, is by limiting the moral sphere.[67] Since the human species is doomed to a mass reduction in numbers in any case, in Hardin's narrative, his focus is on minimising the suffering of all (including, crucially, the non-human realm of living existence) by focusing all efforts for survival on those who have the highest chance of coming through the crisis.

In parallel with his "tragedy of the commons" argument, Hardin prefers that the distribution of means for survival be limited to those who occupy a current position of relative privilege or wealth (those in the United States, for instance, but not those in Somalia). Those who survive will be more likely to protect the goods and resources, including the evolved biodiversity, which has ensured their survival. The end result will be a more protected, more morally (because more socially) intact, population, even if this is achieved at the expense of the vast majority.

Hardin's argument is based on the classical Hobbesian narrative that human extravagance, greed or hunger is insatiable, and that natural human appetite, when coupled with an ethic that fails to acknowledge this appetite, will consume until it burns itself out destructively. The only morally feasible stance for such a creature is to exercise a ruthless plan of moral discrimination, embracing those who happen to belong to one's own community, or group, regardless of whether they are more prepared than anyone else to recognise and restrain their natural capacity for limitless consumption, and excluding all else. Hardin's aim in developing this ethic is laudable: his goal is to see the preservation and protection of what he recognises as delicate and intricate webs of interdependence

---

[66] (Ibid.): 442. This raises the question of what Hardin considers to be morally valuable. In a sense, his ethic implicitly extends to the entire biosphere and his focus on containing human resource consumption is, overall, an attempt to protect the biosphere from human impact. His ethic is not couched in these terms, however, and he maintains his focus only on which human group could be realistically included in the ethical "lifeboat", on the rationale that, by extension, this will have the ultimate effect of protecting more of the biosphere.

[67] Garrett Hardin, "Lifeboat Ethics: The Case Against Helping the Poor", (op. cit.).

among organisms and the conditions that sustain them. However, his method of selecting a group whose interests and concerns may well entirely contradict his own is faulty, at best.

Hardin's training as a biologist implies that he recognises human enmeshment. His approach takes a traditional view of agency, however, and more, a clear attempt to cut off the recognition of interdependence with those who are not morally considerable. There is no discussion of the effects of such social exclusiveness on either the survivors, or on biosystems generally. Disenfranchisement has proved an expensive social strategy in the past and whatever level of impoverishment people are reduced to, there has never been a way of neatly excising an entire population.[68] The practicality of this approach is therefore highly questionable, quite apart from the suffering that it would entail.

Elinor Ostrom also questioned, and, using empirical research into actual practice, demolished, Hardin's argument that holding "goods" in common (land, water, and so on) would always end in their tragic diminishment.[69] Yet Hardin's view represents a widely held perspective and includes an attempt to discuss the unpalatable reality of human population increase (and an accompanying, exponential, increase in demand for material goods and benefits), a discussion that is not easy to dismiss.[70]

Part of the difficulty with Hardin's approach is that any justification for action on moral grounds that also justifies entirely self-centred action is not really, therefore, moral. Ronald Dworkin points out that if we look for "some conception of what it is to live well" that allows us to "understand our moral responsibilities in whatever way is best for us", we are not actually, acting morally, "because morality should not depend on any benefit that being moral might bring."[71]

In contrast, Amartya Sen and Barry Commoner argue that there is no inherent difference between the value of one human life and the value of another. In the context of the ecological emergency, this demands an egalitarian ethic that is close to the Kantian notion of the inherent value of

---

[68] North Korea springs to mind, but even that tightly guarded nation leaks a steady trickle of escapees to tell of the horrors of internment and raise awareness, keeping alive the possibility of change.

[69] Elinor Ostrom, *Governing the Commons:* (op. cit.).

[70] Personal communication, Chris Davies, MEP, EU Commission (Fact Finding Mission with the Irish Environmental Network). (Oct 2013).

[71] Ronald Dworkin, "What is a Good Life?", *New York Review of Books*, (2011).

the life of every individual.[72] Taylor's expansion locates him far from the narrow egotism that, paradoxically, nevertheless recognises that the survival of any recognisably civilised version of the human species relies on a functioning ecosystem. His approach is tempered only by his priority principles that form a weighting system to balance the different interests affected by each decision.

The debate between the "selfish gene" approach of Hardin, and the egalitarian ethic approach of Sen, Commoner et al., presages the concerns that occupied Taylor when he put forward his egalitarian, biocentric ethic. It illustrates the ideological divide between the broad inclusiveness of Hardin's concerns that motivate him to narrow who is morally considerable, and the more traditional concerns with social justice first, and environmental justice arising as a secondary consideration. Taylor's attempt to sidestep this divide by prioritising the entire ecological community may not have convinced the pragmatists or the idealists, but it was a revolutionary way to design the problem.

Narrow anthropocentrism to sentientism

Basing moral principles on rational grounds has unexpected and sometimes undesirable consequences in practice.[73] An egalitarian approach to ethics in general, and to environmental ethics in particular, hits other ideological walls, too. There is the lengthy debate between how current human (moral) agents might include potential future members of the species within this equation. Hardin argues that whatever we do to ensure survival indiscriminately for humans now will impact negatively on the future. Sen and Commoner argue the opposite: by improving conditions for present humans, future human and environmental problems will be more easily addressed. Healthier human populations now, treated more fairly, will be more likely to address population issues,

---

[72] Amartya Sen, "Population: Delusion and Reality" reprinted in David Keller (ed.), *Environmental Ethics: The Big Questions* (op. cit.); Barry Commoner, "How Poverty Breeds Overpopulation", reprinted in David Keller (ed.), (op. cit.).

[73] The classic example is the argument associated with Immanuel Kant extolling a universal principle of not lying. Yet in particular conditions (the most cited is the instance of a Jew hiding from the Nazis) there may be highly undesirable consequences to following such a maxim. An example in the context of environmental ethics is that of the "carrying capacity" of certain land areas for different species: on such a rationally-based understanding, the carrying capacity of the land for the human species is a small fraction of the existing population, with obvious undesirable implications for species size reduction strategies.

the single highest risk factor for the future of both human and all living systems.[74]

From an anthropocentric perspective, we are bound inevitably to witness the world from behind species-specific spectacles and our interests are primarily in what is good for us, first individually, then collectively. If we look after the world for moral reasons, these are ultimately because we are protecting what provides for our own (and that is the ultimate) good. Therefore stewardship is the primary anthropocentric position, laid out by Aristotle ("nature has made all things for man") and extended through the various religious incarnations (the idea that "the environment, as God's creation, must be respected") to contemporary times.

The problem with this extended anthropocentrism (expounded most clearly by Peter Singer in *The Expanding Circle*), is that it is still informed by a hierarchical view of the world.[75] As Holmes Rolston III puts it, "humans are of the utmost value in the sense that they are the ecosystem's most sophisticated product. They have the highest per capita intrinsic value of any life form supported by the system".[76] The problem lies in the circularity of the argument: to judge the worth of any other organism from the point of view of what is worthwhile to oneself merely confirms one's own bias of what is valuable. Making "honorary persons" of dolphins or chimpanzees on the basis that they have capacities that closely resemble those held by humans is still human-centric. Human functioning relies on various sets of capabilities, but it makes no more sense to judge a bat's capacity to sing arias than it does a human's ability to fly through a cave in the dark and yet that is exactly what sentientism does. It is still an attempt to give prime concern to capacities and capabilities which are, by their very nature, anthropocentric.

---

[74] Population increase alone is much less significant as a factor of anthropogenic impact than the accompanying increase in demand for material resources per capita, fuelled by the ideological narrative that accumulating material wealth is good.

[75] Peter Singer, *The Expanding Circle: Ethics, Evolution, and Moral Progress* (op. cit.). Robin Attfield has laid out the spectrum from anthropocentrism to ecocentrism, via sentientism, zoocentrism and biocentrism, more comprehensively than any other author I found on the topic. He has written several overviews of the field, most comprehensively Robin Attfield, *Environmental Ethics: An Overview for the Twenty-First Century.* Cambridge, UK; Malden, MA: Polity Press, (2003).

[76] Holmes Rolston III, quoted in David Keller (ed.), *Environmental Ethics: The Big Questions* (op. cit.): 12.

Anthropocentrism is premised on a rational expansion of our selfishness to include reciprocity, figuring that if we give, we will in turn get. Yet the centre cannot hold, in this scenario, because, as Dworkin illustrated, morality should not depend on any benefit that being moral might bring.[77] There is a moral vacuum at the heart of any ideological argument for founding an ethic on egoism. There must be independent reasons for reciprocating that do not depend on egoistic benefits or the claim that this is a moral stance collapses.

It is not just the short-sightedness of the "own best interests" approach that is the problem. Recent biological research suggests that the survival interests of every holon, whether a cell, a body, a society, a species, an ecosystem, or a whole living planet, must be balanced in the mutual consistency of the whole and all its parts.[78] Egoistic morality is viable if tempered by the survival interests of local and global communities.[79] The problem arises because we rely on there being a centre that is qualitatively unique, yet the only evidence for this is couched in an ideology that depends upon outmoded metaphysical metaphors of a largely Newtonian nature: the persistent reliance on body/soul, human/natural divisions in the general imagination. The grounds for claiming species superiority are somewhat undermined by the best scientific explanation we have for our existence here: evolutionary theory. This theory makes it clear that the human species is a latecomer, and peripheral to living existence as a whole.

When sentience is no longer the key to value

Viewing life as merely instrumental to human flourishing risks a reversion to religious-style exploitation of living systems by the back door, as it were. There is clearly something Berkeleyan in the argument that value is only present when human valuers are in the room to do the valuing. Various thought experiments have been devised to refute this view and show how

---

[77] This also clearly reminds us of John Rawls' approach to a just society: in choosing what is right, we need to be blind to what is good for us, specifically, and therefore the best way to approach a just society is behind a veil of ignorance of our own conditions. See John Rawls, *A Theory of Justice, Revised Edition*, Cambridge, Mass.: Belknap Press of Harvard University Press, (1999)

[78] I am indebted to Ronnie Hawkins, former adjunct professor at the University of Central Florida, for this idea. (Personal email communication via Philos-L, 2010).

[79] Ronnie Hawkins, "Introduction: Beyond Nature/Culture Dualism: Let"s Try Co-Evolution Instead of "Control"", *Ethics and the Environment*, 11 (2006): 1–11.

non-human living systems might be envisaged to have value, regardless of whether or not there was a human there to value them.

"The last man" experiment by Richard Sylvan (Routley) suggested that if there was a last man, and a last tree, and the latter had the capacity for reproduction, it would be morally unjustifiable to chop it down, even if there would be no future humans to enjoy or benefit from it.[80] Therefore, Sylvan concludes, value resides in living organisms, regardless of whether they know it or not, and it is not just a quality conferred by the human perceiver. This argument depends on an intuitionist notion of what is "good" or valuable. However, those intuitions are grounded in the biological conditions that benefit organisms. Taylor's grounds for shifting the centre were couched in reasoning that other organisms had conditions that benefit them, but this foreshadowing of a shift in focus from anthropocentrism is useful because it raises the possibility that value is "out there", rather than "in here". The proviso, from Taylor's point of view, is that value depends on what is in the interest of organisms, or, potentially, systems. This idea is extended in the next chapter in considering the possibility that systems have conditions that are good for them.

Humans may be doomed to perceive existence through human eyes, but this does not imply that we are unable empathetically to imagine life from elsewhere. Rather than considering humans as the "monarchs" of the evolutionary process, the acknowledgement of our evolutionary history entangles us. Human intelligence and capacity for creative, artistic and technological design enable us to relate to existence in a way no other organism can. Our pain and suffering become, in some sense, translatable into the pain and suffering of any organism that pursues avoidance of annihilation. Trees or other plants may have nothing we can recognise as conscious awareness. However, it is still obvious that wantonly or unnecessarily destroying something that actively avoids annihilation is, in some sense at least, unjustifiable.

Being human includes the capacity to step outside the "I", to imagine life from elsewhere regardless of whether or not this capacity is exercised or explored in most cases. This is the capacity that must be exercised,

---

[80] Richard Sylvan (Routley), "Is There a Need for a New, an Environmental Ethic?" Proceedings of the XVth World Congress of Philosophy, 1, (1973): 205-210. G. E. Moore made a similar argument in his *Principia Ethica,* and responses to this have included questioning whether or not humans have a biological propensity to favour conditions that are in their survival interests, which they, therefore, find "beautiful" or "worthwhile" compared to conditions that are not in their interests.

however, if a biocentric view is to emerge. The stretch to imagine what life is like from another point of view does not, and cannot, require that we leave our own experience. Yet recognising that each form of life is driven by evolutionary necessity to avoid death for as long as possible, through autopoiesis, the process of self-organisation that defines living systems, is enough to give us an idea of what life is like from elsewhere. Living individuals are primed, evolutionarily, to reproduce, if that is possible, just as we are (although cultural systems have made it possible to reinterpret this priming through, for instance, the urge to produce a piece of art or literature). Looking at conditions from the point of view of another living organism makes it possible to perceive the conditions that benefit, and those that harm, particular manifestations of living existence. From the biocentric point of view, all living organisms have conditions they value by virtue of having conditions that benefit them.

The problems with biocentrism have already been touched upon: individual organisms are interdependent but also in competition; some individual organisms have lives so transient, in human terms, that they have barely come into existence before they are decomposing. Biocentric egalitarianism faces the same problems that egalitarian ethics faced earlier: moral repugnance as we reduce life to the bare functionality of systems or to indifferent interchange of billions of micro-organisms for a single elephant. Yet moving to include all life at least dethrones the claims to human superiority that underpin anthropocentrism. The idea of agency within this biocentric view rests on an evolutionary understanding of human existence and therefore the individualistic, atomistic understanding could well be revised to better take that into account.

Aldo Leopold and his student, J. Baird Callicott, decentred humans, and even individuals, locating value, instead, in relationships. Ecocentrism is the narrative in which the flourishing of the entire ecosystem comes into focus. The success or failure of the enterprise depends on seeing what that system needs for its self-maintenance (in ecocentric terms, the integrity of the community).

Ecocentrism faces the serious problem of showing how a relationship, rather than an entity (an individual or a species) can have value. Relationships, even within the *oikos*, or home, are not themselves centres, but interactions. Harley Cahen in "Against the Moral Considerability of Ecosystems" concludes:

> Currently, mainstream ecological and evolutionary theory is individualistic. From such a theory it follows that the apparent

goals of ecosystems are mere byproducts and, as such, cannot ground moral considerability.[81]

Cahen is right: it is not possible to ground moral considerability in the relationships that emerge between different points of interest in the matrix of an ecosystem. However, this is not because particular relationships are not "good" or indeed "bad" for those points of interest. As I will argue in detail in the third chapter, talking of "the good" of systems requires revision, just as talking about a "centre" requires revision. Regardless of where the teleology of systems lies, it is still possible to talk of "the good" of systems (in the same vein that Taylor talks of "the good" of organisms). There is still ground, although it is no longer a moral one, for considering what would benefit, or harm, systems, including ecosystems.

Biocentrism locates the centre quite clearly in each individual (something that only becomes problematic when I begin to question the integrity of the idea of individual identity). Ecocentrism is already in trouble: there is no centre of value to begin with. The integrity of the community implies that there is an end point (at which all is in balance and harmony) to which we can aim. This state is unachievable in the dynamism of activity through time when ecosystems are always dying in some respect and being born in some other, and Taylor makes it clear early on that he does not believe that the idea of a "balance of nature" is a useful paradigm:

> Whatever elements of equilibrium and stability may hold among the species-populations of an ecosystem *at a particular time*, these must be seen as general features resulting from natural selection as it occurs among individuals competing in their attempts to survive and reproduce ...[82]

In other words, rather than considering the evolving ecosphere as having an inherent stability, it is more accurate to consider it to be in a state of dynamic transience. Still, this system may be relatively less stable when compared to systems that lack any kind of autopoiesis or self-organisation. In a similar vein, it is inaccurate to consider evolved systems as progressive, in the sense of proceeding towards higher states. Certainly,

---

[81] Harley Cahen, "Against the Moral Considerability of Ecosystems," *Environmental Ethics* 10, no. 3 (1988): 195–216. See also Stanley and Barbara Salthe, "Ecosystem Moral Considerability: A Reply to Cahen," *Environmental Ethics* 11, (1989): 355-361.

[82] Taylor, *Respect for Nature* (op. cit.): 8.

evolution has developed in the direction of increasing complexity for a minority of systems, but mainly, evolution progresses by just going on through time. Both harmony and evolutionary progress, therefore, are ideas that need revising if we are to understand both organisms and ecosystems, and therefore what kind of response we make to them.

Having said all that, it needs to be acknowledged that both ecocentrism and biocentrism are progressive imaginaries in the sense that they take into account a more accurate understanding of evolutionary systems. They both hold that things other than humans can have particular conditions that are "good" for them, even when those other living systems have no way of consciously processing information. You do not have to "know" in the same way that human consciousness "knows" what is good for you, if you are a tree Plants may respond sensitively to avoid drought, toxins, and whatever else is likely to cause their demise even if they do not "know" in the human sense. They certainly grow more roots where there are more nutrients, grow more branches and leaves where there is sunlight, and so on, implying that something more than mere reaction is going on.[83]

Conclusion

I have sought to show that ideological, or righteous, thinking abounds in environmental ethics, not simply at the political level, but in the narratives that underlie the different theoretical approaches. At this more fundamental level, the ground on which responses are built is fragmented and divided on the basis of commitments to narratives that still contain unexamined elements. This has led to a divergence, and entrenchment, of attitudes that further delays or even blocks our capacity to develop convergent theories, and practices, in response to the ecological emergency. More recent moves to decentre moral consideration from humans to a broader array of organisms, or even systems, have certainly opened up some of the previously unexamined themes of our narratives to scrutiny. Yet there are still features that we hold on to, in spite of our changing understanding of the human condition, including the narrative that human responsibility is something separate from physical action. In the next chapter, I will hone in on a revision of this view to show that an ethically neutral understanding of the human context for responsibility can emerge.

---

[83] Pollan, Michael, "The Intelligent Plant," *The New Yorker*, December 23, (2013); Hall, Matthew, "Plant Autonomy and Human-Plant Ethics," *Environmental Ethics* 31, no. 2 (2009): 169–181.

Chapter Two

From Respect for Nature
to the Question of Agency

Introduction

In the last chapter, I worked to set out the scenario, to show how the field of environmental ethics still leaves unquestioned the idea that human responsibility for the ecological emergency is based on a (mental) decision to carry out a (physical) act. In a sense, therefore, this idea implies that the human capacity to respond, and therefore human moral agency, is independent of natural, probabilistic laws. This is the first key idea that I think requires revision if we are to come to a better understanding of our capacity for responsibility. The second is the notion that we are required to become an ideal person (or agent) on the one hand, or even to move towards an ideal, or ideologically pure position, and on the other, that our relationships with both other humans, and other naturally evolved organisms can or should become ideally harmonious. While this may sound as though we should be content with the way things are, it is actually a call for reflection on the nature of idealism, and ideological thinking. Before I tackle that idea, however, I want to set out in more detail how such thinking has been justified in the field of environmental ethics by looking at one particular approach to the issue of how we should see ourselves in the context of natural systems. Finally, I want to argue that we can attune to compassion, and that, relatedly, there is a "good" of systems that we can recognise and respond to from a perspective of compassionate attunement. I will endeavour to explain what I mean by this in the next chapter.

As I outlined in the previous chapter, my approach in considering how to respond to the ecological emergency began with a close reading of key aspects of Paul Taylor's theory of "respect for nature" set out in his book of that name.[1] It is to Taylor's thesis that I turn now as a framework for considering the steps taken so far to revise our self-understanding in the context of environmental ethics. His rational, analytical framework is informed by an Anglo-American philosophical approach. He was a philosopher in the Kantian, enlightenment tradition, basing his arguments on reason, science and humanism. His thesis is based on an evolutionary, physicalist explanation of the human condition. His theory deserves a much broader audience. If even a few people are minded to read his book, and consider his arguments, as a result of my work, I will feel I have done him some justice. However, thirdly, I argue that his own premise, that humans are indubitably a part of, and inherent in, nature has implications that require a much more radical reappraisal of the relationship between human responsibility, moral agency and ideology. While he posited an ethical response as the accepted narrative for responding to the ecological emergency, my own research took me beyond ideology, and beyond ethics.

Taylor's contribution to the spectrum

Taylor's enquiry begins by locating the moral action and its viewpoint within the human organism.[2] That is, he offers two categorisations: moral agents are a subsection of the human species and moral agents are such because they alone decide how to live.[3] Human responsibility (the capacity humans have to decide to respond according to an underlying set of beliefs or values), and therefore moral agency, is clearly related to the capacity intrinsic in Taylor's idea of personhood: the ability to self-reflect, to choose, and to act on that choice.

Personhood belongs are all those who "give direction to their lives on the basis of their own values."[4] This gives a person, and indeed a moral agent, a considerable amount of liberty: she can choose what to value and she can choose what to do, based on what she values. Yet if she understands

---

[1] Paul W Taylor, *Respect for Nature.* (op. cit.)

[2] One revision of Taylor's depiction of human organisms that is not directly relevant to this study, but that I think may make my own position easier to understand, is the idea that we are human animals, in the way that Eric Olson describes us. Eric Olson, "An Argument for Animalism", in R. Martin and J. Barresi (eds) *Personal Identity*, Oxford: Blackwell, (2003): 318–34.

[3] Taylor (op. cit.): 14; 48.

[4] (Ibid.): 33.

what, rationally, she should do, her liberty is, in practice, considerably constrained.

Reconsidering the relationship: moral consideration and responsibility

Those affected by the (rational) moral agent fall into two categories of "moral patients", in Taylor's view. Other moral agents also have the capacity to deliberate, and therefore the relationship between them and the agent is always, in some sense, reciprocal: agents respond to agency with further agency. On the other hand, are reactors, who cannot respond, because they have no awareness of what is going on. Reactivity is, therefore, passive, in the sense that it happens automatically. This category includes other living organisms, or communities of living organisms who, without awareness, react to the action as it is taking place. Taylor does not extend the category beyond the living, but it would be perfectly justifiable to consider including water, air and earth systems, since these underlie and support the existence of living systems, and react (as carbon emissions, for instance, increase the amount of carbon dioxide in the atmosphere) simply as a matter of obeying the (probabilistic) laws of nature.

In contrast to the idea of "moral patients" reacting to events involuntarily, human beings as moral agents in Taylor's sense are of a different order. They have free will: they can choose how to act. They also have the benefit of imagination as a prerequisite for action: they can shift perspective and imagine existence from any other living individual's viewpoint. This means that moral agents can imagine what is beneficial or "good for" both sets of moral patients, and even for living communities.[5] Such entities have "a kind of value that belongs to them inherently."[6] Just as a person is not merely useful or valuable as a means to an end, so a living organism or community of living organisms cannot be reduced to their worth as utility.

I will come back to unpick these contrasting categories in some detail, since this forms the core of my own question: is the distinction between

---

[5] Taylor recognised that his theory had failed to take into account the lives of micro-organisms and in later versions, for instance in the "Preface" to the Chinese edition of *Respect for Nature* (2004), Taylor made it clear that he had revised his theory to take into account not only organisms but also species, ecosystems, or life-communities within ecosystems (see especially, "Holism As Well As Individualism" in the "Preface": 2).

[6] Taylor, *Respect for Nature* (op. cit.).

humans as agents and all else justified, given what we now know about evolutionary theory, and physical systems? For now, however, in continuing to describe Taylor's theory, the next important step is to recognise this very capacity humans have for understanding evolutionary theory. It is precisely this, a capacity that draws a line between humans and other organisms in terms of cognitive ability, that allows them to view the living world in its own terms and also *therefore* demands that humans, responding as moral agents, practice species impartiality: "No bias in favour of some over others is acceptable."[7]

Taylor makes specific reference to Judeo-Christian "mythology" that posits a hierarchy of species, "with humans at the top". Evolutionary biology, however, is blind, a process in which species branch out from a universal common ancestor in any direction that, by happy accident, allows them to avoid annihilation. This process has no direction, no end, no goal, and no one route is inherently better than any other. It is simply a matter of some happy accidents allowing survival, while others, for reasons as trivial as bad timing, lead to the cul-de-sac of extinction. Recognising that all living organisms are driven by forces that push them to avoid drought or toxins, for example and to grow towards, or flourish in conditions that enhance survivability, is a recognition of "the good", or inherent worth, all, if (and we will come back to this) survival is a "good".

This capacity to reason that not just humans have, in Taylor's terms, inherent worth dissolves the human/not-human dichotomy that anthropocentrism relies on. It also makes it inevitable that reasonable people, as moral agents, will follow the rationale that a recognition of "the good" of other organisms implies: human agents will extend moral consideration to them (paving the way, in Taylor's terms, for an ethic of respect).

After all, living existence is not a passive backdrop providing resources for the benefit of active, self-conscious, deliberative moral agents. It is a kaleidoscope of teleological centres of value, pursuing often conflicting sets of "goods", emerging from their evolutionary history.

An anthropocentric approach recognises only one moral realm – the human – and other categories as morally relevant only instrumentally to human, moral agents. In contrast, Taylor proposes that we consider there to be no moral difference between humans, as organisms that can perceive themselves, and organisms with no capacity for self-perception,

---

[7] (Ibid.): 45.

or self-reflection. The former are aware that they have interests in things while the latter have things that are in their interest, though they do not know it, but both have conditions that benefit, or harm, them.[8]

There is one further feature of this method of understanding moral considerability and its relationship with having interests, or "goods", to which I will return because it has important implications for human responses to the ecological emergency. That is that humans (and perhaps members of some other species) can have an interest in something (say, eating particular foods, getting enough exercise, keeping secure from threats of violence, warmth and shelter, and so on) and nevertheless fail to pursue those interests. There is a difference, in this case, between pursuing interests that are in one's interest, and interests that one is interested in, but that are evidently harmful. Taylor characterises being able to distinguish this difference in terms of strength, or weakness, of (mental) will.[9] You can either choose to follow through on your rational decisions, or you cannot.[10] That is the exercise of moral agency, or not, in Taylor's terms, and it represents a widely-held, largely unreflective view of free will. We, as human agents, can choose to do the right thing, but whether we do or not depends firstly on our access to sufficient information, because the right thing is also the rational thing to do, and secondly, on our strength of will. This, along with the idea of moral patients reacting involuntarily, while moral agents choose what to do, is the view of moral agency, and therefore of free will, that I will challenge below.

Three degrees of human impact

Moral agency entails, for Taylor, a kind of "noblesse oblige". The capacity to choose is linked to the capacity to shift perspective. It is because human moral agents have the capacity to understand that all living organisms

---

[8] (Ibid.) "Moral concern is the ability and disposition to take the standpoint of animals and plants and look at the world from the perspective of their good": 203.

[9] Taylor never explicitly labels this weakness of will as a mental or otherwise non-physical characteristic, but he does talk of two aspects of character, the deliberative and the practical, and in both cases he refers, in turn, to "dispositions", "strength of character", "powers of will", "self-mastery" and self-control" all of which imply mental states over which the moral agent is believed to have some level of control. (See Taylor (Ibid.): 199).

[10] This is sometimes called "reasons-responsiveness" and can be weak, moderate, or strong. See, for instance, Todd R. Long, "Moderate Reasons-Responsiveness, Moral Responsibility, and Manipulation", in J. K. Campbell, M. O'Rourke and D. Shier (eds), *Freedom and Determinism*, MIT, (2004).

have "goods" that they pursue, for the same (evolutionary, biological) reasons that humans have goods that they pursue, that this elicits the response to "respect nature". Having human consciousness, and being able to "see" from other viewpoints, elicits a "moral concern" for other organisms. However, this is not because being human marks a particular kind of existence out as being of higher value, or, if it has a higher value, it is precisely in its capacity to choose a response, to act appropriately on its awareness. An appropriate response depends upon the strength of character of the moral agent, but Taylor maintains that above all, this is an exercise in authenticity, in integrating the response with the recognition.

Exercising her agency is "good for" the moral agent because it ensures that she fulfils the capacity she has to live "the kind of life one *would* place supreme value on *if* one were fully rational, autonomous, and enlightened."[11] However, she cannot fulfil the conditions for living this kind of life without considering organisms other than human individuals as ends in themselves. In Taylor's impartial, egalitarian view, the human agent must consider each individual as equally valid, since the evolutionary, biological branching that has given rise to their being where they are was random: there is no hierarchy of interests. Moral patients may not know what is good for them, but they nevertheless have conditions that will benefit, and conditions that harm them, just as human agents do. I will use this idea of "good for" as the basis of my own argument that if there are conditions which are inherently "good for" organisms, or even systems, this implies that "good" as a quality, or value, in some sense at least is inherent in the universe.

Before engaging in a critique of Taylor's view of agency, and by extension, free will, and then taking a different slant on the idea of "the good" of systems (and organisms), I want to mention a final area he focuses on. That is, he divides the class of moral patients into categories: wild nature, "the bioculture" (farms, zoos, genetically modified organisms, golf courses and parks, all that has been heavily influenced by human interference), and human-to-human ethical relationships. His focus in the original edition of *Respect for Nature* was firmly on the first, on what he called "nature", but what I might more specifically define as the evolved systems, including living systems, of the planet that have not been impacted by human activity. He warns that unless we curb the "dominant trends" - over-exploitation of resources, a cultural acceptance that more

---

[11] Taylor, *Respect for Nature* (op. cit.): 64. Taylor contrasts this with other bases for the "Human Good": "human flourishing", "self-actualisation" and "true happiness".

stuff equals more happiness, treating wild places as a human playground, there for our entertainment - we will see wilderness "turned into a vast artifact."[12]

His three categories are not strictly separable, even in Taylor's view, but I would contend that the categorisations collapse for other reasons. No region of the planet is unaffected by human impact, which collapses the first two. In Taylor's terms, there is no justification for treating human to human ethical relationships as different in principle from human to non-human ethical relationships (although in practice we are, inevitably, more focused on human-to-human relationships) which collapses the first two and the third.

Taylor is worth paying close attention to. His importance lies in his challenge to the anthropocentric narratives that have allowed humans to justify their turning the natural environment into just the kind of vast artefact he warned against, a process that continues to threaten the integrity of systems to this day.[13] For Taylor, the problem lay in the hierarchical view of organisms – humans at the top of the evolutionary ladder – that is still pervasive, and leads to the idea that humans are particularly privileged when it comes to ethical consideration.[14] Other, earlier attempts at challenging anthropocentrism met with difficulties of dilution (when the circle of considerability was expanded) or of definition (the conflation of different senses of "intrinsic value", for instance).[15] Taylor, by contrast, gave us a rigorous, step-by-step argument, that led from a recognition of the evolution of all living organisms, to the concept of "respect for nature" by human moral agents, not as a logical, but as a rational, necessity (as a matter of "supervenience").

---

[12] (Ibid.): 5.

[13] "Perhaps most remarkably of all, humans, who only represent roughly 0.5% of the total heterotrophe biomass on Earth, appropriate for their use something around one third of the total amount of net primary production on land." Andrew S. Goudie, *The Human Impact on the Natural Environment: Past, Present, and Future* Oxford: Wiley-Blackwell (2009): 296.

[14] Paul W Taylor, "The Ethics of Respect for Nature", in David Keller (ed.) *Environmental Ethics: The Big Questions*, (op. cit.): 176.

[15] John O'Neill, "The Varieties of Intrinsic Value", in David Keller (ed.) *Environmental Ethics: The Big Questions*: 120-129.

Taylor compared

Taylor's biocentrism fits between that proposed by Robin Attfield, on the one hand, and James Sterba's, on the other.[16] To put it crudely, Attfield's biocentrism is consequentialist, and non-egalitarian, while Sterba's is pluralistic. Attfield is concerned to develop an all-inclusive ethical code which would guide us in our responding not only to the ecological emergency but also to the problems we have in human relationships, problems such as injustice and unfairness in the distribution of wealth, violence and greed, population issues and the like. Relatedly, Attfield sees the capacities for self-consciousness of most humans and some nonhumans as superior to those of organisms that are either conscious but not self-conscious, or neither.

Attfield, like others, dismisses Taylor's biocentric egalitarianism as impracticable.[17] He also questions whether or not "respect for nature" is really an ethic, because it fails to consider sufficiently the conditions of autonomous beings (persons) who require extra moral signification, and its priority principles do not flow from the egalitarianism on which it is based. He says, instead, that Sterba (a deontologist) in "A Biocentrist Strikes Back" and Attfield himself, present viable arguments for biocentrism.

Sterba's concern is to show how a pluralistic ethic might be developed that is situationally responsive, prioritising different values depending on the circumstance[18] This is important because while Sterba, like Taylor, acknowledges that there is no inherent ground for prioritising human over other interests, working out how to prioritise interests in practice, based on the principled approach that both take, remains a problem for both thinkers. Sterba's attempt is perhaps more ambitious than Taylor's, since he works to create an ethic that combines individualistic biocentrism and holistic ecocentrism, along with a reconciliation of environmental ethics

---

[16] Robin Attfield. "Biocentrism, Moral Standing, and Moral Significance," *Philosophica*, 39, 1, (1987): 47–58; Attfield. "Biocentric Consequentialism: Pluralism and the 'Minimax Implication': A Reply to Alan Carter", *Utilitas* 15, 1, (2003): 76–91; Attfield, "Biocentric Consequentialism and Value-Pluralism: A Response to Alan Carter." *Utilitas* 17, 1, (2005): 85–92; James P. Sterba, *From Rationality to Equality.* Oxford: Oxford University Press, 2013; Sterba, "A Biocentrist Strikes Back", *Environmental Ethics* 20, no. 4 (1998): 361-376.

[17] Karann Durland, "The Prospects of a Viable Biocentric Egalitarianism", *Environmental Ethics*, 30 (2008): 401–16.

[18] See, for instance, the "conflict resolution principles" that Sterba discusses in "Kantians and Utilitarians and the Moral Status of NonHuman Life" in David Keller (ed.) *Environmental Ethics: The Big Questions*, (op. cit.): 184.

with related fields. Taylor, on the other hand, fits his environmental ethic into an existing framework that contains human-to-human ethics, based on treating humans as ends-in-themselves.

Returning briefly to Attfield's approach, this could be open to the same kinds of criticisms that political emphases on universal rights meet: that they are in fact the impositions of a particular culturally embedded set of values and belief systems which ignore certain (generally the global South's) histories and values.[19] Thus, the approach smacks of imperialism. Alan Carter calls Attfield's position "inegalitarian biocentrism", but Attfield maintains that he has simply returned the debate to the field where ethics is normally discussed and that he is not inegalitarian with respect to humanity.[20] Yet Attfield maintains that he remains a biocentrist, calling his position "biocentric consequentialism", in spite of his hierarchical view of humans.[21]

The second approach, the one taken by Sterba, to develop a pluralistic ethic, risks the accusation that there are too many potential areas for conflict between principles that attempt to honour, on the one hand, human interests, and, on the other, non-human ones. There are, of course, millions of instances of such conflicts, but in one account of his ethic, Sterba gives the real-life example of Nepalese subsistence farmers making

---

[19] The idea of granting "rights", first to humans, and then, by extension, to other organisms, systems and so on, is a history grounded firmly in the philosophical and cultural traditions of the global North, from Greece, on. To illustrate the extent of bias in how rights were exercised, see, for instance, Carole Pateman and Charles Wade Mills, *Contract and Domination*, Cambridge, UK; Malden, MA: Polity Press (2007).

[20] This is difficult to reconcile with Attfield's own words, since he claims, on the one hand, that "complicated and sophisticated" capacities (such as those belonging to humans) do not automatically take precedence over the capacities of less complex creatures when it comes to developing their good, but that they do take precedence when there is a conflict of interest. "In short, Attfield's inegalitarian biocentric consequentialism may well enjoin us to bring into existence billions and billions of humans with their capacities developed ever so slightly in preference to the existence of many other species – a bizarre conclusion indeed for a supposedly environmental ethic." Alan Carter, "Inegalitarian Biocentric Consequentialism, the Minimax Implication and Multidimensional Value Theory: A Brief Proposal for a New Direction in Environmental Ethics", *Utilitas*, 17 (2005): 66.

[21] Expounded in Robin Attfield, *Environmental Ethics: An Overview for the Twenty-First Century* (op. cit.), where biocentric consequentialism is defended against criticisms from Alan Carter relating to population, quality of life and environmental sensitivity.

incursions into a national park (Chitwan National Park) and endangering, in the process, the survival of a number of threatened and endangered species, including the Bengal tiger and the one-horned rhinoceros.[22] Sterba proposes that we ask other humans who are existing above subsistence level to provide for the Nepalese subsistence farmers in some way (he does not make clear how exactly) and guardians of the endangered species "should use force against such rich people rather than against poor people."[23] Quite how this force might be exercised without further endangering the national park and its species is not at all explicit, and Sterba admits that he recognises the practical difficulties with getting rich people to "make the necessary transfers" so that poor people are not "led to prey on endangered species in order to survive."[24]

Taylor and the limits of reason

Taylor's work to discover a principle-based ethic that is practical enough to allow for the prioritisation of some values in some circumstances, and others in different ones, was an attempt to overcome the shortcomings of both the alternatives. Unfortunately, Taylor's delineation of an environmental ethic from one which applies to humans alone does not seem entirely justifiable, by his own reckoning: if we have an equal worth with all organisms, then we need to bring our ethical codes in line with that understanding. This means that we need to revise existing ethical codes so that they reflect a recognition that in fundamental and morally significant ways (because of our common evolutionary heritage) we are no better than, and deserve no more consideration than, other organisms. If we are significantly different (and Taylor maintains that human-to-human ethics can coexist with his environmental ethic), then human interests

---

[22] See Sterba "Kantians and Utilitarians and the Moral Status of NonHuman Life" (op. cit.): 185.

[23] Sterba, (Ibid.): 186.

[24] The evidence suggests that enforcing a ban on poaching or killing alone is not particularly successful as a strategy, but that political will, a reduction in international conflict, tourism and, to a surprising extent, changes in the behaviour of the endangered species themselves, combine to give more successful outcomes. (In global terms, of course, tourism requires energy inputs from elsewhere (particularly for the energy-demanding costs of flying) but these are thought to be substantially less significant than the energy costs of military aircraft during war). See Neil H. Carter and others, "Assessing Spatiotemporal Changes in Tiger Habitat across Different Land Management Regimes", *Ecosphere*, 4 (2013).

need to be clearly segregated from those of other organisms, and they are not in Taylor's thesis, nor is it clear how they ever could be.

Taylor evidently wanted to ensure that existing obligations based on our cultural development were honoured. Not to do so would be to threaten cultural stability and integrity. For pragmatic reasons, then, rather than just for rational ones, it does, after all, make sense to have a human-to-human ethic and an environmental ethic that dovetail together in the relatively coherent way that Taylor proposes, but only if an ethical system is necessary in the first place, which, I will argue, it is not.

Taylor's concern in the 1986 version of his theory was to show that because all organisms that are alive have inherent worth (as opposed to the two alternatives he considers: intrinsic value and intrinsic worth), they are not instruments of human good. It is the "life force", as Sterba lightheartedly puts it in his essay, which gives certain conditions "value" for individual living organisms.[25] As I mentioned above, Taylor's ethic applies to the sphere of natural communities of living organisms that have evolved (largely) without human intervention. He fully recognises, and explicitly states, that this ethic has to dovetail with a human-to-human ethic, and his purpose is to develop grounds (his five "priority principles") on which to perform this dovetailing. This means that there may be circumstances in which the ethic of respect for nature modifies the dominance of human considerations, given that humans, as organisms, are only as relevant as any other living individual of any other species.

Taylor's biocentric approach is rooted firmly in evolutionary theory: humans are latecomers "... while we (*Homo sapiens*) cannot do without

---

[25] James P. Sterba, "A Biocentrist Strikes Back" (op. cit.). I am sure that Sterba is being lighthearted because otherwise we are back in the problematic realm of attributing to a mysterious, non-physical quality ("the life force") some guiding sentience and this leads straight back to a dualistic separation of something non-physical from mechanistic, inert material structures it operates on. Sterba's account is comparable, therefore, with Christopher Stone's conclusions on the idea that we use the word "want" or "need" in quite obvious and unambiguous ways in association with other organisms, even when we do not necessarily attribute a knowledge of those wants or needs to the plants, animals or systems in question: see, for instance, " I am sure I can judge with more certainty ... whether or not my lawn wants ... water, than the Attorney General can judge whether and when United States ... needs... to take an appeal from an adverse judgment by a lower court." Christopher D. Stone "Should Trees Have Standing? Toward Legal Rights for Natural Objects" reprinted in Louis Pojman and Paul Pojman (eds) *Environmental Ethics: Readings in Theory and Application,* (op. cit.): 242.

them (all other living things) they can do without us".[26] Given this, he
sought to relocate an ethical approach in our evolutionary biology. The
risk was that he might be committing the naturalistic fallacy:

> Is our biological nature at all relevant to the choices we must
> make as moral agents, and, if it is, in what ways is it relevant?[27]

What is morally relevant in the choices we make as rational agents? The
forces that drive us to survive (roughly equivalent to what Sterba terms
"the life force" in shorthand) are translated, through rationality, into a
motivation to live at "optimal well-being".[28] "Our normative guides" as to
whether or not we are doing so are "survival and physical health". Taylor
admits that we are dependent upon "contingencies and accidents, forces
and processes" and that this puts us in the same existential situation as all
other organisms. And yes, he claims, we still have the ability to act as
moral agents.[29] Even though this gives us the freedom that other living
organisms lack, for Taylor, our agency has the potential to be constrained
by the very capacity that it emerges from: our conscious awareness of our
place in the world, including our ability to understand what this place is.
For Taylor, this capacity to realise what kind of creatures we are, alongside
our ability to understand the commonality this gives us with other living
creatures, creates a context for one reasonable response: respect.

Taylor observes that we have ethical codes that we apply across the
human board because we realise that all human individuals are an "end in
themselves". This means that we respect individual humans' efforts to
pursue their own optimal well-being. If we then add to this the
understanding that all other living individual organisms have conditions
that they pursue, that are good for them, then for consistency's sake, we
must agree to extend the respect that we show to the efforts made by all
other organisms too. Respect is the only attitude we could adopt towards
the biotic community that would be coherent with our existing rationale
for human ethics.

---

[26] Paul Taylor, *Respect for Nature* (op. cit.): 100, 114.

[27] (Ibid.): 49.

[28] (Ibid.): 103.

[29] (Ibid.): 104.

Taylor and moral realism

Taylor observes early on in his work that we cannot "read off" moral norms from a certain way of conceiving of the order of living things. We must engage, rather, in what he calls "ethical enquiry". Morality is not "out there", in other words: it is in what we do with the information "in here".[30]

His reasoning that we can root ethics in our membership of the living community stems from the idea that we, like it, evolved and therefore are a part of that living community. As humans, we have the capacity to understand this, just as we have the capacity to organise our knowledge of the world into internally coherent arrangements, narratives that are self-consistent, and form a framework that shapes how we respond to our experience. Taylor's argument is that it is not this capacity (to understand, to organise or conceive a framework) that is primarily of value to humans, however. What our acknowledgement that we are members of the living community tells us is that what is of value to us as humans is living (actually, living well, flourishing, and reproducing[31]) - the same thing that is also of value to the rest of the biotic community, regardless of whether or not it knows it.

It is because we belong within, and, therefore, are fundamentally of the same kind as, the rest of the living community that we owe it, and ourselves, Taylor's version of the golden rule: respect. If we conclude that treating individuals in human communities reasonably demands that we respect their right to pursue their own well-being, then, because non-human communities also have well-being that they pursue, we owe it to them to show them the same kind (or its species-specific equivalent) of respect. Our moral agency is the tool that we use to work out a coherent position, in this context.

Carlo Filice has pointed out that Taylor's position is very similar to Rawls' "veil of ignorance" view: we could have taken any other route through the evolutionary maze and ended up as a buzzard or a bacterium.[32] The fact that we ended up being human is contingent. The fact that we can reflect on our humanity and see it in context gives us the

---

[30] (Ibid.): 14ff.

[31] Reproducing in human terms can also take a metaphorical turn, in the sense that we seek to leave some trace of ourselves through art, literature, ideas that change paradigms, wealth creation, architecture, and so on, as well as or sometimes instead of children.

[32] Carlo Filice, "Rawls and Non-Rational Beneficiaries", *Between the Species*, 13 (2006).

capacity to see how to live, including seeing what is right and wrong, based on the idea that we are only contingently where we are, individually or as a species. Acting morally is an extension of natural action, once we acknowledge that some conditions benefit, while others harm us, and that therefore that some conditions benefit, while others harm other living organisms too. Yet the contention that moral agency could arise from our evolutionary condition – that we could come to have a "moral sense" because we are evolved, rational creatures who need to tell ourselves self-consistent stories – commits a fallacy. Just because we can see the situation we are in does not mean we are free of the same constraints - reactivity to all the micro- and macro-conditions that shape our lives and experience - as all else in existence.

We realise that we fit into the evolutionary picture as members of the biotic community, in the same way as other organisms. They, like us, have "goods" of their own. Having a good of its own does not necessarily imply that we should extend moral consideration to any organism, however. For this to happen, Taylor introduces the idea of "supervenience". It takes a factually informed, rational, reality-aware moral agent for the condition of moral considerability to arise. When this person is introduced, then the "good" of any organism becomes a condition for inherent worth, and for "respect".[33]

David Hume famously pointed out that deriving an "ought" from an "is" is logically illegitimate since the realms to which the two concepts apply are separate: the first is prescriptive while the second is descriptive.[34] Harris has questioned this analysis and more and more evidence suggests that values are, in fact, inherent in our evolutionary nature: some things just are good for us.[35] However, Taylor's thesis of moral agency depicts something that arises out of, but is independent of, natural laws: moral

---

[33] Paul Taylor outlines this relationship most clearly in a *Letter to Professor Claudia Card,* (op. cit.). In the same letter, he raises the issue of "moral realism" to which he is sympathetic.

[34] "… that the distinction of vice and virtue is not founded merely on the relations of objects, nor is perceiv'd by reason." 3.1.1, Hume, David., *A Treatise of Human Nature, (1793),* L.A. Selby-Bigge (ed.), Oxford: Clarendon Press, (1896).

[35] https://www.ted.com/talks/sam_harris_science_can_show_what_s_right/transcript?language=en

"There are truths to be known about how [human] communities flourish whether or not we understand these truths." I don't agree with Harris that we therefore need to call what happens next "morality": our response to this understanding is better conceived of, in my view, as a realisation, which then elicits compassion.

agents can decide for themselves what decisions they are going to make about how to live, based on the strange alchemy of complex human-evolved capacities that lift them beyond simple, probabilistic laws. According to Taylor, humans' abilities to reason and to integrate that reasoning with an understanding of how to live give them moral agency: they are natural, but they are also moral (agents).

In addition to depending on an evolutionary account of the human condition in order to develop his environmental ethic of respect, Taylor also relies heavily on the idea that we can make sense of "the good" of organisms as grounds for respecting them. Oliver Curry has developed the most convincing defence of Taylor from George E. Moore's naturalistic fallacy. Moore's "good" is indefinable and irreducible. It is not interchangeable with pleasure or virtue or anything else. There is nowhere else to go with "good" as a descriptor, and therefore to consider that it might be a natural property discoverable in the world is simply wrong (Moore is something of an intuitionist, in this account). Taylor's understanding of "good" is played out through the evolutionary forces that have made some conditions of benefit, while others are harmful, to living organisms. "Good" is, therefore, in Taylor's account, what arises as a matter of interest for living organisms, even if they do not know it, or think about it. Some conditions are, therefore, naturally "good" for organism, regardless of whether or not there are moral agents around to discover what is good for a particular organism. This appears to conflict with Moore's idea of how we should think of "good":

> Moore used "natural" to refer to properties of the external world. He contrasted "natural" with "intuitive" ... "objects of thought" such as good. Hence when Moore claims that good is not a natural property, he is simply restating the point that good is ... not an objective feature of the outside world... [36]

Curry, similarly to Harris, points out that no one, anywhere, has demonstrated that the natural and the normative inhabit two entirely separate realms: there is nothing to show that a mental realm exists separately from a physical realm and therefore, nothing to demonstrate that a qualitative world of ideas, including the idea of "good", could exist separately from the physical world of quantifiable objects. In Taylor's terms, it is a moral agent's rationally-informed reflection on the empirical situation of organisms that engenders the idea that we have moral

---

[36] Oliver Curry, "Who's Afraid of the Naturalistic Fallacy?" (op. cit.).

obligations associated with recognising that some conditions are "good for" organisms. "Good", in a moral sense, therefore, does not arise out of the organisms themselves: it is a human agent's idea, demanding a human agent's response. In a sense, then, we have to separate out two senses in which Taylor is using the term "good": what is "good for" organisms only becomes morally relevant when it becomes an "object of thought" for human moral agents.[37]

Teleology in Taylor

Taylor is at pains to be clear that other organisms, not just humans, are goal-oriented creatures, pursuing or seeking out (variously and at different times) survival, reproduction and well-being. The image this gives rise to is of a metaphorical "pull" towards some end, or goal. Yet evolutionary theory, which is also central to Taylor's narrative, provides us with the opposite kind of image: an image of blind, unconscious avoidances. Living organisms are far more driven by the many situations that they must escape - pain, negative stimuli like toxins, drought, the threat of annihilation - than they are drawn towards the few circumstances that ensure their continuance. "What survives from one generation to the next is just what happens to work ... what worked just happened to happen and was preserved because it did".[38] Having a goal, being drawn towards a particular condition, implies a degree of awareness of ends and there is little, if any, evidence to show that most creatures have this kind of awareness.

It is misleading, therefore, to think of teleology in Taylor as a set of conditions that an organism pursues because they are "good for" the organism. A more accurate way of considering Taylor's idea that conditions are "good for" organisms, and that therefore organisms are teleologically motivated, is to reverse the imagery and consider how (and even why) living organisms avoid the inevitable pull towards entropy that

---

[37] Taylor's moral agents recognise "the good" of organisms and arising from this, as an "object of thought", their inherent (moral) worth. However, this is not the same as Moore's intuited "good", even though he describes that as an "object of thought". The difference is that Moore's "good" is non-rational, and cannot be analysed. Taylor completely rejects intuitionist "hunches" when it comes to assessing "the good", or what to value, more generally. See Taylor concluding that " we cannot use either our own or anyone else's moral intuitions as grounds for accepting or rejecting a theory of environmental ethics." in *Respect for Nature* (op. cit.): 23.

[38] Samuel Harris, "Can Science Show Us What Is Right?" (op. cit.).

this narrative (the Big Bang theory within which evolutionary theory nests) implies.

If conditions that are "good for" organisms are those that allow them to avoid entropy, to avoid the chaotic breakdown of patterns of autopoiesis that characterise living individuals and communities, then we need to start asking how we can understand living creatures in terms that are consistent with other physical processes. If living creatures are, teleologically, avoidance processes, then it is worth asking what kind of characteristic features of living organisms are consistent with such avoidance, since these will be key to understanding better what conditions are "good for" living communities.

One of the main arguments used in debates about the "naturalness" or otherwise of life (particularly human life) by those who point to supernatural causation, is the idea that the evolution of life runs counter to the second law of thermodynamics. By this logic, any organised system should immediately dissipate energy and reach a state of entropy. Yet that is not what we see in the universe around us, or in other living organisms, or in ourselves. Proponents of intelligent design point this out as irrefutable proof that the system is being conducted by forces larger than natural, probabilistic laws: a god, or gods. Yet this is not the only possible explanation for this apparent anomaly, and examination of this feature of living things is very instructive in our attempts to see what conditions might be "good for" living things in the reversed image of teleology that I have outlined.

Evolutionary development is consistent with the development of patterns of existence in many systems in the universe. The dissipation of energy gradients from more energetic, more organised states to less energetic, less organised states, culminating in total chaos, is largely consistent with what we see unfolding around us. However, instead of a simple, direct correlation between time elapsing and systems collapsing, we see the graduation of energetic flows, including the creation and maintenance of structures that cohere, although the energy that they consist of is constantly dissipating, for many millennia. These structures include objects like stars and planets and, of course, living organisms and communities.

The avoidance of non-existence that we see as characteristic of living organisms can be interpreted as a graduation of the solar flow of energy (since that is the particular, dominant source of energy flow for our planet) through as many dissipative structures as happen to have come into existence at any one time. The more complex biodiverse systems become, the more intricate the energy flows and therefore, the more effective the global system of energetic dissipation becomes. This is Taylor's teleology couched in physicalist terms. It is a point I will return to in some detail when considering how to understand conditions as "good for" organisms, or communities of organisms, in chapter three.

From reason to the ideal "good"

Taylor's argument is that not just survival, but optimal well-being, is "good" for organisms. He does not examine the question of why it requires reason to work out what is "good" for humans when most other organisms pursue their "goods" blindly and without thinking about it. Perhaps optimal well-being is a pre-rational, or even a non-rational goal to pursue, if, as I have suggested in the previous few paragraphs, there is some link between living organisms' pursuit of life, or avoidance of annihilation (for as long as possible, through, amongst other things, reproduction, as well as through survival attempts) and the second law of thermodynamics. Perhaps this pursuit is motivated by more general forces that are connected to, for instance, the particular energy dissipation systems on this planet, rather than the capacity for rationality. This accords with Haidt's view of intuition being the elephant, and rationality, the rider, justifying actions in rational terms that have actually already been caused by pre-rational, intuitive motivations.

Taylor points out that evolution itself has no purpose, and therefore no reason or rationale, other than its own blind pursuit of survivability. This brings us back to the question of the degree to which human agents are conscious choice-makers rationalising decisions that, in many cases, undermine their survivability, and the degree to which they act as living organisms and pre-rationally avoid conditions that threaten to annihilate them. Since it is our capacity to reflect rationally on what is "good for" other organisms that allows us to include them in the sphere of our (moral) consideration, there is something singularly ironic about our doing this with the very same capacity that we use to justify actions that steer us away from what is "good for" us, individually (and, as I will later argue, as a species).

Taylor relies on moral agents' capacities for rationality as the foundation on which to build his ethic. People are both the only living organisms with the capacity to be moral agents, and the only living organisms with the capacity for rational reflection (Taylor recognises that this requires that we screen out some other perfectly good candidates, but since it is the response to a human-induced ecological emergency that is at issue here, it makes sense to focus on the human capacities to respond). Yet this very capacity to be conscious has also led to our making risky decisions that lead us towards, not away from, annihilation (from smoking, drinking and unsafe sex to pollution, deforestation and desertification). Biocentrism, doing what is in the interest of all members of the biosphere, is in the ironic position of extending a singular capacity to the consideration of other species that is rarely used in the consideration of its own.

The "good" of human agents, unlike the "good" of other living organisms, has a self-reflective character. It can include the pursuit of something extra, or even contrary, to the agent's gain. Significantly, it shows that the capacity for an agent's awareness that a thing is right beyond its benefit to the agent is the source of her moral motivation.

For Taylor, the evolved biological character of living existence creates the context for conditions that can harm or benefit all living organisms. Biological organisms have inherent worth on the grounds that they have these conditions - "goods" - that are recognisable by conscious human agents. This recognition, which is also an acknowledgement of commonality, elicits a certain kind of response. I have sought to show that this response is not something that already exists "in the world": it is not an automatic reaction generated by the conditions we find ourselves in or the knowledge we get from the world. It is the creative reaction of a reflective organism, recognising and then responding to something in the world that it also recognises in itself. It is what we do with the information that is the response: how we process it is a measure of our capacity to exercise our potential for reasonable action, which is what moral action is, for Taylor.

Developing an attitude of respect is, for Taylor, the sign of successful processing of our current state of knowledge. The attitude we develop involves acknowledging the full depth of our capacity to exercise consideration and extend reasoning so that our actions and our narrative match. Therefore for Taylor, respect for nature is a sign of authenticity: we both understand, and respond to that understanding.

Rational deliberation about our own capacity for flourishing, and seeing that this is a capacity we have in common with any and all other living organisms, leads us to an attitude of respect. From our biological "goods", we are educated to reason out our moral "good": respect for naturally evolved organisms, or, respect for nature, is the endpoint of this reasoning. With the hefty proviso that there is no direct conflict of interest, the attitude of respect for nature, manifested towards the existence of all current living entities, will govern all the decisions (and actions) of a reasonable person.

The origin of this perception that an action is right even if it is of no benefit to the agent is at the heart of Taylor's philosophy: it stems from the rational process of connecting a biological, evolutionary sense of self with the biologically necessary conditions for survival, and linking those with the idea that this implies a teleological directionality to organisms, an ideal way of being that moral agents can respond to. This, then, is Taylor's account of moral agency: it is confined to persons, it is realised rationally and it is driven by a sense of common origin and purpose.

For agents, rationality is the key. It has a pivotal role to play in the ability of agents to develop opportunities and make choices towards a "life worth living".[39] Rationality can be developed, along with factual knowledge, and even autonomy, through both increased education and increased access to resources. For all other organisms, rationality is irrelevant in the pursuit of their good: what is in their interest is sought blindly, without prejudice or judgement; what is in moral agents' interests, by contrast, is open to development, and the development is very much on a scale on which "best" is at one extreme, dependent for its realisation on rationality, while "worst" is at the other, dependent on moral weakness.

Taylor's agents are expressly moral and this is what allows them to make ethical choices. Moral agents are deliberative and practical. They can think clearly about a moral problem, particularly when they have some guidelines, and they have reasoned things through, and they can carry that deliberation into effective action. If they do both - deliberate clearly, and act on the deliberation - then they can call themselves virtuous.[40] To be virtuous is to have deliberated on a rational basis for an ethic – in this case, an environmental ethic which focuses on the non-human, and non-humanly influenced, natural environment or, to put it simply, nature – and to act on that deliberation. Not to do so is to exhibit weakness of will, which he defines as " a tendency for one to become confused or irrational due to the influence of one's non-moral interests, wants, needs and emotions."[41]

Taylor's account, so far, is that of virtue developing from a purely rational understanding and appreciation of humanity's situation in the environmental, particularly the non-human, living, environmental, sphere. From this basis, he concludes, in an echo of Kant, that, just as particular rules apply if we are to meet the requirements to pay due

---

[39] Paul Taylor, *Respect for Nature* (op. cit.): 64.

[40] (Ibid.): 87.

[41] (Ibid.): 87.

respect to persons, so there are parallel rules that apply to our relationship with other species, and thus with nature. Only when we follow these rules can we consider ourselves to have the "character traits of moral agents".[42]

Being "worthy of respect"

If human moral agents are worthy of being considered as "ends in themselves", then so are all living organisms. Taylor's careful untangling of the definitions of inherent worth, intrinsic worth and intrinsic value is worth pausing to examine at this point, since this process of delineating precisely what it means to be worth consideration is at the heart of Taylor's effort to show that humans are not alone in being valuable. It is this process of delineation that is at the heart of the shift from an anthropocentric to a non-anthropocentric ethic.

Even though I will move to show that ethical neutrality is a preferable approach to the ecological emergency, without Taylor's careful work to clarify how to locate value, it would not be possible to make the revisions necessary. It underlies a process that I want to focus on in the next chapter: the process of connecting the idea of conditions being "good for" a situation with the idea of a motivation to act on that knowledge.[43]

Taylor defines intrinsic worth as something that is worth doing for its own sake as evaluated by a particular perceiver. Practicing medicine or even the job of executioner could be seen, from some perspectives, as worth doing both for the sake of the job (both activities could be considered of benefit to a particular group) and for its own sake (an executioner can take pride in the line of a cut, just as a surgeon can). Taylor differentiates intrinsic worth from intrinsic value through the locus of perception: a job can have intrinsic worth from the point of view of the person doing the job. To have intrinsic value, an object, a state of affairs or an organism would be widely considered to exemplify excellence, uniqueness or rarity. To have intrinsic value, the perceiver has to be external, whereas to have intrinsic worth, the perceiver might be self-assessing a situation or activity.

Organisms or objects are more likely to be taken into consideration and protected or looked after if they evoke the response that they are intrinsically valuable but that does not make them objects of moral concern. To be objects of moral concern, they must be considered as ends

---

[42] (Ibid.): 89.

[43] (Ibid.): 72.

in themselves, beyond any utilitarian, aesthetic or emotional response they elicit. That is, they must have conditions that are "good for" them and which they can pursue, at least potentially. A job that has intrinsic worth is not an object of moral concern because even though there can be a perceiver, a doer of the job, the job itself is morally neutral – a surgeon can murder just as well as an executioner, if he chooses to – and it is only in considering the surgeon or the executioner as having inherent worth that we can begin to respond to them morally.

Taylor's division of the worthy from the valuable into these three categories challenges the view that has morality arising at the epicentre of what is good, or beneficial, for the individual, and spreading in ever-widening circles from there. Just because humans have a seemingly exclusive ability to measure their experience qualitatively, based on what they perceive as valuable because it is pleasurable, or beautiful, rare or unique, gives the experience no moral content.[44] Something else has to happen to make it necessary to consider another: the other has to be worthwhile in its own right.

Taylor's call is that respect for nature be an ultimate attitude for all moral agents based, as it is, on an impartial recognition of empirically verifiable facts, and not on intuitions or "hunches".[45] This grounds respect more fundamentally, he says, than, for instance, "love", which is partial. Respect, on the other hand, when it is understood in Taylor's sense, is, "we ... believe... binding on all moral agents'.[46]

This challenges the utilitarian ideal of pleasure as the ultimate source of good (and hence of suffering as the ultimate source of harm) and brings into focus the ideological divide between a moral sense that emerges from the idea of what is good or right for the individual, and the ideal that we can have laws or principles that are based on what we know, objectively and rationally, about the world. Taylor's philosophy is rooted in a belief that we can persuade ourselves to obey laws, codes or principles if we can only see the reasons clearly enough for doing so.

Morality and norms are here contrasted by Taylor: respect takes priority because all other norms are reasons for actions which are neither general, universal (or universalisable), disinterested, approved (in the Kantian

---

[44] (Ibid.): 73.

[45] (Ibid.): 90.

[46] (Ibid.): 91.

sense of willed to be universal) or supreme.[47] Respect is the basis of person-to-person ethics, and it is also the basis of a biocentric ethic, an ethic that decentres human interests. Taylor's resolution of these two ethics is intricate and sophisticated but the question of whether or not it is coherent is the central motivating factor for the revisions I propose.

In one sense, Taylor is expanding an existing (rule-based, Kantian-style) ethic which is anthropocentric and which applies only to the human species, to one which is biocentric and which applies to the parallel environment over which we have least influence: what he calls "wild" nature. Therefore, for instance, he examines the existing, exploitative attitude with which nature is viewed at present and contrasts it with the implications for action of the attitude of respect for nature.[48] His conclusion is that we have to look at underlying belief systems in order to recognise the framework within which either exploitative or respectful attitudes to nature develop.

However, while demanding what is essentially a justifiable foundational shift, Taylor omits to account for the seminal role of emotion in the development of beliefs or attitudes. This omission requires revision: without it, we are left with an idealised version of how human agents ought to act but a gap between the kinds of agents we are and the kinds of agents we would be if we were motivated by reason alone.

Secondly, Taylor's limiting of the environmental ethic to wild nature is unduly conservative. With his proviso of five "priority principles", there is no reason why he could not have included all spheres of human engagement, from person-to-person relationships, through the bioculture (that realm of the non-human world over which humans have already exercised considerable influence, from agriculture to animal experimentation), to the "wild" nature that is his actual focus.

We may be able to escape our human, or even our individual, interests when considering moral relationships, but to ignore them entirely is to deny an element of our biological existence: our closest relationships, human and non-human, are amoral.[49] To treat every living individual with equal status is an ideal few of us would desire to strive for.

---

[47] (Ibid.): 27, 28, 29, 31.

[48] (Ibid.): 96.

[49] Hans-Georg Moeller makes this vital point in *The Moral Fool* (op. cit.) when he argues that we do not conduct our relationships with our nearest and dearest on moral terms; we conduct them on the basis of love or other strong emotions.

The challenge of Taylor's thesis is that it demands that we question any ideological base from which to approach the ecological emergency. Taylor's approach is based on unimpeachable principles, principles that recognise the human as a part of the living community. Yet questions arise over the ethical basis of his approach, and we need to ask if an ethical basis for responding to the emergency is ever going to be valid.

Either we return to Hardin's approach and limit the moral circle to a chosen few, or we question the validity of an ethical approach to the issue of the ecological emergency altogether. Hardin's approach, for all its consideration of the wider biological world, nevertheless amounts to little more than an advanced form of extended egoism, arbitrarily selecting a group to survive on the basis of their relative position of power (in or out of the lifeboat as a representation for being in or out of the nation state or race that happens to be in a position of power when the emergency begins to cause serious loss of life). There is very little reason to believe that such an approach is moral in any meaningful sense.

To return to the issue of the affective, or emotional, dimension in ethical decision-making, Taylor does point out that a particular feeling is elicited when a moral agent truly understands the implications of their capacity to empathetically imagine themselves in another's place.[50] This is all very well when considering chimpanzees, pandas or elephants. It is less obvious that most agents will become disposed to "act for the relevant reasons" when the organisms under consideration are viruses, beetles or worms.

Including affect as a disposition deposes emotion from the intuitionist's primal position, or even from the empathist or the utilitarian's recognition of the fundamental role feeling plays in motivating actions. We can shift our standpoint and still act on principles we have reasoned out but for Taylor, the virtuous agent is the one motivated by reasonable beliefs about how they fit into existence, and able to focus long and hard enough to act on those beliefs. Being positively disposed towards other organisms might shore up the motivation, but it is an accompanying effect, and not the elicitation of the response: the starting point is reason.

The ethic Taylor offers is overtly idealistic, designed for a utopia where "respect for nature is fully expressed in the character and conduct of all moral agents."[51] This implies a recognition that he is asking for human

---

[50] (Ibid.): 84.

[51] (Ibid.): 89.

agents to act rationally all of the time. The reality is that human agents act emotionally, aesthetically, counter-rationally, intuitively, and on a number of other motivational bases, none of which are less motivational than ethics, most of the time.

The biocentric outlook offers the potential for developing an attitude that better reflects our place in the world. Taylor's insistence on egalitarianism offers an impartial, non-biased standard for adjudicating between conflicting interests. However, individuals as the focus of value are impossibly diverse and numerous: we cannot take them all into account. This makes the principle unworkable. Not only that, but many individual lives are simply too transient to feature as a chronologically relevant factor in weighing up interests. The problem, then, of centring value on individual organisms, is the problem of the human imagination which has only conceived of organisms which parallel the life-cycle of the human organism. In this sense, Taylor himself has become a victim of the surrounding culture of anthropocentric thinking.

The standards demanded of moral agents by Taylor's ethic are idealistic, and idealistic expectations create problems: if a social system is overly demanding, there will either be an acceptance of hypocrisy, in which case the system will be perceived as corrupt, or else there will be a sense that the system is inauthentic, in which case the system will be a sham, an emperor with no clothes. In particularly unfortunate circumstances, the system will be enforced, creating oppression. Other ideologies that demand impossible standards, like absolute truth, or a state of constant submission, have faced these problems in the past and the problems have not been resolved except, perhaps, in the unsatisfactory case of repressive regimes.

Despite these criticisms, Taylor's role in laying out a robust rationale for questioning anthropocentrism is admirable. Taylor's ethic, if acted upon, would not be likely to create an oppressive social system, at least to the extent that a faith-based system could. This is because Taylor's ethic is based on, and can be discussed on, rational grounds, whereas a faith-based system cannot.

Persons' relationships

For Taylor's ethic to work, there needs to be a set of rules for how to respond practically to this secularised, rationalised understanding of our place in nature, and of our respect for living organisms and communities.

We cannot simply react intuitively: there is too much partiality involved. Respect must be disinterested for it to form the basis of an ethic.[52]

He sets these rules out as: no maleficence (no deliberate harm); no intervention (no unnecessary intrusion into the lives of others); fidelity (not to break a trust – this implies no more hunting, shooting or fishing, all of which involve deception) and restitutive justice, when an agent has broken a valid moral rule and by doing so has upset the balance of justice between himself and a moral subject, and must make this balance good.[53] These rules represent general moral virtues which are aspirational rather than attainable: "no one's actual character ever fully exemplifies [them]".[54] The rule of justice, for instance, demands the virtue of fairness (in an echo of Rawls), while fidelity demands trustworthiness. Nonmaleficence requires considerateness and non-interference demands impartiality and regard, a feeling of antipathy towards intrusion.[55] These rules, then, all form the groundwork for understanding how an attitude arising out of reason can form the basis of a moral agent's response. Respect, "the ultimate attitude", is the reflective recognition that is elicited by any moral agent "in an ideal set of epistemic conditions". These include being informed of all the relevant facts, and being capable both of reason and sufficient awareness of reality.[56] Respect itself is filtered through the medium of the five principles outlined below.

Two key problems Taylor faces with his rule-based conception of environmental ethics are the problem of rights, and the problem of conflict of interests. Rights, he says, are unnecessary: he dismisses them on the grounds that, while particular societies might (and sometimes ought to) grant living organisms legal rights, these are entirely relative to the mores and norms of the societies. Moral rights, on the other hand, while conceptually feasible (moral patients are as "entitled" to the pursuit of their interests as are moral agents) fall foul of Occam's razor: they add nothing to the existing obligations which moral agents already owe other living communities or organisms. Once they are held "worthy of respect", the motivation to act ethically towards non-human organisms is already a strong enough duty to require nothing additional. The rules for engagement are laid out on the basis of a rationally-inspired attitude.

---

[52] (Ibid.): 202.

[53] (Ibid.): 172, 174.

[54] (Ibid.): 202.

[55] (Ibid.): 208.

[56] Paul Taylor, *Letter to Professor Claudia Card*, 15 April 1994 (op. cit.): 2.

When it comes to the second question, that of balancing interests, Taylor once again relies on a set of principles, or a schema, by which, he suggests, competing claims can be assessed. The five principles are: self-defense, proportionality, minimum wrong, distributive justice and restitutive justice and, as can be seen, there is an increasing level of intervention in each principle. Self-defense, for instance, involves the agent being under attack, and therefore, on the principle of reciprocity, a proportionate response is appropriate. This leads to the notion that the response must be equal and opposite, but that no extra force is used than is necessary to defend the individual agent or agents. The principle of minimum wrong implies that when moral agents' non-essential interests require serving (for example, through the building of an oil terminal in an area otherwise relatively unaffected by the impact of people), then account must be taken of the amount of harm which will be done to the organisms in an environment that is, to date, relatively pristine. Every effort must be made to minimize this harm and the effect on individual organisms will count cumulatively (the more individuals harmed, the greater the breach of this principle).

The final two principles involve a further analysis of what the invasion of moral agents into pristine environments means in terms of what is owed. Again, reciprocity is the easiest way of conceiving of these principles: distributive justice involves an equal balancing of the interests of moral agents and other living organisms, when essential needs of both are in conflict (for instance, when people need to kill wild animals for food). Taylor manages to avoid the morally questionable, directly reciprocal implication which springs immediately to mind: that is, if it is morally permissible for people to kill whales for food, for instance, why is it not permissible, in equally severe environmental conditions, for tigers to kill humans? Instead, he suggests four ways in which a balancing of interests might take place, including allowing agents to have a rotational access to wild areas, thus sometimes leaving them free of humans; leaving other areas entirely free of humans all the time; creating as much sensitivity as possible in the interventions that take place in wild areas; and sharing areas between humans and non-human, evolved communities in what he calls "common conservation".

Restitutive justice has become an important principle in European approaches to the tensions created by pressures on land use and access. The problem with attempts at re-wilding, or attempts to put things back to the way they were before humans intervened, has been extensively explored.[57] Robert Elliot's conclusion is that the interruption of evolved systems with human synthetic systems, even if an attempt at reversal is made, still results in artifice. Taylor also admits that what has been lost requires "a special duty of compensation" that brings about "an amount of good that is comparable ... to the amount of evil to be compensated for".[58]

This approach, which is an attempt to restore a "balance of justice", fails Elliot's test to take into account the impact of human agents per se, meaning that what has been lost – the continuous natural evolution of an ecosystem over millennia – can never be restored, only "faked". It also introduces the idea of "evil" which, as a quasi-religious concept and one Taylor has not used up to this point, strikes a jarring note in a naturalistic approach. Finally and most importantly, however, it is at this point that Taylor admits that the focus in restitutive justice needs to be "on the soundness and health of whole ecosystems and their biotic communities, rather than on the good of particular individuals". Taylor has moved away from biocentric atomism even as he defends it, demonstrating the increasing difficulties he meets in maintaining individualism as a coherent position.[59]

Conclusion

Taylor's biocentric approach is empirical and firmly physicalist, based on the premise that humans, as an evolved species, are just as interdependent, and in no way inherently more important, than other species. It acknowledges that a decentralisation and a deprioritisation of humans must take place in the context of anthropogenic impact on other species and communities of living organisms. In addition, it accounts for moral agency in terms of an additional capacity from that possessed by other organisms (the same capacity that entitles humans to term themselves "persons") and concludes that this implies added responsibilities. The capacity to decide how to live entails a duty to embody our understanding in our moral action.

---

[57] For an in-depth analysis, concluding with the currently unpopular view that re-establishing native flora and fauna lacks authenticity and does not represent a bridge to an evolutionary continuum, see Elliot, Robert, *Faking Nature: The Ethics of Environmental Restoration*, Routledge, (1997).

[58] Taylor, *Respect for Nature* (op. cit.): 304 - 305.

[59] (Ibid.): 305.

His outline of the origins of our morality implies that we evolved with this capacity for a moral sense. However, it is because we have the capacity for self-awareness, and for the organising principle of rational thought, that we have the additional and associated capacity to develop as virtuous characters, enlightened by our ability to act impartially and consistently. This argument is weakened when he acknowledges that, in common with all living organisms and communities, we pursue conditions that are "good for" us. What this omits is the acknowledgement that humans appear to pursue conditions that are in direct conflict with our "goods", sometimes in full awareness, sometimes in ignorance. This leaves us with the conclusion that it is a weakness of will that has left us where we are, in relation to the ecological emergency. Weakness of will only makes sense, however, in the context of an agency that is somehow supra-physical, and Taylor's own account disallows this. If we are to respond as effectively as we might, then we need to revise both our understanding of organisms, and our understanding of the primacy of ethics in response to the problems our impact has created.

Taylor's contention that individual living organisms alone are possessors of inherent worth begins to unravel when considered in the light of the very theoretical premise – evolutionary theory – that underpins his approach. Evolutionary theory makes it clear that organisms do not simply act as atomistic individuals but interact within both living and non-living relationships. Empirical evidence shows that individual organisms are, themselves, amalgams, in evolutionary terms at both the micro- and at the macroscopic level. Inter-reliance and interdependence are not just features of organisms; they define them. No organism acts in isolation. While it is also true that fierce competition for limited sources of available energy is a driving evolutionary force, the relational nature of organisms makes it meaningless to treat them as individual entities. This somewhat undermines an atomistic understanding of the worth of living organisms but I will attempt to revise the idea considered from the perspective that organisms behave more like systems than they do atomistic individuals.

Taylor's five principles demonstrate the problems with an approach that recognises that it is aiming for a utopia it can never realise. Agency is contextualised within systems that are imperfectible because unfinished, always in a state of flux, and therefore not able to come to a state of harmony.

I want to take some of the key points made in Taylor's thesis - the distinction between human moral agents, and all other organisms (and systems) as moral patients, firstly; the confusion around the understanding and prioritising the status of rationality in the context of depicting a moral theory, secondly; the potential for extending a much broader, more coherent notion of "the good" from the idea of conditions that are "good for" systems, thirdly. I want to show how agency itself is subject to this interdependence; that we are not, therefore, free to choose what to do in the way that Taylor implies. Seeing agency from the perspective of beings that are interwoven within one another's contextual space gives it an entirely different set of referents. Indeed it makes talking about agency in any traditional, and particularly in any dualistic sense, confusing. If agency is to have any clear meaning after this revision has been completed, it will have to be with some reference to systems themselves, rather than to individualism or to any dualistic understanding of some extra-physical entity, like mind.

Taylor's framework gives a comprehensive basis from which to revise what might be left to talk about when discussing human agency, and therefore free will. It leads to the question, what would mean to act, and respond, if we were to accept a different concept of freedom? Is there a need for any ideological basis for action (or at least, should we reflect on the intuitive nature of our ideological commitments? If we approach an understanding of context from the perspective of systems, rather than atomism, we find a different way to explore what our responses, and responsibilities, might look like. If we understand our capacity for freedom as entirely enmeshed in our capacity for our awareness, or realisation, of context, our perspective on where our responsibility lies shifts fundamentally.

Taylor's thesis provides a valuable antidote to the push to treat individuals as means, to be used as objects at the whim and behest of others, and the extension of this to the non-human realm is an important step in re-framing our responsibilities. In the next chapter, I will show how individuals are more complex and more interdependent than this atomistic account shows, and are therefore better considered as systems. The narrative of being enmeshed involves viewing the ecological emergency as an inseparable aspect of being human. It therefore allows us to re-envision our idea of agency and that gives us the potential to see ourselves in a different kind of relationship with the rest of existence than is available through any idealised account.

Secondly, an enmeshed view allows us to acknowledge and accept our fallibility, and therefore to work from a more pragmatic basis than that proposed by Taylor. This is important if we are to have a workable ethic, and not simply another set of principles that are aspirational, rather than practicable. The final revision flows from the previous two: the relationship between humanity and its biophysical enmeshment is neither separable, nor ideal, so we need to find a different way of assessing what kinds of relationship we can focus on, given a much more radical interpretation of our capacity for agency, and therefore for responsibility. Adding to these the idea of certain conditions being "good" for systems, and therefore of systems having "goods" brings us back to the language of value, which is now seen not as a human imposition upon systems, but as an inherent element of existence: values are in the universe, just as facts are. They are out there to be discovered. From this perspective, a whole new vista opens, one that both demands much more of us, since it is our perception of ourselves that shapes our response, but one that is inherently compassionate, and therefore creates the resilience we will need to mitigate at least some of the suffering that the ecological emergency implies.

Chapter Three

From agency as respect
to agency as realisation

Introduction

Taylor's work is important and ground-breaking for a number of reasons, not least because it dares to create an entire ethic (of respect for nature) from a non-anthropocentric basis. However, his theory does not go far enough in its work to devolve power from the human centre. I unpicked his theory in some detail to show the reasons for this in the previous chapter.

Firstly, moral agency does not make sense if we take the theory of evolution, and therefore our own enmeshment, to its logical conclusion. We simply do not have the kind of freedom required to be able to act as independently as moral agency requires. I will discuss the implications of this in more detail below.[1] Secondly, the kind of relationship we have with the rest of existence is as enmeshed organisms in a probabilistic universe that is in a state of motion towards entropy. This means that we can never be fully empirically informed in the way that Taylor suggests, in addition

---

[1] I have attempted to show that the narrative that "moral agency" is an ontologically distinct category crops up again and again in the literature relating to environmental ethics. A different understanding is given, for instance, in the work of Simon James: "it 'locates' the value of a thing, not in the thing itself, but in the agent who is 'ennobled' by valuing it," in Simon P. James, "Human Virtues and Natural Values", *Environmental Ethics*, 28 (2006): 339–53. For an extended exploration of moral agency in the context of environmental ethics, see, also, Lawrence Vogel, "Does Environmental Ethics Need a Metaphysical Grounding?" *The Hastings Center Report*, 25 (1995): 30–39.

to which our intuitive response precedes our reason.[2] If we review what agency, and therefore free will, might consist in, we also need to review the basis on which we call our actions "moral". The notion that humans are not in any meaningful way separable from context undermines the idea that we humans are rational, responsible agents who act in some objectively definable way on the wild, relatively unimpaired, natural world that is the focus of Taylor's concern. As an extension of the second point, harmony in nature does not exist (Taylor is clear about recognizing this), harmony in human nature does not exist, and aiming for a harmonious relationship between two entities that are inseparable, and inharmonious in as far as one can talk about them as entities, is problematic, to put it mildly.

In essence, I am contending that Taylor's biocentric approach (even in its more complex form as Taylor revised it later) is insufficiently radical to take into account all the implications of the principle premise – that we are evolved beings – that he uses as its foundation.[3] Biocentrism relies on the kind of individualistic atomism that, I will seek to show, is no longer viable if we are "reality-aware", in Taylor's terms. If we take the ideas of evolutionary biology, and indeed of what we know of physics as a science that describes a probabilistic, and fluctuating, universe, to their logical conclusion, then we cannot claim to have the kind of human agency, and particularly not the "free will", that we generally take for granted.[4] On top of this, if we are as enmeshed as Morton claims, and I will argue that we are, there is no "one" to do the valuing. Enmeshment precludes the freedom to act independently of the system within which "we" take place. Finally, the idea that we could aim to have an ideal, harmonious relationship with the environment, or ecological systems, or even enmeshment itself, breaks down as we come to understand ourselves as part of a system that is constantly in a state of dynamic adjustment to the complex interplay of matter and energy dissipating within and around us. There is no ideal, harmonious state.

---

[2] Jonathan Haidt's work on describing the prerational basis on which we make decisions is important here. He outlines this in *The Righteous Mind* (op. cit.).

[3] Paul Taylor, "Preface" to the Chinese translation of *Respect for Nature* (op. cit.).

[4] Samuel Harris has made the most popularised case for the illusion of free will. His assessment of the consequences are perhaps less radical than those I draw, since my conclusion - that realisation, and subsequent attunement with the elicitation of compassion - owes more to my introduction to Zen, and in particular to the work of Dōgen, as well as to other non western traditions, than it does to Harris' approach.

However, there are states which are "good for" the systems that created and sustain us, and that are also good for us. This becomes rather nuanced, since evidently not all states are good for all systems, but there is a pragmatic balance. How we come to this pragmatic balance, given we are not free to choose, is the work of the remainder of this book.

Even from a systems-based perspective, there is still an aspect of our cognitive capacity that we can exercise that better fits the definition of "agency" (and is morally neutral) than the moral agency Taylor defines. This means there is still a response that we can make, though this is not aspirational, since in this revised view we are not striving towards becoming ideal respondents, or seeking to respond in an ideal way. Since our relationship cannot be one of harmony, for the reasons given above, we do better to explore the relationship with our context (rather than just with Taylor's wild nature). By exploring what we know about physical systems, we find there are still ways of discerning what is "good" for the systems we are enmeshed in. Although these cannot be captured as principles, since they, too, are dynamic and interactive, there are enough clues from what we know about biophysical systems to provide us with some guidance on how to respond. Our response is not that of the "mental" act preceding a "physical" action. It is a realisation, a meta-event which alters our relationship with the rest of our experience, and that allows us to attune to what it elicits, through the effort of direct attention.[5]

These, therefore, are the possibilities I want to explore in the context of the ecological emergency that we currently inhabit, and in order to develop a better understanding of what kind of response, and responsibility we have for the emergency. The consequences what follows are more far-reaching than Taylor's reading implies, but give us a more

---

[5] I am aware that this definition is unsatisfactory and begs a number of questions in the field of philosophy of mind. However, very loosely, I take it that we are biophysical organisms, broadly in the way that Eric Olson describes, for instance, in "An Argument for Animalism" (op. cit.). Therefore I would surmise that our mental states are directly mapable onto physical, physiological states. Because we are living organisms, the mechanistic descriptions of this correlation utterly fail to do them justice and this has created confusion. However, if I may use this as a premise, it explains how I think realisation as agency works: it arises, spontaneously in some circumstances, or through meditative or mindfulness techniques in others, as a physiologically identifiable phenomenon that has an effect on all the conditions out of which it has arisen, including on itself, and this is why I describe it as a meta-system. I will, obviously, lay this out in detail (since it is pivotal to the entire theory) in a section below.

realistic foundation for proposing that we can respond to the ecological emergency, and that we can find the basis for a convergence in our response.[6]

First, I spell out the criticisms each idea elicits from the perspective of internal coherence with one of Taylor's main premises: evolutionary theory. Then I use a systems-based approach to address the objections levelled against Taylor's ideas, and show how, in each case, this allows for a revised idea of human responsibility. Finally, I explore an alternative view of "the good" of systems to show that there are ways we can realise, in two senses, our agency, but that these involve a very different kind of agency from what we are accustomed either to describing, or experiencing.[7]

Reviewing individualism

Taylor locates value (in the complex way I described in the previous chapter) in individual entities. He does this on the basis that evolution proceeds through gene mutation and natural selection, both of which occur at an individual level.[8]

However, factually aware individuals with information about recent research in evolutionary biology know that living organisms do not, in fact, evolve independently or atomistically.[9] Locating value in individual

---

[6] I note, as have others before me, that Taylor's views changed since writing *Respect for Nature* and the revisions I make here merely extend the direction of this change further: "Since writing *Respect for Nature*, some of my views have changed. Perhaps the most important one is that I no longer accept my strictly individualist account of what entities have inherent worth (and so are "morally considerable"), have moral standing in their own right, or are proper moral subjects toward which we have direct duties." *Letter to Professor Claudia Card*, (op. cit.).

[7] The inspiration for this idea came from multiple sources. One important one was Robert Elliot's 2008 paper, "Instrumental Value in Nature as a Basis for the Intrinsic Value of Nature as a Whole", *Environmental Ethics*, 27, 1, (June 2010): 43–56; other physicalist approaches to understanding energy dissipation within systems, including work by Scott Sampson, Ibrahim Dincer, Daniel Botkin and Stanley Salthe, details of which appear later in this chapter and in the bibliography.

[8] Paul Taylor, *Respect for Nature* (op. cit.): 6.

[9] See, for instance, Daniel C. Fouke "Humans and the Soil", *Environmental Ethics*, 33 (2011), 147–61. (especially 155); Jerry A Fodor and Massimo Piattelli-Palmarini, *What Darwin Got Wrong*, New York: Picador/Farrar, Straus and Giroux, (2011); Judith Korb, "Termite Mound Architecture, from Function to Construction", in David Edward Bignell and Yves Roisin (eds), *Biology of Termites: a Modern Synthesis*, 2nd Edition. Dordrecht ; New York: Springer, (2010): 349–73.

organisms encounters further difficulties when we consider the time scales of the existence of different organisms. It indicates that the implicit focus of Taylor's concern was macro-organisms – from earthworms to whales – rather than micro-organisms, the importance of which in biological evolutionary terms is only now becoming apparent.

There are further grounds for believing that macro-organisms were Taylor's implicit focus: countless species, particularly of micro-organisms, have not yet been identified or classified by humans. Even those that have been identified interact in complex ways, making it difficult to know whether to classify them as individuals, or as interdependent parts of larger organisms. We cannot value them as individuals because they do not fit into the categories we normally use for classification. There are two revisions necessary to the individualistic account Taylor has given us: we need to review the idea of individualism, and we need to review the idea of a locus of value (since if individualism is not as widely applicable as we have formerly understood it to be, then locating value at the individual level is also not as widely applicable).

The arbitrary uniqueness of being human

Taylor locates responsibility for human impact in the mental decisions humans make as moral agents and he says that both human-centred and life-centred theories agree about "which beings in the world are moral agents".[10] While I agree with Taylor that human impact is the source of the emergency, and that being human is unique in important ways, I would like to offer a revision of the idea that the human capacity to "exercise the necessary resolve and willpower to carry out ... decisions" takes place in the way that Taylor describes, and therefore I am offering a revision of the idea of human moral agency.[11]

Part of the uniqueness of being human lies in our capacity to (mentally) imagine what it would be like if conditions were different. We may not know what it is like, in Nagel's famous phrase, "to be a bat" or anything else on a different evolutionary branch, but we have the capacity to imagine different future scenarios, and to empathise with other humans, and even to understand that other organisms and ecosystems "need" particular conditions to survive.[12] It is reasonable to conjecture that this

---

[10] Paul Taylor, *Respect for Nature*, (op. cit.): 14.

[11] (Ibid.): 14.

[12] Thomas Nagel, "What Is It Like to Be a Bat?" *Philosophical Review*, 83 (1974): 435–50.

kind of capacity arises as a result of our own evolutionary conditions: it happened that we developed different cognitive capacities, which are based on the physiological make-up of our brains, and other organs. Other organisms developed different sets of capacities: this happened to be one set that we developed, but it is not inherently different in quality from those developed by others.

Yet the narrative that accompanies our uniqueness is one that also tells of our superiority. The narrative is that human cognitive capacities (along with opposable thumbs) have directed the kind of impact that humans have had on other organisms and planetary systems. However, human cognitive capacities, in evolutionary biology terms, emerge as a result of our biophysical conditions, and give us no claim to superiority.[13] The narratives that we tell ourselves about our relationship with other organisms and planetary systems shape how we understand this relationship.[14] Our methods of communicating this understanding are amplified through the use of signs and symbols (religions are obvious ones), metaphors in language, and technology which speeds up and further disseminates commonly held understanding. The effect of this amplification is to further alter and potentially distort our understanding. Because we believe we are superior, this attitude feeds back into how we use our cognitive capacities (like empathy and imagination). We limit what we include, and what we respond to, which further drives the negative effect of our impact, as a species.

For human moral agency to be a completely unique capacity, it would have to be of a different order from the capacities of other organisms. It

---

[13] Wendell Berry gives an explanation of this that is clear and precise in *The Landscape of Harmony* where he describes human impact in terms that could be construed as "extravagance", in the sense of "wandering from the path" of straightforward survival aims. Seen from this angle, human technological developments are increasingly over-sufficient for ensuring the continued survival and reproductive capacities of the species and this situation has gone on developing, in the way that evolutionary situations do, just because of the accidental success of the strategies (tool-making, forward thinking) that contributed to the process in the first place. We are mainly "dependent upon reflexes, instincts, and appetites that we do not cause or intend", but humans also have the capacity to think, to plan, to imagine futures for themselves, to create "this artifact, this human living" Wendell Berry, *The Landscape of Harmony*, Hereford; Five Seasons, (1987): 35.

[14] Simon P. James, "Finding - and Failing to Find - Meaning in Nature", *Environmental Values*, 22 (2013): 609–25.

would have to involve a process that was uniquely independent of the biophysical conditions we have evolved in. If human moral agency is not unique in this way, then what is happening, when we act, is just like what is happening when all other organisms act. We are responding to circumstance and the ideas of resolve and willpower as capacities that we impose independent of circumstance do not come into the equation at all.

If this is the case, then human impact on other organisms and planetary systems has been unintentional. Moreover, the reason that such an extreme level of impact has arisen is as a direct result of the narratives we have told ourselves, and our consequent understanding, of our inherent superiority and independence. Our impact will therefore continue as long as we maintain this attitude, and this reliance on a dualistic understanding of our relationship both to the rest of existence, and to our own capacity to act, our agency.

Our impact has also manifested itself in the way this sense of superiority allows us to withdraw our attention from particular facets of our relationships. To summarise what I have said so far in this section: we are biologically evolved, and so are our cognitive capacities, which means that they are not inherently superior to those of other organisms, since they were the result of a process of (blind and impartial) evolution that has no hierarchy. Yet we have told ourselves that we are inherently superior, and even that these capacities are unique and distinct, and give us independence from the biophysical conditions we have evolved in. This means there are two views to correct: our view of our superiority, and our view of our independence.

Harmonious relationships

Taylor makes it clear, as I mentioned in the last chapter, that stability, and therefore some end-state of harmony, is not a feature either of individuals or of ecosystems. It makes no sense, therefore, to strive for stability when considering either the responsiveness of systems or the ecological emergency. The view of systems that I am taking for the purposes of this discussion is one based on a biophysical understanding of how systems operate.

Effectively, this is an extension of Taylor's understanding of organisms as having evolved. If organisms evolved, then they evolved in accordance with scientific laws. These laws are probabilistic, and falsifiable, therefore any explanation they facilitate is only theoretical. However, they are the best description we have for empirical evidence of what is taking place in the universe – they require the least complex explanation, they accord best with the evidence, and their falsifiability allows us to discard any theory we have if evidence disproves it. Biophysical systems are, in this sense, informational exchange systems, where relations between different sets of information (in the form, for instance, of "packets" of energy – quarks – or at a larger scale, electrons and protons) are in dynamic interplay, moving (according to the second law) towards entropy (a state where there is less information to exchange, because less organization, and therefore more chaos).[15]

James Ladyman describes the universe as being made up, not of things, but of mathematical relations. Scott Sampson, from a different perspective, talks of a relational universe.[16] There are not distinctly unique interchanges of energy or information. At the purely physical level, one can reduce this to a mathematical metaphor: the interchange is an equation, working itself out, but in doing so, it changes the balance of all other equations which then have to work themselves out, and so on. This process is effectively infinite (at least from a human point of view) and paints a picture of the universe into which our understanding of biophysical systems can be worked.[17] We can think of this interchange as directional, using the "big bang" metaphor: at an earlier time, more concentrated exchanges take place, and these become progressively less concentrated. So, in a sense, there is a "flow" to this systematic process.

There is no ideal or harmonious relationship within these systems and the interchanges they involve are dynamic. However, the patterns of

---

[15] I have kept this discussion as brief as possible, in order to sketch it in as the scientific premise that underlies Taylor's premise, and therefore show how a fuller understanding of the implications of biological evolution give us more interdependence than Taylor's theory allows. This brevity includes some potential misunderstandings. I do not mean, of course, that the early universe was organised, and the later universe will be disorganised. Rather, I mean that the early universe had a higher potential for informational exchanges, and the later universe has a lower potential. We could sum this up poetically, with Yeats, by saying, "things fall apart". Scott Sampson, "The purpose of the universe is to disperse energy" in *What is your Dangerous Idea?*, ed. John Brockman, New York, Harper Perennial, (2007).

[16] As discussed by James Ladyman in, for instance, in James Ladyman, James Lambert and Karoline Wiesner, "What Is a Complex System?", *European Journal for Philosophy of Science*, 3 (2013): 33–67.

[17] Stanley N Salthe discusses in detail the connections between living systems and the laws of thermodynamics in "Purpose in Nature", *Ludus Vitalis: Journal of Philosophy of Life Sciences*, 16 (2008), 49–58; and again in Salthe, "Maximum Power and Maximum Entropy Production: Finalities in Nature", *Cosmos and History: The Journal of Natural and Social Philosophy*, 6, (2010): 114–121.

existence that maintain themselves for a certain length of time include biophysical systems and one notable feature of biophysical systems is their ability to develop this "whirlpool"-like character of systems still further by self-replicating, or reproducing, in order to maintain the pattern.

In reviewing the ideas of the harmoniousness within systems, and the prospects for harmoniousness between humans and other systems (or more accurately, their enmeshment), a further point is that very often we cannot know, with any certainty, the results of anthropogenic impacts. The interrelationships are too complex, or not enough research has been done to establish the effects on the interrelationships of human activity. Responding from the context of being enmeshed is more complicated, and involves more unknowns, therefore, than if human responses could be calculated atomistically. Systematic enmeshment implies that if something acts, reacts or alters its trajectory, then the entire mesh shifts. We need to assess what clues there might be in the conditions we find ourselves in for discerning what kind of responses accord with, and which ones interfere with or obstruct, the "flow" to this systematic process.

Taylor's approach is based on the demand that we acknowledge our peripheral status as a species and on challenging the narrative of human superiority. I agree with Taylor on this count. Taylor recognises that humans are latecomers. He concludes that the human capacity for deliberative action confers responsibilities towards, rather than privileges over, other species. The problem with this is that if we conclude that humans are peripheral, we push ourselves into a kind of inverted inegalitarianism in which human systems are sidelined in favour of non-human systems.[18] This position might satisfy a "deep green" philosophy but it is imbalanced from most human perspectives.

Instead, and given that our enmeshment dissolves the requirement that we see ourselves as either central or peripheral, I recommend that we take

---

[18] What I mean here is that to say that we are peripheral, because we are, evolutionarily, latecomers, could be interpreted (and for some, has been interpreted) as meaning that we ought to reduce our numbers to a very low level, relative to the current human world population. I am not advocating this position, although the logic that our rights are subordinate (if rights are really universal and non-anthropocentric, in the sense implied by deep ecologists) to those who have been here longer (almost all other species apart from some micro-organisms, since very few known new species have evolved since the evolution of *Homo sapiens*) is, from an allocentric viewpoint, hard to dispute..

an allocentric view to resolve this tension.[19] In other words, if the focus of our attention is on our relationships within our enmeshment, then we need not concern ourselves with our peripherality. We may be latecomers, but we are host to ancient microbes, our virally derived RNA links us back to some very early life-forms, and, of course, we are more than biological, we are also physical organisms made of the same stuff as everything else in the universe at the current time.

We can therefore consider the argument that what we value, what is "good for" us, is independent of us, as valuers. This means that there can be a centre of value outside a valuer. Holmes Rolston III, quoted in Simon James, uses the "light in the refrigerator" analogy:

> ... what values would exist in the world, not as it appears from the viewpoint of the subject picturing such a world, but as it would appear independently of human experience.[20]

By admitting that values, as conditions that are "good for" different entities and systems, do exist, independently of those entities and systems, we can make sense of the idea that there can be a centre of value outside the valuer. Neither a bacterium nor a forest needs to know what is good for it in order for those conditions to exist.

A final important criticism of Taylor is that raised by Karann Durland: Taylor's proposal lacks credible practicability.[21] This needs to be dealt with as an issue of practice and therefore I will discuss it in the next chapter since it links the problem of thinking about the ecological emergency to the practical applicability of any systematic, intellectual approach.

---

[19] The use of the term "allocentric" to describe a view point that is "other-centred" I first came across in the work of Ronnie Hawkins, "Extending Plumwood's Critique of Rationalism Through Imagery and Metaphor", *Ethics and the Environment*, 14 (2009): 99–113; and "Introduction: Beyond Nature/Culture Dualism: Let's Try Co-Evolution Instead of "Control" (op. cit.).

[20] Simon P. James, "Human Virtues and Natural Values" (op. cit.): 346.

[21] Karann Durland, "The Prospects of a Viable Biocentric Egalitarianism", (op. cit.). Another major source of responses to this level of criticism with some suggestions for how to address the critique comes from Jason Kawall in "On Behalf of Biocentric Individualism", *Environmental Ethics*, 30, Spring (2008): 69-88.

Revised responsibility

While Taylor's assertion that evolution proceeds at the genetic level is a reasonable one, it begs the question both subjectively, for humans, and objectively, for the other organisms within Taylor's sphere of consideration. The most general form of the question ("what am I?") is one that philosophers are prone to ask more frequently than most. The evolutionary answer ought to be that I am a primate, yet the biophysical answer is that "I" am largely (over 65 percent) water.[22] Of the remainder, around 15 percent dry weight is made up of mitochondria whose DNA has more in common with all other mitochondria found in the bodies of all other multicellular organisms than it does with the primate DNA with which I tend to associate my "I".[23] This results in the absurd conclusion that "I" am less than 20 percent "me" and over 80 percent "everything else". It is just as absurd to claim that human evolutionary progress is made by the 20 percent "I" am willing to admit as "me" while everything else follows along in its wake like a bridal train.[24] The fact of natural selection implies that the other 80 percent will have an enormous effect on the way that the 20 percent is realised, or expressed, or whether or not mutations take place.

There is a new area of biology, Metagenomics, that seeks to explore the evolutionary interactions between multicellular organisms and the microbial communities that both colonise, parasitise and symbiotically evolve with them. Metagenomics considers humans as communities of organisms containing microbes that harvest, for instance, nutrients and energy from food that primate digestive enzymes lack the capacity to

---

[22] "Water is the most abundant chemical compound in living human cells, accounting for 65-90% of each cell." Raymond Chang, *Chemistry*, 9th edition, Boston: McGraw-Hill (2006): 52.

[23] Extensive work by philosophers on identity is relevant in this context. Primarily, however, I refer the reader to work on the microbiome within the human (that is also relevant to other multicellular organisms).See, for instance, Charles S. Cockell, "The Value of Microorganisms", *Environmental Ethics*, 27 (2005): 375–90. Graham Parkes, "Voices of Mountains, Trees, and Rivers: Kūkai, Dōgen, and a Deeper Ecology", in Duncan Ryūken Williams and Mary Evelyn Tucker (eds), *Buddhism and Ecology: the Interconnection of Dharma and Deeds*, Cambridge, Mass.: Harvard University Center for the Study of World Religions, Harvard University Press, (1997):111–28; Daniel Fouke, "Humans and the Soil" (Ibid.) (2011).

[24] "What we call our "selves" are not individuals but whole communities living in symbiosis, and this is true not only of ourselves, but of all organisms". Daniel C. Fouke, (op. cit.): 153.

metabolise. Any understanding of human biology must view human organisms as microbiomes, "mutualistic human-microbial interactions" that allow one another to survive and indeed flourish.[25]

It is more accurate to describe evolution as a process of gene transfer that is complicated by the interactions between the various systems that go to make up multicellular organisms, single-celled organisms, and the surrounding conditions, than it is to describe it as gene transfer alone. If the complexity of the interrelationships between multicellular and microbial communities and organisms modifies gene transfer in humans, then it does so in all multicellular organisms. The situation is more complicated still: microbial communities depend upon, interact with and modify the conditions for multicellular organisms, and vice versa. It is much more accurate, therefore, to consider both multicellular organisms, microbial communities and even the background conditions of temperature, hydration, geology, pressure and so on, as systems, than as entities.

We need to make further revisions to an atomistic, individualistic approach when considering single-celled organisms. Not only in evolutionary time, but in each instant of our existence, trillions of microbial cells overwhelm the number of human cells in a human body, making it more of a bipedal colony than an isolated individual. As scientists frequently observe, "By numbers of cells, a human being has ten times as many bacteria as human cells."[26] In addition, even the so-called "human genome" is disproportionately comprised of ancestrally viral fragments, "fragments that were vital to evolution of all organisms."[27]

Single-celled organisms, or microbes, do not behave as individual organisms, whether in their entwined relationship with multicellular organisms, or while acting in apparent independence in the soil.[28] This

---

[25] National Research Council: Committee on Metagenomics: Challenges and Functional Applications, *The New Science of Metagenomics: Revealing the Secrets of Our Microbial Planet,* Washington, D.C.: National Academy Press, (2007): 37, quoted in Daniel Fouke, "Humans and the Soil". (Ibid.): 153.

[26] James Gorman, "Aliens inside us: a (mostly) friendly bacterial nation", *The New York Times* (1 April 2003).

[27] Frank Ryan, *Virolution,* London: Collins, (2009).

[28] Nicola J. Holden and others, "Prevalence and diversity of *Escherichia coli* isolated from a barley trial supplemented with bulky organic soil amendments: green compost and bovine slurry", *Letters in Applied Microbiology,* (Nov 2013). (This is one of an increasing number of papers demonstrating the results of recent research

implies that humans cannot claim even at the organic level to be boundaried individuals whose evolutionary trajectory relies solely on the mutation of genetic material and natural selection. While it is reasonable to acknowledge the importance of the role of individualistic genetic transference in evolutionary progress, it is unreasonably reductionist to extend an assumption of this importance to a consideration of how living organisms interact, and therefore to how we weigh up organisms' interests.

Given all this, we should be sceptical of an entirely atomistic approach. It is useful to think of living organisms, including ourselves, as unique, boundaried entities, especially, for instance, when deciding who will pay for dinner. However, in considering a human condition imaginary of the kind described in the last chapter, it is equally important to recall that we and they are also "dissipative structures," to use Ilya Prigogine's term, maintaining a coherent integrity while energy and matter continues to exchange.[29]

Organisms do not evolve in empty space but in relation to other organisms and the systems which contain them, and even in close co-evolution with those systems. We are ourselves examples of such co-evolution. We depend, absolutely and essentially, upon the microbial communities, as well as the non-organic, chemical interchanges, that make up the internal and external context of our existence.

It could be argued that when we change the level at which we reflect on our identity as entities, by considering ourselves as "persons", for instance, then our ability to see ourselves as separate individuals within a world of other separate individuals makes sense. To a degree, of course, it is practically necessary that we perceive ourselves in this way. However, when the stories that we use to make sense of our condition so distort our understanding of our relationship with the context that we are no longer able to understand that we are reacting completely within context, and that our agency, our capacity to respond, lies elsewhere, then this perception of separation becomes an obstruction instead of a facilitation.

---

into microorganisms (*E. coli*) that co-exist with non-living matter (slurry) and non-organic matter (minerals in the soil).

[29] Scott Sampson, "The purpose of life is to distribute energy" (op. cit.). While I disagree fundamentally with the statement in the title of Sampson's essay (there are significant problems with the idea that "life" should have a "purpose" in this sense), the imagery of patterned distribution of energy has been extremely useful in envisaging the nature of the graduated flow of energy through systems..

The narratives themselves need to be revised, updated and questioned in the light of new information if we are to be able to realise where our response facility lies. We can only respond, with agency, when we become aware, at the time, of the conditions of our enmeshment. We cannot rely on a distorted sense of our own agency as a mental act exercised on physical conditions since it is exactly this that holds us rigidly within a reactive context. While the revised explanation of agency given here, like any narrative, is undoubtedly incomplete, and while our ability to integrate this information will also, therefore, be experiential and exploratory, a kind of feeling our way, this is still preferable to not updating the narrative at all.[30]

Morton's word "enmeshed" and its different forms (enmeshment, "the mesh", and so on) is a useful metaphor for the interrelationship between what we think of, traditionally, as "the human", on the one hand, and "the environment" or "the other" outside of "us", on the other."[31] This way of perceiving how we interrelate leaves no room for separation of entity from the background "hiss". We are not exclusively, or even statistically significantly, "human" in make-up and nor is there anything "outside" this "us" to which we can refer for measurement or scale. It is, therefore, only human cultural systems that create the context within which we measure.[32] They demand a story about our relationship with the world in order to find some way of drawing a line between "us" and "them". Without a story, there is no culture. Without culture, there is no "human".[33] As Wendell Berry has it, we are not human until and unless we are encultured.[34]

---

[30] For a detailed exploration of the role of meaning in our understanding and relationship with the rest of the evolved context, see Simon James, "Finding - and Failing to Find - Meaning in Nature", (op. cit.).

[31] Timothy Morton uses the word "enmeshed" frequently throughout his work, including, for instance, in *The Ecological Thought*, (op. cit.): 124. See also "Environmentalism", published in Nicholas Roe, (ed.), *Romanticism: An Oxford Guide*, OUP, (2005): 696–707.

[32] See, for instance, Timothy Morton, "Ecology without the Present", *Oxford Literary Review*, 34 (2012): 229–38.

[33] Another clear description of the interrelationship between being human and being enculturated, is given by Berry: "But humans differ from most other creatures in the extent to which they must be made what they are – that is, in the extent to which they are artifacts of their culture." Wendell Berry, *The Landscape of Harmony*, (op. cit.): 37.

[34] Wendell Berry, (Ibid): 37.

Being encultured is another aspect of our systematic approach to our own survival, and involves seeing ourselves as contextualised within culture. Berry wants to emphasise our naturalness, but this, too, has to be seen in the light of human enculturation:

> We and our country create one another ... our land passes in and out of our bodies just as our bodies pass in and out of our land.[35]

Human enculturation creates the land but the land also creates human enculturation and the two are inseparably interrelated. Nature, and "the land" as its representation, has become, in a sense, "our artifact".[36] We can go further than Berry, though, because what creates the land is not just the "we" of the human species, but a much broader set of interactions between multiple communities and systems within which we, and they, are enmeshed. From Berry's context of enculturation, we can extend the implications to wider and wider systems.

This idea of interrelated creativity is hugely filtered, now, at the level of human enculturation, through synthesised artefacts. At the scale of our existence, neither those of us who claim a stake in human culture, nor any of the less intimately involved systems, are now outside the human cultural net. In the sense that we have used these synthesised artefacts to probe internally and externally to the limits of the known universe, there is no longer any outside-human context.[37]

Our enmeshment and the context of our perception is further complicated by prosthesis, or what could be described in more radical terms as our evolution into biophysical organisms dependent upon, but also, potentially, rendered vulnerable, or endangered by, technological artifice.[38] An extreme view might remark that the soles of our feet use the

---

[35]Wendell Berry, (Ibid.): 22.

[36] Wendell Berry, (Ibid.): 40.

[37] This is an extension of Timothy Morton's remark in "Ecology without the Present" (op. cit.), that "there is no outside-human text": 231. I understand this to mean not that we know everything there is to know about the context, just that we have encompassed everything we do know within the bounds of the technologically synthesised products we have created to measure it. While we will no doubt continue to synthesise technological means to probe further, for now, what we do not know is potentially knowable within this context.

[38] What I really mean is more than prosthesis: it is the idea that we alter our experience internally and externally and with conscious deliberation through the

prosthesis of shoes to deal with walking on potentially hazardous ground. More conventionally, and increasingly, prosthesis extends, prolongs or replaces the function of limbs or sensory perceptual devices (from artificial knees to dental implants, spectacles and pacemakers). However, deliberately altering our experience is broader than these physiological adaptations through the use of synthesised artefacts.[39] We ingest substances, legal or illegal, to alter our mood, and sometimes our perceptions, from coffee to Prozac to cocaine, and sometimes these synthesised products artificially extend our lives by changing our blood pressure, countering terminal illness, or even altering the rate of our decay. Yet we also breathe in and ingest the accidental by-products of bio-technological dependency, from fertilisers to effluent from factory farms. These internally or externally applied synthetic artefacts shift the balance between what we are as evolved organisms, and what we are, as human, synthetic systems.

We have altered the make-up of ecosystems within which we are only distantly involved. Even before genetic engineering, artificial selection altered the evolutionary trajectories of targeted species and, by extension, of those (particularly single-celled organisms) that interacted most closely with them. Even those systems we have not targeted in any way are affected by the by-products of synthesis. We can find traces of human (encultured, synthetic) activity laid down and contained (as a thin layer of carbonated by-product) in the ice caps and on the ocean floors and in places no human has ever set foot or laid eyes upon.[40]

---

use, for instance, of caffeine, and, in the more conventional sense of prosthesis, through the use of artificial limbs. I wanted to capture the global, internal and external extent of this manipulation of our experience using these deliberated responses, in order to contrast this with the lack of attention we pay to the ecological crisis that is emerging, as it were "just out of sight" because we are so adept at distracting ourselves from the additional consequences of our impact, when it is difficult to consider them.

[39] Synthesised artefacts can actually enable us to feel, and this is likely to become a more common experience (if we do not experience the collapse of human civilisation through the ecological emergency first). See, for instance: https://www.ted.com/talks/todd_kuiken_a_prosthetic_arm_that_feels?language=e n; http://www.ted.com/talks/amber_case_we_are_all_cyborgs_now.html

[40] "At the very moment at which nothingness was making its way via Buddhism through Hegel into the thinking that resulted in Heidegger's *Destruktion*, a thin layer of carbon was being deposited in Earth's crust ... the Anthropocene was and is and shall be". Timothy Morton, "Ecology without the Present", (op. cit.): 231.

Violence

One other characteristic of our encultured systems is that they are, in many respects, extremely violent.[41] I will return to a consideration of this characteristic when I consider the practice implied by realisation as agency. For now, I want simply to point out that some human cultures have ritualistically noted, and even begged forgiveness for, some of the violent relationships we exist within (including killing to eat, warfare, clearing of land for planting and so on).[42] While philosophers (and academics and thinkers from other disciplines) have questioned the effectiveness and the impact of such rituals, the unacknowledged violence that is so central to the twenty-first century's globalising consumer culture is markedly different in at least two respects from earlier manifestations of violence in human cultures, and from violence exhibited by other species. In the first place, it remains an opaque, barely examined feature of the current globalising, product-heavy, consumer-creating system and in the second, the scale of the violence and the mindlessness, or lack of attention, with which it is carried out, is of a different order from violence or aggression in other times or in other species.[43]

---

[41] This point is made by Morton extensively in *Ecology without Nature: Rethinking Environmental Aesthetics*, Cambridge, Mass.: Harvard University Press, (2009). He makes a related point in a paper, "Environmentalism" : "...it is not so much technology and language that are at issue as oppression and suffering." Timothy Morton, "Environmentalism", (op cit.): 705. Wendell Berry has also written about our aggressive nature: "... our history reveals that, stripped of the restraints, disciplines, and ameliorations of culture, humans are not "natural", not "thinking animals" or "naked apes", but monsters – indiscriminate and insatiable killers and destroyers. We differ from other creatures partly in our susceptibility to monstrosity." Berry, *The Landscape of Harmony* (op. cit.): 40. There have, of course, been many other writers and thinkers who have observed and commented on the aggressive nature of humanity. My point in drawing attention to this is to question whether or not the ideas we have of our agency either exacerbate these aggressive tendencies, or mitigate them. Obviously, this is a deeply complex question but by slicing it differently will, I hope, reveal new insights.

[42] A point made specifically by Thomas Duddy in "Walking Respectfully Upon the Earth", in *From Ego to Eco*, presented at the *From Ego to Eco* conference, NUIG, Galway, (2011).

[43] I mean mindlessness, of course, in the context of the human capacity to be mindful, or notice, not in the sense that other species could be mindful or otherwise of their actions: some probably could, some certainly could not.

In the end, other systems will kill (exploit, destroy and pollute) the ones we depend upon, and us, ourselves.[44] We cannot avoid our own end. Yet we have largely failed to grasp the extent to which our own destructiveness has created the conditions that threaten to undo the very fabric upon which our own continuance as human encultured beings depends.

It is our sense of distinction, our separateness, and the accompanying tendency to withdraw attention from our involvement, that is really at the heart of this matter. The violence of humanly encultured systems looks directional, in the sense that there is an apparent level of purpose to it (war to gain land, exercising ideological control to gain power, intensive farming to increase profitability and production, factory worker exploitation for profit) and yet this purpose may be motivated by factors entirely outside human encultured control (fear, hunger, perceived lack of space or security, on the one hand; extravagance, the unintended consequences of synthesising artefacts, on the other). In the context of the culture that enmeshes us, attention, and the awareness to which such attention gives access, is directed away from questioning. Partly as a result of the narratives of independence and superiority that I mentioned earlier, we fail to question the manner in which factory farmed animals are bred, housed and killed. We do not pay attention to the profit-driven justification of miner's work conditions, particularly in countries in the global South. We do not question the cultural addiction to cheap, non-renewable energy causing the destruction of irreplaceable habitats. We do not pay attention to the tacit arrangements for tax breaks and subsidies, legitimising the otherwise prohibited activities of oil and gas companies whose enormous profits are rarely publicised. In allowing ourselves tacitly to accept the narratives of superiority and independence, even when we become aware of their hollow ring, our attention is distracted, or withdrawn, and the inherent violence of the Anthropocene continues.[45]

The debate around whether or not human cultural activity is more or less violent than that of any other species or system, then, becomes a question of where, how and why the human system directs attention from the violence and, relatedly, the suffering that it generates. This is also, in

---

[44] This is the second of Wendell Berry's seven elements of "harmony" in his "landscape": "This wilderness, the universe, is somewhat hospitable to us, but it is also absolutely dangerous (it is going to kill us sooner or later), and we are absolutely dependent on it." Wendell Berry, *Home Economics*. San Fransisco: Northpoint, (1987): 138.

[45] Timothy Morton makes this point in "Ecology without the present" (op. cit.).

effect, a question about the capacity we have, as perceivers within these systems, to redirect attention. We are not mechanistically determined by our enmeshment. We have, for instance, the capacity to realise the condition we are in. This realisation interacts with our enmeshment: it is a response that engenders other responses. We recognise distraction and withdrawal from paying attention to what we are involved. We allow ourselves to experience what paying attention elicits in us, and thus we sense an emerging set of possibilities that will reorientate, however minimally, our interaction with our involvement.[46]

I cannot leave the issue of violence without alluding to the propensity of human systems to depend on war for their development. Since 1945, for instance, the capacity for violent destruction through nuclear bombing has radically increased. Morton observes that "the bomb occupies the human". Even though Plutonium 239 has a phenomenally slow half-life of twenty-four thousand years, and no one around by then (if anyone is around) will be meaningfully related to me, it illustrates that current actions have measurable, meaningful consequences into the deep future.[47]

This idea that the slightest thing I do now will have grave consequences is true not just of bombs, of course. We are bound to be consumed in the end, but our hunger for energy, including nuclear energy and energy from non-renewable, carbon-based sources, has impacts that reverberate through unimaginable spans of time. The infinitesimal scale of human influence in universal terms may incline us to scoff at the idea that current acts have significant future bearings but, if we put Morton's words in the context that we do not act atomistically but as systems, we can see how a reverberating effect is possible. In five hundred years, seventy-five percent of climate change effects will still be happening. In thirty-one thousand years, twenty-five percent, and even in one hundred thousand years, seven percent of the effects will still be measurable. This is true, too, of the effects of the human species on the rest of the biota of the planet in all the

---

[46] It looks as though being complicit has to mean that what we are doing is morally wrong. I will argue, later in this chapter, that this is not the case. Being complicit just means being involved in something that is obstructing the gradual flow of energy through systems, as I will show below.

[47] Timothy Morton, "Ecology without the Present" (op. cit.): 233.

other ways, from pollution to farming, that we have had an impact.[48] Of course, it would be equally easy to point to prokaryotic and other early cells and their influence on the atmosphere which brought about the conditions, including vastly increased levels of atmospheric oxygen, that allowed the trajectory of multicellular life, including our own, to evolve.[49] However, understanding the difference between then and now requires that we revise how we consider biophysical systems as enmeshed within human systems, and the impact, upon these systems, of awareness.

When we think of ourselves as separable from other organisms, then, this is largely a perceptual trick, one of the many illusions associated with our (accidental, evolutionary) development of conscious awareness, a story that requires reflection and, periodically, revision. In addition, our enmeshment means that we use, as reference points, the points that were used by previous generations and, as these became more dominated by dualistic thinking, the capacity to see ourselves as systems within systems became quiescent. We rest our sense of ourselves on the development of stories, myths and metaphors that have evolved, historically, to explain changing experience. Platonically, for instance, there is a realm of absolutes, only the shadows of which we can perceive, or, in Christian terms, there are hierarchies, the physical ones atop of which we straddle, bipedal, dominant. If our realisation of these relationships is subjective, then each point of self-aware perception is a possible generation point for the perceptive system to understand itself.[50] Realisation as agency implies that the act of realisation creates a new narrative, an experience that then becomes a part of, and therefore interacts with, what is going on throughout the mesh.

To consider organisms as systems is as much a social construct as any other culturally relative idea. After all, the concept depends upon a historical trajectory of ideas that came about as a result of the flourishing of the scientific method, and ultimately, as a result of how we understand

---

[48] (Ibid.): 233. There are difficulties with Morton's interchangeable use of terminology (it is inconsistent of him to claim that there is no "me", yet then go on to talk about "I" as an active entity).

[49] See Cooper, G, *The Cell: A Molecular Approach,* Sinauer Associates, (2000). https://www.ncbi.nlm.nih.gov/books/NBK9841/.

[50] This does not imply that any point of perception is in a privileged position with regard to direct awareness. All perceptual awareness is filtered by the context out of which it emerges. This "realist" position implies that there exists a state of reality in the sense described as "structural realism" in James Ladyman, "What Is Structural Realism?", *Studies in History and Philosophy of Science Part A,* 29 (1998): 409–24.

evolutionary biology. We need not dismiss the model of evolution progressing through individual gene replication (or mutation) and natural selection. But a revision of this atomistic understanding is necessary if we are to construct a narrative that takes into account how intertwined human systems are with those within which they have evolved, and how organisms respond more like systems than like atomistic individuals.[51] In addition, now that we are recognisably in the Anthropocene, a significant proportion of our interactions are with human artefacts. This is changing the relationship between ourselves and the microbial and physical systems that inhabit and surround us and this, therefore, has to be incorporated into our story of ourselves.

This is the first major revision of the predominant narrative, and the one implicit in Taylor's approach: we need to take into account the degree to which our enmeshment changes the boundaries of how we see our actions. Perceiving ourselves as enmeshed is a more empirically accurate metaphor for our condition. It implies that the separation of our agency into a category on its own needs re-examining too. While it still makes sense for individual humans to consider ourselves as boundaried within our skins for the purposes of most of our day to day activities, it is equally valid, and empirically more accurate, to acknowledge that we interact more like systems than like atomistic individuals. More generally, living organisms are not necessarily or even workably separable from the systems within which they are enmeshed. Conceiving of ourselves as atomistic individuals is empirically valid on one level but we must also recognise the interdependency of individuals, and when considering the ecological emergency, it is vital that we acknowledge the degree to which our enmeshment creates our potential to respond. The problem of how to weigh up which systems to support, and how, remains, but is not insurmountable. It ought to be possible to generate an understanding of

---

[51] This reflects Lynn Margulis' endosymbiotic theory of eukaryotic cell development which revolutionized the modern concept of how life arose on Earth but should also cause us to reflect on realisation as an aspect of evolution, a way for an evolutionary system to reflect back on itself, and thus come to some conclusion about the role of the will as "willingness", or voluntarism, or the capacity to elicit compassion and thus collaboration, or symbiosis, or cooperation, that could allow for an evolution of us, as primates, from individualists, or species-only survivors, from selfish gene, to an evolutionary success story that encompasses a much broader understanding of self-interest that includes other species, and indeed that develops in us a deep appreciation of our existence, and our enmeshed natures. See, for instance, https://lecerveau.mcgill.ca/flash/capsules/articles_pdf/endosymbiotic_theory.pdf

the nuanced checks and balances between how much energy we can sequester for our own needs, and still live rich, fulfilled lives, and how much support we need to allow for other, more distal systems, like forests or oceans, to rewild themselves, and thus allow our more immediate systems, as organisms, to survive and flourish.[52]

The cognitive capacity to realise

We are not the only organisms with at least some level of self-awareness. Other members of the family Hominidae, including, particularly, gorillas, chimpanzees and orangutans, show many parallel cognitive capacities, as do many other mammals, but also octopi, with their unique perceptual abilities and communications structures.[53] The unique character of human self-awareness depends on our capacity to decide how to live, to decide on what is right and wrong, and to follow that through with action. This, at least, is what we have learned.[54]

---

[52] Simon James makes this point: "Consider a proponent of materialism, someone who subscribes to the notion that everything, she included, is made of matter. She might be. But she might be a terrible scourge of the environment". And again: "Such an individual clearly believes that we are at one with nature (for her, the material universe) but there is no good reason to think that she must be moved by a positive moral regard for the natural world." both in Simon P. James, "Against Holism: Rethinking Buddhist Environmental Ethics", *Environmental Values*, 16, (2007): 447–461.

[53] For a comprehensive exploration of the idea that animals can be considered conscious organisms because they exhibit a spectrum of capacities (including memory, emotions, learning, thinking and communicating) see, for instance, Gary E Varner, *Personhood, Ethics, and Animal Cognition: Situating Animals in Hare's Two Level Utilitarianism*, New York: Oxford University Press, (2012); David DeGrazia, "On the Questions of Personhood Beyond Homo Sapiens", in Peter Singer, (ed), *In Defense of Animals*, Blackwell, (2004); Oliver Sacks, Tim Flannery, Caspar Henderson, H. Allen Orr, and Richard C. Lewontin, "The Mental Life of Plants and Worms, Among Others", The New York Review of Books, 24 April 2014. Peter Godfrey-Smith's *Other Minds*, New York : Farrar, Straus and Giroux, (2016) is the seminal text on octopus consciousness.

[54] The prioritisation of individualistic over relational conditions in the perspectives of those in the cultures of the North is well-documented but the alternative view has been less well set out. Karyn L. Lai, "Conceptual Foundations for Environmental Ethics: A Daoist Perspective", *Environmental Ethics*, 25 (2003): 247–66, illustrates how a symbiotic relationship between individuals and wholes gives an entirely different perspective of our experience and allows the focus of motivation to

In some senses, we are bound to see from a single perspective. However, if individual organisms are not single organisms but complex systems, then they cannot exhibit the purely individualistic, teleological pursuit of ends that Taylor relies on to give them a locus of value. We are not moral agents in the way Taylor envisaged because we, too, are not individual organisms, but complex systems, pursuing ends at a variety of levels (and sometimes for contradictory goals). In addition, human moral agency is not that different from the responses of other kinds of organisms (or systems), and therefore calling what we do "moral" is simply not justifiable.

In revising the idea that humans have a unique kind of agency, namely moral agency, I want to reflect on why we consider human agency in general to be unique. My sense is that human agency is considered to be unique because we still labour under the illusion that humans make decisions about their lives in a way that other organisms do not. Taylor maintains that moral agents are alone in their capacity to decide on the right way to live, and in having the wherewithal to pursue such a decision with action. This is an extremely strong and persistent view, but it relies on the highly questionable Cartesian narrative that the human will is some kind of supra-physical entity that can control and direct physiological or physical matter from somewhere else. As I have just attempted to show, if we are entirely enmeshed, human systems are as subject to natural laws and processes as all else, and therefore any claim for a directional force that exists outside the mesh is unjustifiable. Instead, I suggest we consider what agency might mean if we take the point of view that we are indeed enmeshed, and that any ability to respond that humans have takes place in the context of interactive, dynamic systems, that are intimate with human enmeshment.

For Taylor, respect is the attitude that living organisms, or communities of organisms, elicit from reasonable moral agents. The closer these moral agents come to the ideal of being fully factually informed, reality-aware, rational beings, the more likely they are to respond appropriately. Taylor's moral agents, like moral agents in the environmental ethics literature in general, are unique in the animal world in that they can "engage in moral deliberation", "form judgments about right and wrong", and so on.[55] These are not the kinds of cognitive capacities that other organisms have.

---

become maintaining a flow of energy between relationships, rather than preserving individualistic identity and space.

[55] Taylor (op. cit.): 14.

Yet if we allow that human moral agents have these unique capacities, we cannot, at the same time, claim that humans are just like everything else, unless we also claim that these capacities are no more or less special than a bat's echolocation or a nightingale's song. The logical extension of Taylor's idea that humans are fundamentally a part of the evolved community is that there is nothing particularly special about being human. Yet the capacity for human moral agency is distinctly unique if it gives humans the ability to choose what to do, because this is distinctly not the case with having the capacity for echolocation or birdsong.

If we are biologically evolved, along with everything else, then the claim that we have an ontologically different level of choice from everything else is a suspect claim. I maintain that we think we have the level of choice that would allow us to call ourselves "moral agents" because we have inherited an unreflective narrative about our own superiority. If we are just the same kind of thing as everything else that has evolved, and if we are as enmeshed as everything else, then it is very unlikely that we have evolved a capacity that gives us a wholly different kind of relationship to the decisions we make from other organisms. In other words, when we think we are responding voluntarily, we are actually reacting. Harris has made a strong case for this, asking us to reflect on the context in which our next decision occurs. We did not choose our family, or the time, place or conditions of our birth, early environment, or all the accidental and unique events that shaped our character and quirks. Yet our brains make choices and decisions based on:

> …preferences and beliefs that have been hammered into it over a lifetime - by your genes, your physical development since the moment you were conceived, and the interactions you have had with other people, events, and ideas. Where is the freedom in this?[56]

The process of decision making is, of course, highly complex and non-linear, in addition to which it is not even particularly predictable. So many variables are at stake. It is, however, as subject to probabilistic laws as everything else in the universe. Therefore, I think it makes sense to agree with Harris and others who have drawn similar conclusions, and dispense with the idea of thinking of our wills as being "free" and therefore also of our being "moral agents" in the sense of freely deliberating beings who are either strong or weak-willed.

---

[56] Samuel Harris, *Free Will*, (op. cit.).

Where I go beyond Harris, perhaps, is in suggesting that we have one element of cognitive capacity that is, if not unique to humans, particularly well developed in us compared with any other species we know about. That is our capacity to self-reflect, to be self-aware, to be able to see ourselves in action (even if there is less we can do about it than we might previously have thought).

Understanding that we are in the emergency, that the emergency is in us, and that it is arising precisely because we are entirely enmeshed and reacting to everything that has happened to us, can, because of our self-awareness, our capacity to reflect, and to realise, elicit a response. I would beg to differ from Taylor that the response it elicits is "respect", but I do agree that an attitude can arise as an appropriate response to a realisation of our human condition when we understand our evolutionary and current context. I am not sure, however, that calling this attitude "moral" is justified although there are grounds for deliberating over the question. The attitude that I think arises, or rather, is elicited by a reflection on our circumstances, and indeed on the circumstances in which any entity or system finds itself, is compassion.

Morality may simply be the wrong word for what arises, although there is certainly the implication that the compassionate attitude that is elicited by a full realisation of our circumstances has a connection to moral value. Self-reflection and self-awareness are crucially important and primarily, if not uniquely, human phenomena. They, and not things like the mental determination to carry our a physical act, or other supposedly "moral" phenomena, are the source of our uniquely human agency.

Plants do not sway in the breeze because they have decided to do so. By the same token, human activity is a direct reaction to the physical, environmental conditions (temperature, access to shelter and food, security and so forth), genome, early years and cultural conditioning, and so on, that go up to make the current context of individuals and groups.[57] If plants sway, so, in some important senses, do humans. Plants, microbes, and other living systems maintain and regenerate an integrated organisation, responding in evolutionarily appropriate ways to the forces, breezes, and other conditions that make up their context. In this sense, plants, microbes and any other living system, exhibit agency - responding, repairing, regenerating as organisational structures – just as humans do.

---

[57] Matthew Hall, "Plant Autonomy and Human-Plant Ethics"(op. cit.).

"The good" of systems

If we transpose Taylor's original idea that "the good of an individual non human organism [consists] in the full development of its biological powers" to the sphere of living organisms as systems (for instance, trees as communities of both symbiotic (e.g. tree/ root fungus) and parasitic (tree/ trunk fungus) relationships), then we can see how teleological or goal-centred activity is a characteristic not only of human systems but of all living systems.[58] This is the transposition of the Aristotelean sense of teleology as the actualisation of potentiality.[59] In this account, all organisms have a potential (to grow, flourish, reproduce, protect and maintain themselves) towards which they aim (teleologically). Whether they do this "to the full development of their biological powers" or not is a moot point. There is no "intention" behind the flourishing, in the sense that there is no ideal towards which a system or individual living organism is pulled. Instead, from a systems-based perspective, this potential can be much better understood as the inherent tendency of systems to dissipate energy in a particular, and well organized, way, while attempting to maintain, and reproduce themselves, like vortexes in a stream.

"The good" as the graduated flow

Just as growth, reproduction, and so on, are organising processes, so the systematic distribution of energy is an organising, patterned process that graduates, rather than randomly increasing or decreasing, the flow of energy towards entropy. The difference between human and other systems does not lie in their capacity to exercise this potential, but in their capacity to realise that they are exercising it.

Daniel Fouke, in discussing microbial life, remarks that the soil itself can be validly viewed as a "self-organising system which can be disrupted by changes to soil structure as well as soil biota".[60] This directional organisation is motivated by

> ... a flow of energy produced by photosynthesis in plants that converges with energy produced by decomposers of dead organic matter at higher trophic levels. The two energy pathways are also linked by the nutrient cycling of mycorrhizal

---

[58] Paul Taylor, "Ethics of Respect for Nature" (op. cit.): 176.

[59] David Keller, "Introduction" to *Environmental Ethics: The Big Questions* (op. cit.): 14.

[60] Daniel C. Fouke, "Humans and the Soil" (op. cit.).

fungi and nitrogen-fixing bacteria in symbiotic relations with the roots of plants.[61]

Human encultured systems include extremely complex energy flows, including linguistic capacities that can be passed through time (like books) or through space (like conversations on a mobile), and the communications, manufacturing, distribution and power processes that create and maintain them. We, as dynamic self-organising systems, characteristically exhibit self-awareness, both through the use of these artefacts, and through the exchanges of information that we broadcast and receive via their use. Yet, in considering ourselves as systems, we need to accept that our responsiveness, even at the cognitive level, takes place in the context of dynamic, interacting responses at the microscopic and at the macroscopic levels over which, in terms of agency, we have no control.

Soil underlies the boundary between organic and inorganic processes and understanding this brings to light the problem with perceiving systems as mechanisms. Such an approach fails to acknowledge this continuum between living and non-living systems. It does not allow for recognition of the complexity, sensitivity and reactivity of evolved systems. Systems are processes, full of uncertainties and probabilities that are not at all linear or mechanical in character. Human conscious responsiveness gives all the appearance of self-aware reaction to biophysical events but unless we deliberately draw our attention to the extent of our enmeshment, our agency is equivalent to a root's avoidance of nutrient-poor soil.

The metaphor of a systems-based approach allows us to view ourselves as occupying the same conceptual space as the context within which we are enmeshed. More complex systems have exponentially more potential outcomes, but all evolved systems are inherently probabilistic, and therefore flexible. In revising the idea of what is exclusive about human agency, we can see that from the point of view of a highly complex system of interactions and responses that nevertheless still obey probabilistic natural laws, it is consistent with all other kinds of agency exhibited across biophysical systems.[62]

Human agency is both the highly complex, but nevertheless consistent, response system to events and conditions within larger dynamic and

---

[61] Fouke (Ibid.): 149.

[62] Laws in this sense express the activity within a relationship involving exchanges and can be written in the form, "if...then..."

complex systems. It is not free from those systems, and it is not driven by some exclusively human will. However, there is one sense in which human agency is different, and perhaps somewhat unique. That is in the sense that humans have the cognitive capacity that we exercise, sometimes by chance, sometimes through the use of techniques like meditation, which allows us to perceive our responses and reactions, as though from a perspective beyond them.[63] Because this capacity takes place within the same biophysical arena, it is interactive: exercising this capacity alters the processes of other systems. This alteration is usually quite subtle but it is nevertheless highly significant, since it interacts throughout the system. This is significant because it is such a unique and profound effect.

Human systems are driven, as all evolved systems are, to maintain themselves in the temporary vortices that give them what we see as their identity. As with all biophysical systems, it is their complexity that makes them effective systems of energy dissipation.[64] In revising the view of agency, I suggest we reverse the traditional teleological metaphor that Taylor uses, that describes human and non-human organisms as actualising their potentiality in Aristotelean terms. As I said earlier, Taylor's use of the Aristotelean idea suggests that "the good" of the organism is a future state towards which it is mysteriously pulled. This does not fit well with the evolutionary thesis. Instead of the image of systems being driven (or pulled) towards an end, or goal, we can see that systems are pushed by myriad minute processes, all of which are flexible reactions of activity dissipating and redistributing energy flows in order, however temporarily, to maintain themselves in existence, or reproduce themselves so that in some sense they, or we, go on. The distinction is important because it accords better with a picture we have of energy dissipation from a narrow base at a higher concentration to a less concentrated, much broader set of potential outcomes.

The criticism that human agency is "determined", from this perspective, is shown to be false since the unique aspect of human agency is the capacity to reflect, or realise. In the context of the narratives, we tell ourselves, our capacity for realisation is also our capacity to alter the narratives and this, in turn, shifts how we relate. This allows us to see

---

[63] This specific phrase, "to see ourselves see", is used by Beau Lotto in his talk on perception at *Beau Lotto: Optical Illusions Show How We See*, (2009). <http://www.youtube.com/watch?v=mf5otGNbkuc&feature=youtube_gdata_player>.

[64] This idea comes from Scott Sampson in "The purpose of the universe is to disperse energy" (op. cit.).

human agency, in the sense of realisation, as a meta-system, driven by the same conditions that drive all systems - energy dissipation - yet able to reflect and so (to a degree) alter them.

In this revised sense, human agency is the capacity to self-reflect, to become aware of context and interrelationships, to explore and question metaphors, and so to shift relationships. Human cultural systems depend utterly on the fact that agency in the more general sense of response-reaction exists at every level, from the ability of plants to photosynthesize, to the capacity of some systems to live 10,000 years, to the ability of some species to produce 20 million offspring, or regenerate after being put in a blender. In this understanding, we are response processes because we are like, and even because we are reliant upon, other systems, not because we are the species, *Homo sapiens*.

The difference between response processes across most other systems, and response processes in human systems is that the latter have the unusual additional capacity to reflect on the processes themselves. From a systems-based perspective, the human, encultured ability to avoid threats is general agency, not agency as realisation. However, the capacity for human systems to perceive themselves, and to allow an attitude of compassion to arise, is agency as realisation. That this capacity for reflection, or realisation, gives us access to the elicitation of a particular attitude opens up possibilities that would otherwise remain latent. This is what I mean by realisation as agency.

Realising "the good" of systems

In Christian and other faith narratives, if we fail to respond to the demands of the practice of the faith, we call ourselves sinners. There is an acknowledged gap between principle and practice, between what we aim for, and what we do. By the same token, in Taylor's development of the idea that an ethical response is necessary, a gap develops between the elicited response and the duty that it imposes.[65] This gap poses difficulties

---

[65] Taylor overtly sets up the ideal as something we can make a closer and closer approximation to (see Taylor *Respect for Nature* (op. cit.): 307-312). This criticism was also laid against Peter Singer's ethic proposed in Singer, Peter, *The Life You Can Save* Pan Macmillan, (2010), since it demands too much of individuals (that we reduce our consumerism to bare existence and give everything else away to those who are living in extreme poverty). Singer since amended his ethical approach but freely admits that he himself does not live up to the ethic, since he owns more than

even in its own terms since it means we can never achieve the ideal status of complete compliance: we are bound to fail to fulfill the code of ethics because it is too stringent to adhere to. Ethical codes create the conditions for hypocrisy: even the most ardent practitioner is going to falter, and this means that there will be some who justify their actions on the basis that they could not succeed. We have seen many examples of this, from recent scandals in Catholic institutions, to forced "marriages" of young girls to Sunni soldiers on the battlefield.

However, in the terms I am proposing, those of an evolved enmeshment, our responses emerge from the context of our conditions, and not as a result of our degree of compliance to ethical codes. We reflect on our own enmeshment, and this alters how we see ourselves, and what options for action arise as a result of this shifted view. The narratives that we absorb, along with the information we are exposed to, shape how we view our relationship with other organisms and planetary systems, and this, too, shapes and alters how we respond. To call what is elicited by reflection "ethical" is a strange use of the word. However, the space that opens when reflection, or self-awareness, mindfulness, or "waking up" to our situation happens, fills, if we are open to the elicitation, with compassion.

Imposing an environmental ethic on a cohort of discussants who hold different sets of ideological beliefs, whose narratives about the human-nature relationship vary and conflict, causes divergence. The narrative it implies is a direct challenge to existing narratives, and this causes further entrenchment in viewpoints, and obstructs opportunities for discussion and negotiation that could lead to the possibility of a convergent response. Putting aside ethical demands in considering how to respond to the ecological emergency and instead, focusing on the capacity we have to see ourselves in context opens us to the possibility of dialogue and discussion based on looking for connection, not attempting to prove that we are right, and the other is wrong.[66]

Taylor's reasoning, from the point of view of seeing the human condition in the context of evolutionary biology, is an effective starting point, as is his general idea that humans are not alone in responding to conditions that benefit or harm them. However, to then demand that we act with

---

minimal goods and lives on more than a subsistence income (although he does give a substantial portion of his income to causes that work to alleviate global poverty).

[66] See Hans-Georg Moeller, *The Moral Fool* (op. cit.): "...foundational ethical statements are not factual but, so to speak, ideal.": 3.

respect for nature as an ethic creates an insurmountable – and unnecessary – gap between theory and practice.

The problem with an ethical approach multiplies, though, because it contains within it the potential not for a universally applicable set of guidelines, but for conflict. This is because ethical guidelines, as opposed, say, to agreed rules in sport, or even to laws, are dependent on underlying ideological commitments that are carried, usually with deep emotional commitment, as a matter of personal identity rather than simply as a matter of fact.[67] Basing a response to the ecological emergency on an ethical demand to respect nature is like adding another layer of potentially contentious conditions to an already over-burdened framework. This is true of any ethical response to the ecological emergency, since an ethical response is based on a defined set of values and beliefs. An ethically neutral response may face other problems, because there is an inclination to distrust one who does not carry an ideological banner. However, it will only be by circumnavigating the divisiveness of direct confrontation, looking for common ground, exploring connection, that a convergent response can emerge.

There is another, equally important, argument for not responding to the ecological crisis with an ethical demand, and that relates to the systems-based approach I alluded to earlier. As I showed when I revised Taylor's idea of atomistic organisms, the divisions he attempts to uphold have all disintegrated around us. Human and nature, like organisms and systems, are not two separate realms and neither are humans unnatural. What human systems lack in failing to respond effectively to the ecological emergency is not authenticity but awareness, reflectiveness or, to put it more precisely still, realisation. Realisation, the idea of both coming to an awareness of a state of affairs and creating or "making real" some additional state, is quite different from moral agency: it is attunement to a quality that exists outside and beyond human values: some things "just are" good, for us, and for other systems. Cooperation, from its most fundamental sense as the interaction between entities to its more common use in terms of symbiosis within evolutionary systems, or in human terms, to the seeking for common ground, is manifest most clearly

---

[67] For a detailed treatment of this argument, see Hans-Georg Moeller, (Ibid.): 45ff. We do not, on the whole, become attached in any emotional sense to rules in games or sport (although we might well become emotional if people break them). They are not a part of our identity. However, belonging to a religious or a political, or even a "social" group like "Polyamory Ireland" generally does become part of one's identity, since it represents one's moral, social or political values.

in humans as compassion, the ability to view what we are and do from an attunement to what the most loving, or compassionate, act might be.

Eliciting compassion

If we allow ourselves to view uniquely human agency in the way I have just described, we begin to notice how our activity responds and is responded to in its enmeshment. Not only do we become more sensitive to the feedback processes we are inevitably involved in, but the very process of noticing shifts how we relate, both physiologically, and in the kind of attitude we have to our interrelationships. The systems respond to each other and we can see that, while it would be ambitious to believe this system of reflectiveness could disentangle itself from the system entirely (to exist, a reflection, after all, must be a reflection of something), the reflection itself is not passive. It offers the possibility of actively engaging with other systems, shifting the relationships between them and becoming a force, in itself, for altering the trajectory. It also generates a shift in the framework so the narrative that we use to describe our relationship to the context we are in shifts and this alters our attitude and responses to the relationship.

One example of this is in how we talk about our relationship with other biophysical systems. From viruses to tsunamis, we talk as though the universe was against us. Yet, on reflection, what our language reveals is how keenly we still hanker for a directional agency "out there", even a malignant one, rather than accepting the much more probable scenario that these forces are entirely indifferent to human systems. Within a revised narrative, therefore, there are neither forces that are "for" us, or "against" us.[68] However, when we attune ourselves to a less judgmental, less evaluative view of what is going on, we realise that there are forces that allow energy to dissipate and matter to cycle, and there are also conditions that create interference, or resistance to these energy flows and matter cycles. So, in a sense, there are still conditions that are good for, and conditions that are less beneficial, or even harmful to, the flow of energy. We might easily find ourselves calling those conditions "good for" or "bad for", if, in the context of the system, they benefit or impede processes of energetic flow.

As soon as we realise the kind of agency we have, we allow it to exercise itself and it becomes an active process. Because it is a system that arises out of our biophysical system, it interacts with all the biophysical relationships we are involved in and each is shifted on its trajectory, minutely or profoundly. Each realisation is an opportunity for more possibilities for beneficial exchanges to arise, although there are degrees of attention and full realisation requires tremendous effort. This is not the effort of willpower, but the effort of keeping attention on all the interactions one is involved in which requires that trauma, thirst, hunger and other conditions are incorporated and acknowledged but do not overcome this state of watchfulness. Such an effort requires practice, though from the first realisation, the interactions within the system alter and there are more options for new, compassionately guided, interactions to take place.

The impact of this (as far as we know) uniquely human capacity is potentially as profound as the capacity to synthesise matter into arrangements that can no longer interchange information or energy. Different traditions view this capacity in different ways. The Daoists considered that the ability to self-reflect leads to all kinds of problems. Knowledge of this capacity, combined with the failure to exercise it, is irresponsible, yet it is hard work to keep attention on what is going on. Exercising this capacity without humility, or compassion, is also, potentially problematic and may simply create scorn or indifference. I have attempted a brief exegesis and I will attempt to explore more fully below how an attitude of compassion and humility is elicited by this process. However, the fuller one's awareness of one's condition is, the easier it is to see that one is neither as worthy of reward (hence humility) nor as culpable (hence compassion) as one is led to believe by the narratives of independence and superiority.

We are far more subject to the circumstances we find ourselves in than traditional agency allows, and compassion arises when we realise that all systems respond interdependently, including others that, like us, can suffer. While humans are interdependent with everything else, they are also peripheral. Other, older systems like bacteria and microbes have been maintaining the dissipation of solar energy and cycling matter for long millennia before the creatures that would become human evolved lungs. When we understand and appreciate this, we see that other systems do not rely on us nearly as much as we rely on them. A reasonable response to this realisation is a sense of humility, and empathetic resonance (perhaps

---

[68] A very old idea that is extensively used and described in the Daoist tradition and is well explained by Moeller in *The Moral Fool* (op. cit.).

as awe, gratitude, or at least appreciation) for older, wider ecosystems, which create the foundations of what allows our existence.

This may make us less inclined to let our attention be as easily distracted by that other uniquely human capacity, the artificial synthesis of material that rigidly fixes energy into conditions that cannot easily interchange information or participate in regulated dissipation. In stepping back from our enmeshment within artificial systems, our awareness extends beyond them, back to the deeper interrelationship with the systems that steward our existence.

This position could be criticised as anthropocentrism by the back door: after all, a good reason to pay attention to how we behave within systems that steward us is so that our responses allow the latter to keep maintaining us.[69] But there are other reasons why this approach is worth taking that do not benefit the human species at all. Central to this approach is the recognition that the human species will not exist indefinitely. Even taking into account the possibility that we are potentially threatening our own existence now, there is a longer view. Taking this approach is a response that allows us, where possible, to mitigate some of the more destructive features introduced by anthropogenic impact, but that will long outlast our species.

It is from Scott Sampson that we get the suggestion to imagine the flow of energy through time as a vast river, within which whirlpools are created, representing patterns of existence that maintain themselves for a particular length of time.[70] These whirlpools are concentrations of energy that conform to a certain pattern and then dissipate back into the river of energy flowing all around them. Examples of these whirlpools include such vast and, from our perspective, long-lived systems as stars, galaxies or constellations, but they also include much smaller, more temporally minute systems, like living systems, or even molecules or quarks. These concentrations of energy involve the exchange of information, in a Poincarean sense.[71]

---

[69] Richard Watson gives a good account of the reversion of biocentric to anthropocentric positions in his paper Richard A. Watson, "A Critique of Anti-Anthropocentric Biocentrism" (op. cit.).

[70] Scott Sampson, "The purpose of the universe is to disperse energy" (op. cit.).

[71] John Baez has done extensive work to coordinate mathematicians' and physicists' research on this. See, for instance, *Creativity in the Face of Climate Change*, (2009). <http://www.youtube.com/watch?v=in5F3OfbtUA&feature=youtube_gdata_player >; also the Azimuth forum (www.johncarlosbaez.wordpress.com).

From the universe as a system, we can pan in to focus on the biophysical systems of the planet. Taylor's "good" of planetary organisms was something he developed to show that more than humans have inherent worth. To have a "good", an organism has to have conditions that can be to its benefit. In this sense, a wheelbarrow or a tractor cannot be benefited or harmed, only damaged.[72] However, a close reading of Taylor suggests that his analysis of "the good" of organisms is, in the end, instrumental.[73] For instance, "the good" of plants includes water, but water is, therefore, only instrumentally good for plants if the end of plants is to continue to survive and reproduce. Survival and reproduction is also only a "good for" plants if they serve some other structurally related end.

Taylor's conclusion is since we would not ask what a human being is "good for" and yet we would agree that humans actively pursue goals, we must accord the same level of worth to other organisms, since they act in a parallel fashion. However, from a systems-based perspective, it is perfectly legitimate to ask what humans are "good for" since we are envisaging them as relational rather than as atomistic. If we are not entities in this way, then we are not "ends", at least not individually. In a similar way, if we are not evolving towards some "higher" state, then there is no ideal towards which our lives are directed. So our sense of being moral agents acting to realise some ideal is no longer justified.

Autopoiesis is a phenomenon exhibited by all systems that self-organise, and in particular, by living systems. In revising what we might understand by "the good" of systems it is worth reviewing Peter Singer's idea that, in order to be valid contenders for moral consideration, organisms or systems must have "intention". Singer considers that all language related to talking of what is "good" or "intentional" for systems and entities is metaphorical. One could say that rivers pursue their own good by striving to reach the sea, but one would not be talking about a conscious process, just as one is not talking about a conscious, intentional process in plants

---

[72] See Simon P. James, "Buddhism and the Ethics of Species Conservation", *Environmental Values* 15, 1 (2006): 85–97, and Warwick Fox, "Forms of Harm and Our Obligations to Humans and Other Animals". In Evangelos D Protopapadakis (ed.), *Animal Ethics: Past and Present Perspectives*, Berlin: Logos Verlag, (2012); 197–221.

[73] I am not using this word in the sense that Simon James uses it, as a way of expressing instrumental value to humans. I am using it in the sense that the processes of energy dissipation I have described are instrumental in allowing systems to flow, or, when they are not allowed to flow, in obstructing those systems.

or most animals.[74] Singer's question is why should we respect one process when it is as equally automatic and unreflective as the other.

Taylor maintains that there is a difference between those things (organisms, or living systems) that actively pursue conditions that benefit them, and non-living systems (like rivers) that do not actively pursue those conditions.[75] From a systems-based perspective, we can revise the differentiation on an alternative basis. Processes that are pursued automatically and without awareness have no capacity to shift the system's trajectory whereas processes that can reflect upon the system do.

The relationship between this capacity for awareness, or realisation as agency, and the directional flow of the universe, is easier to establish now that we have left aside any attempt to locate moral value in the system. We can begin to consider what it might mean to say that some kinds of activity are "good for" systems, and in what sense this could be true, without the distracting search for a moral response. This, in turn, will give us an idea of how our understanding is itself a realisation, and therefore interacts with the information we manage to collect.

Viewed from a physicalist perspective, our experiences are dynamic, relational information exchanges. We are able to perceive the experiences both as someone involved in them, and as an observer. We can see ourselves as relationships, therefore, but we can also see ourselves as interacting with those relationships through our attention. This idea is useful for visualising the directional flow we can facilitate or obstruct by drawing our attention to conditions, or withdrawing our attention from them.[76]

As Sampson points out, the boundaries between the whirlpools and the river are highly permeable, although, of course, we experience them as significant. Skin, for example, is a permeable membrane, constantly exchanging matter with the external environment and yet it marks the boundary between the systems that are concentrated around the genetic activity that maps and sustains each organic structure and the wider systems that feed into and dissipate energy from this patterned form. Particularly at microscopic scales, it is difficult to determine with any

---

[74] Warwick Fox, "Problem 14 in Human Relationships, Nature, and the Built Environment: Problems That Any General Ethics Must Be Able to Address", in *Sage Handbook of Environment and Society*, London, Sage, (2007): 107–23.

[75] Taylor, *Respect for Nature* (op. cit.): 63.

[76] James Ladyman,, "What is a Complex System?" (op. cit.).

precision where the organism ends and the external world begins. As Sampson puts it:

> Even apparently dense and unyielding things, like rocks, trees, bones and mountains, turn out to be fluid at atomic levels and/or on geologic timescales, their internal make-up shifts like river currents.[77]

Biodiverse systems are some of the richest, most complex examples of energy dissipation systems that we have yet come across. This implies that the energetic exchanges that occur in richly biodiverse systems increase the dissipation of energy more effectively than their poorer, simpler counterparts. This matters to human systems because such complex systems reduce the solar gradient by "filtering" energy through the various systems, extracting as much energy as possible to dissipate, leading to a relatively graduated, and therefore relatively more stable, system of informational exchanges. This is the picture of the world, from an energetic point of view, that humans evolved in.

Energy flows are directional, therefore anything that facilitates the tendency to dissipate energy through systems is "good for" that flow in the instrumental sense that it maintains it, although ultimately entropy is not "good for" anything. This does not imply that a simple arithmetic increase in entropy is "good for" us, but since biodiverse systems maintain the graduated flow of energy, they are "good for" human systems. So, if we have an interest in our own survival (and most of us do), we also have an interest in maintaining, restoring or mitigating the damage to biodiverse systems.

Biodiversity is a vanishingly rare occurrence, as far as we can discover so far, but the evolution of biodiverse systems has been a chance affair. It may be argued, therefore, that any system that graduates energetic flow will be good for us but the fact is that we evolved in the very specific context of the milieu of biodiversity that sustains us, and synthesising a system that imitates what we have evolved in, "faking" evolution, cannot capture the complexity, sensitivity or sophistication of the interactions that evolved systems exhibit. Evolved systems are self-supporting, in the sense that all biodiverse systems benefit from the graduating presence of all other biodiverse systems. On a universal scale, this dissipation is neither beneficial nor harmful. But it is "good for" us, in the sense that it

---

[77] Scott Sampson, "The purpose of the universe is to disperse energy"(op. cit.).

forms the foundation for our survival as a culturally sophisticated species and that underpins any other "good" we might decide to value.

From the best descriptions we have of how the universe operates at the moment, the idea that energy is dissipated through systems is widely accepted. Biodiverse richness is "good for" more than humans, therefore. It is good for energetic dissipation within the context of life on the planet, as a whole. This gives us grounds for considering not just what is "good for" human flourishing. To hold energy in states that cannot participate in the flow of energetic dissipation is to hold them outside the exchange of information and flow of cycles of matter that allow graduated dissipation to proceed. All the systems within which we are enmeshed are actively dissipating energy "in order to" return to the relative inertia of non-living existence.[78] It is in this dissipation that we are maintained.

Humanly synthesised artifices cannot participate in energetic exchange of information because the molecular structures are locked in non-participative forms (like plastics, or synthesised radioactive isotopes). Likewise, our increasing inroads into habitats destroy evolved and richly biodiverse systems and replace them with systems that are much less diverse (monocultures) or that do not symbiote (cities, where individual trees are planted as decoration but fragmented from the ecosystem they would have evolved with).[79] This creates gaps in the graduation of energetic flow and steepens dissipation, causing other knock-on effects, like systematic collapse. Simpler biophysical systems are much more vulnerable to sharp changes in conditions than richly complex, biodiverse ones, but even richly complex systems are unlikely to be able to sustain themselves if the gradient of energy dissipation becomes too steep.

If we recognise that the systems within which we are enmeshed have conditions that are "good for" them, instrumentally, because they allow energetic dissipation, then we have the beginnings of a response-base from which to direct our agency as realisation. But we still need to establish whether or not agency as realisation can be directed.

We can do this by becoming aware, to whatever extent is available to us, of the vast web of interconnections within which we are enmeshed. With

---

[78] Timothy Morton, *The Ecological Thought* (op. cit.).

[79] It is easy to point to such apparently non-living structures as cities here, although in microbial and invertebrate terms, recent research suggests that cities do develop complex biodiverse systems and it is worth remembering that little research has been done into the ability of evolved systems to recover when human enculturation becomes more self-aware.

practice, we can hold ourselves in that state of awareness or attention, and by doing so, elicit an attitude of compassion and humility in the face of the vast whirlpools of energy that create and sustain us. It is through this process that the compassion we elicit, or attune to, alters the trajectory of what responses become available to us, or, if you like, come to light. Through compassionate attunement, the latent qualities that make up systems, particularly those of cooperation, and symbiosis, become options that otherwise remain hidden, and since compassion is inclined to cooperate, it alters the trajectory of our existence to better either our own systems, and chances of survival, or the systems that maintain us, and theirs.

Realisation as directional

In revising Taylor's idea of agency, I have shown that it is possible to see agency as a process of realisation, as the exercise of a capacity for self-awareness, and to consider the possibilities that arise when this realisation, which is itself a system, feeds back through other systems. It seems clear from what I have shown so far that being able to exercise agency is still possible, and indeed desirable, as a system of compassionate attunement that interplays with and thus influences the interactions other systems.

Human perceptions come to a perspective on existence as a result of myriad physical interactions and influences, but also through cultural narratives that are filtered by the particular, dynamic conditions of each person. Sometimes, identity can be tightly bound up with a particular cultural narrative (when, for instance, it is accepted without reflection, or when there are particularly strong motivations for the identification). When this is the case, any discussion about the narrative is also a discussion about an individual or group identity and this can be seen as threatening or undermining. This is the core problem of attitudinal divergence.

If we can see ourselves as a part of biophysical and cultural systems, systems over which we have no control except through the process of realisation, we come to a somewhat different sense of identity. The idea we develop of ourselves is less tied to a particular commitment to a cultural narrative. We can also see that much of the sense of moral agency that we might have had, much of the sense of being responsible for a set of actions, or of being a victim of another set of actions, no longer makes sense. Instead, we begin to recognise that in reacting, we were responding within context, without having paid close attention, and therefore without meaningful responsibility. This is not to let us off the hook: we have the capacity to respond by paying close attention and seeing what opportunities emerge through compassionate attunement. We can begin to acknowledge that it is only through this kind of attentive attunement that compassion itself, as a kind of qualitative pattern, shows us how to mitigate the anthropogenic impact that has been so massively destructive and threatens our own species cultural and civilisational survival. Blame or guilt, however, are not appropriate or useful attitudes in attempting to motivate a response. We must keep stepping back and allowing compassion to arise and allow the attitude it elicits to guide our response.

In this picture, there is no ideal which will allow us to rest or stop having to make the effort to respond to the situation, to realise that our agency is this act of paying attention to see what options emerge. Each state we find ourselves in is dynamic, changing and in all senses impermanent, as the biophysical description I outlined earlier relates. To aim for a particular state is to imply that it is possible to hold one position indefinitely, and that contradicts a fundamental condition of this perspective. As I said earlier, it is better to picture ourselves as being pushed, as biophysical systems, to avoid the steep gradients of energetic flow that imply the collapse of systems, species, or individual death. We are not being pulled, teleologically, towards the top of an evolutionary ladder. However wonderful it would be to enter the perfect state, to aim to do so is to divide the frame of reference into this now and some other then. On the contrary, what we respond to, as human systems, realising as agents, is always an unfinished dynamic.

Many cultural narratives, including the dualistic narrative that underpins much of globalising culture, reject the idea that this imperfect, dynamic state is all there is. Yet by adopting the approach to agency I have described, this is the most obvious conclusion: we are in a dynamic state because biophysical systems are dynamic, transient, and impermanent.[80] Taylor himself clearly rejected the idea that the natural world was a harmonious place, and that therefore humans could mimic nature in order to live in harmony with it. He stated that modern biology has shown that in evolved communities of living systems, no state of harmony exists, since all are always in a state of flux, or change.[81] Taylor did, however, posit an ideal state towards which humans could strive, while recognising and acknowledging

---

[80] This narrative is agnostic about any other kind of existence.

[81] Paul Taylor, *Respect for Nature* (op. cit.): 8 "... what has been called the "balance of nature" can no longer be assumed as a kind of basic norm built into the order of the natural world."

that this state was unrealisable. In revising Taylor's thesis, I think we can respond to the ecological emergency much more effectively if we put aside these attempts to strive for an ideal state and focus, instead, on making the effort to realise what state we are in and how we can better allow the gradual flow through our relationships.

In revising how we imagine "the good" of systems, I am rejecting the idea that we need to locate value within any entity. I am suggesting that there is no ideal state towards which we can aim, and no atomistic entity to posit value, so we can only get guidance on how to respond by paying attention, and then discerning whether or not systems (including ourselves) obstruct or facilitate the graduated dissipation of energy, and what options are available to us to mitigate any obstruction.[82]

Comparisons with Asian traditions of thought

This process parallels the work of many non-dualistic philosophies, in which we are able to see how the particular bias, attractions and aversions of our current perspective come about as a result of the conditions we find ourselves in and the conditions that have brought us to this point. The process of awareness is also the process of realising, a system that allows us to reflect, impartially, as it were, on all the engagements we are involved in.[83]

There is a difficulty with language that arises in this attempt to describe a self becoming aware that it is not, after all, a self. The non-dualistic idea that we can "forget the self" as a specific perceptual location is notoriously difficult to describe without using esoteric language or imagery.[84] Yet agency as realisation is precisely this activity of stepping back from the relationships and interactions we are all involved in and being able to see them, and ourselves within them, as transitional and dynamic rather than as fixed identities.

The more deeply this process is engaged in, the more a motivation develops to maintain, as far as possible and whenever possible, openness to the insight that this perspective gives. Attention to the autonomous

---

[82] This does not imply that any point of perception is in a privileged position with regard to direct awareness.

[83] "One simply refrains from attaching any value judgements to one's perceptions," and,"The indifferent and amoral mind sees more clearly than the emotionally and morally afflicted one." Hans-Georg Moeller *The Moral Fool* (op. cit.): 58 and 59 respectively.

[84] Dōgen, *Shōbōgenzō: Treasury of the True Dharma Eye*, (op. cit.).

processes, including those of the body, the breath and, of course, any sensations and experiences, including cognitive experience, creates an understanding of the connections and interdependence of the internal and external, or the self and the other. This capacity for reflection is not cognitive, in the sense of intellectual, but is the raw experience of the network of enmeshment and it generates both beneficial and relaxing sensations, and so offers its own reward, but also empathy as a result of the revelation of interconnectedness. This empathetic sense is not limited to (but includes) the understanding and appreciation of the involvement of all other organisms, human and non-human, in this vast web of reactivity and also of the appreciation, and awareness, of the inevitability, or involuntary nature, of action and reaction.

This is the motivation to pay close attention to systems of engagement that we have, through cultural narratives that obscure them, or through our own personal trajectories, ignored or denied. The broadest, most prevalent and urgent of these is the ecological emergency.

Leah Kalmanson in "The Messiah and the Boddhisattva" points out that Eihei Dōgen's *Shōbōgenzō* gives guidance on how the meditative techniques he describes, which this process parallels, can provide a motivation to respond to critical situations.[85] Rather than simply making people feel good about themselves, the practice of meditative awareness has the feature of generating inspiration to pay more attention and so shift engagement within relationships that are not "good for" systems. Realisation as agency gives us the capacity to shift our attention within, and thus how we engage with, systems and relationships themselves, so it offers, potentially, a profound and powerful way of responding.

This approach contrasts markedly with a call to moral action. The field of environmental ethics developed out of a narrative that proposed that a moral response was necessary to generate sufficient impetus in the face of the environmental crisis. Personal moral obligations, translated into ethical social codes for action in the tradition of Rawls, Kant, Bentham and others were seen as a counter to alternative, non-ethical approaches. The alternatives to ethics, from economics to aesthetics, were condemned for being likely to lead to fear, exclusion or violence in the short term, or to the long-term damage to society resulting from greed for profit, regardless of

---

[85] Leah Kalmanson, "The Messiah and the Bodhisattva: Anti-Utopianism Re-Revisited." *Shofar: An Interdisciplinary Journal of Jewish Studies* 30, 4, (2012): 113–125.

the human or environmental costs.[86] Taylor and others founded their ethics on narratives that suggested our capacity to respond depended on developing a strong moral will. I agree with Taylor that the response we need to generate often requires tremendous effort. But this effort is not willpower but the effort of becoming completely aware of what is going on, in and around us.

It is increasingly difficult to see how any ethical strategy has improved our response to the ecological crisis. Ethical approaches to contentious issues (ecological destruction, migration, land rights, and so on) have, time after time, created, instead of unity, increasing fragmentation, polarisation, acrimony and even conflict among the different groups involved.[87] Even within groups that have similar concerns (religious organisations, political communities, scientists) the ideological and ethical positions quickly create discord quite contrary to their avowed intentions.[88] Basing the response to the ecological emergency on ideas of

---

[86] For a description of the fear that violence increases during ecological crises, see, for instance, Garrett Hardin, "Lifeboat Ethics: The Case Against Helping the Poor" (op. cit.). For an overview of the ethics to aesthetics debate, see, for instance Daniel B Botkin, *Discordant Harmonies: A New Ecology for the Twenty-First Century*, New York, NY.: Oxford Univ. Press, (1992). For additional arguments see, also, James C. Anderson, "Species Equality and the Foundations of Moral Theory", *Environmental Values*, 2 (1993), 347–65.

[87] For work that illustrates in great detail the negative effects of imposing what is thought of as an ethical benefit - aid (in the form of food, money and human intervention) - on communities that have their own traditional systems of reciprocal relations, see Barbara Harrell-Bond, *Imposing Aid*, OUP, (1986); Jason Brennan gives a useful account of the prevailing attitude in "Dominating Nature", *Environmental Values* 16, 4, (2007): 513–528; Dale Jamieson explores the political aspects of self-interest in the negotiations on climate change in "Global Warming and the Ethics of Climate Change", http://www.youtube.com/watch?v=_pPnc-ocQOA; Paul Knights investigates the cultural relationships within embedded and less embedded cultures in "Native Species, Human Communities and Cultural Relationships", *Environmental Values* 17, 3 (2008): 353–373.

[88] An obvious example is the climate change debate in which the ideal of determining to find objective data in relation to anthropogenic impact quickly fell foul of underlying ideological commitments to fit data to various existing ideological frameworks, with disastrous consequences for the perceived integrity of the scientists involved, and the ensuing polarisation of the debate.

how things ought to be actually closes off the possibility of responding authentically to the situation as it is.[89]

Realising compassionate attunement creates a very different scenario.[90] In asking participants to step back from, and fully realise their commitments to a particular set of values as the prime mover in debate and discussion, a deliberate attempt could be made to pay attention to an assessment of the impacts of various activities without recourse to justification or evaluation. Drawing attention to the historical, cultural and other local and distant factors that shape the commitments themselves would provide another useful way of stepping back and engaging with an observational process rather than a process that depends on where one is located in the mesh. Understanding why people have the ideological commitments that they do, and that I, too, am situated in a particular cultural and ideological context, allows a breathing space to develop around this, a recognition of the complex of connections that contains me, and that also contains other points of view. When we relate from this point of realisation, we are much less invested in what Jonathan Haidt calls "the righteous mind": we can look for ways to connect with the other person, as someone like us, neither good, nor bad, but simply enmeshed, and highly likely to be looking for ways to eliminate their own, and perhaps others' suffering.

Attention to the findings of empirically conducted research, like research into the history of evolution, will result in the attitudes of compassion (because it is no one's fault) and humility (because none of us can take credit for IQ, or colour, or nationality) and these, in turn, will allow the relational flow of information to become more graduated, less abrupt. In the context of how attitudes become entrenched, this kind of elicited response makes it easier to imagine engaging in discussions and negotiations, and searching for convergence in views. The problem remains, of course, that not all those who can, do make the effort to realise their enmeshment, which raises the question of what to do about those who are unprepared to step back in this way. Haidt has recognised that free riders, sociopaths, and other "non-cooperators" do in fact exist as a

---

[89] Andrew Chitty makes a case for more detailed work into exploring the "human condition imaginaries", or narrative frameworks, in "Ideology and Climate Change Convictions", (op. cit.).

[90] For a detailed argument on this, see Hans-Georg Moeller *The Moral Fool* (op. cit.).

significant proportion of the populace (though they will also always only be a minority)[91]

One major difference between the two approaches is that, in Taylor's original approach, and in deontological approaches generally, being morally weak is deplorable, a position from which each individual must lift themselves or lose their status as a moral agent. In the scenario of a systems-based approach, those who make no effort are unable to realise themselves: they remain blind to their condition. Those who do realise their agency also realise the relationships they have with these others, and this means that they extend their awareness to those relationships, doing what they can, through the process of paying attention, to graduate the flow of energy through these relationships. This might mean disentangling from the relationships (for instance, by divesting any holdings in companies that refuse to recognise or acknowledge how they contribute to anthropogenic destructive impact). Or it might mean drawing attention to obstructions to this graduated flow (through, for instance, paying close attention to the kind of language and mannerisms used in interactions, working to develop connections with people who hold different ideological positions, working on compassionate communication and seeing how communication is facilitated by this close attention). However, it makes no sense to blame others for their lack of awareness or to resent them for their denial or refusal to pay attention: they are part of the system that is being realised and they are not separable, entirely, from whoever is doing the realising.

In realising that each individual perception of the situation comes about as a result of events that are almost entirely beyond the control of the individual, any judgment of another's perception is inappropriate. It may still be appropriate to defend oneself, or to evade any attack from a person or group that is unwilling or unable to realise their own agency, but engaging in reciprocal violence just generates more systems of

---

[91] Both Jonathan Haidt in *The Righteous Mind* and Samuel Harris in *Free Will* describe psychopathology as being inherent in the human genome: some free-riders exist. For some, it's an evolutionary advantage to have no empathy. Like dealing with activity that harms while also recognising that "free will" has nothing to do with why people do what they do, we still need to protect societies' members from harm and to do this, we must both learn to recognise free-riderism and psychopathology, and allow ourselves to develop strategies, like disempowering, or if necessary isolating, those who display these characteristics, certainly if they have already caused harm or suffering.

engagement with violence. In this larger sense of "self", it is violence against the self.

Realisation as agency requires effort, because paying attention requires effort, and eliciting, and fostering, the attitudes of compassion and humility is also effortful. It is remarkably easy to forget and to take credit for events that were due to activities over which we had no control whatsoever. Nevertheless, collecting data, undertaking research, gathering falsifiable information and other associated activities are all acts that require us to pay close attention, as are many artistic, literary, cultural and other more obvious activities like traditional meditation and yoga practices that are practices of paying complete attention. These activities do not involve coercion, proselytising or the use of force. They are ideologically and ethically neutral. And yet the way that they reflect on unfolding situations gives them importance in the ecological emergency since they create a way of engagement that is itself a system of realisation.

Addressing criticisms

In revising Taylor's ethic, I have already mentioned Richard Watson's argument that if humans are natural and there is nothing we can do that can be deemed unnatural, then there is no point in attempting to alter the trajectory of human evolution, even if this means our own destruction. This argument is widely cited in different forms in discussions about the ecological emergency, and I have attempted to show how a systems-based account of agency as realisation counters this argument. Since the capacity to realise is itself a natural system, it feeds back into the processes and systems within which it is enmeshed. Our capacity to realise is an evolutionary fact. Our realisation (in the sense of understanding) that we have this capacity may be a matter of luck or chance: we may simply have stumbled upon the realisation independently, or we may have been given access to forms of engagement, like meditation, mindfulness, yoga or other practices and philosophies that deliberately focus on fostering awareness, and compassion.[92] When the capacity is realised (in the sense

---

[92] It may be something that happens as a result of our interactions, or it may be because we are encouraged to question, or reflect, or are naturally curious. This is an area for further scientific research. It relates closely to the field of research into the effects of meditation that begun to show results consistent with the theory that a feedback system comes into effect that influences the physiological (and the psychological, social, and other) systems of the meditator (as point of perception). For instance, Richard J. Davidson and Antoine Lutz, "Buddha's Brain:

of brought into being), it requires an effort to maintain awareness of the trajectory of our interactions, to look for emergent options to alter our engagement. The tendency to revert to ideological and cultural bias, to shut down to others instead of reaching out with the attitude of compassion, is enormous. Yet this is a practice, both in the sense of a way of doing things, and in the sense of repetitive habitual actions that improve performance.

The "naturalism" argument is also sometimes used to promote the idea that humans should not change ecological systems (excluding, presumably, any "natural" actions we might take). Yet this position falls in on itself when we acknowledge that the process we are involved in is akin to one of "waking up" to where we are within the mesh of systems. We are not alien systems who must somehow minimise our interactions with other evolved systems. In this narrative, humans have evolved in the context of evolution of life on Earth. Richard Watson accused Arne Naess of inconsistency in this context, since he argued that Naess implies natural states only occur when an ecosystem is left untouched by humans.[93] I hope I have shown through pointing to Morton's work that this narrative cannot be sustained in a system that recognises how intimately human systems have evolved within systems in general.

Taylor uses the arguments from naturalism - that humans were an evolved species, for instance - to conclude that humans have moral duties towards (wild) nature. He concludes that it is a matter of "supervenience" that we adopt an attitude of respect for nature on the basis of a rational understanding of "the good" of organisms.[94] In the revised approach I am arguing for, we need not depend upon our agency being moral in order to respond effectively to the emergency. However, in a sense, the scenario I have proposed is still vulnerable to the accusation that human subjects, even if we are systems, are still treated differently from other evolved systems. Realisation as agency can only come about in the context of systems that have evolved the capacity for self-reflection and these, as far as we know, are necessarily human. It is no coincidence, however, that they are the same systems that have created the artificial syntheses that caused the Anthropocene. We have the capacity to respond to the emergency, but we also had the cognitive and physiological capacity,

---

Neuroplasticity and Meditation", *IEEE Signal Processing Magazine* 25, 1, (January 1 2008): 176–174.

[93] Richard Watson, "A Critique of Anti-Anthropocentric Biocentrism" (op. cit.): 3ff.

[94] Referred to in a *Letter to Professor Claudia Card* (op. cit.).

including the capacity to frame our understanding of ourselves as superior and independent, that created the emergency in the first place.

This position could be criticised as anthropocentric – we are still responding for our own benefit, and realisation as agency has additional benefits, including generating a sense of deep interconnectedness that is profoundly moving - yet I have attempted to show that the division between anthropocentric and non-anthropocentric approaches cannot apply in a systems-based narrative. The only sense in which humans are of a different order from other systems is in the degree to which they have this capacity to pay more attention than they are currently paying to the impact of their actions. This difference does not give humans superior powers. It only means that we have the capacity, at least potentially, to mitigate anthropogenic impact through eliciting an attitude.

The idea that, as perceivers, we are moving and transitory brings me to the criticism raised by Roger King in his contribution to Light and Smith's *Space, Place and Environmental Ethics*.[95] King says that biocentrism - and this extends to the allocentrism I have proposed here - has an "epistemological" difficulty. He quotes Donna Haraway, who says that it is, "a way of being nowhere while claiming to be everywhere equally".[96] This implies that viewing the process objectively rests on a trick of relativity: how could a human, encultured perspective ever know what counts for anything but human encultured systems?:

> Relativists are in the paradoxical position of being able to value all normative positions equally only by erasing their own positions. Were the relativists to take their own moral or epistemological beliefs seriously, these beliefs would begin to structure their evaluations of competing beliefs and the relativist strategy would evaporate.[97]

This criticism can be met by the contention that humans are perfectly capable, indeed, have evolved with the specific capacity, to "step outside" the perspective of an organism boundaried by a skin and anticipate

---

[95] Roger J. H. King, "Critical Reflections on Biocentric Environmental Ethics: Is it an Alternative to Anthropocentrism?" in Light, Andrew and Smith, Jonathan M., *Space, Place and Environmental Ethics*, Rowman and Littlefield, (1997).

[96] Roger J. H. King, "Playing with Boundaries: Critical Reflections on Strategies for an Environmental Culture and the Promise of Civic Environmentalism." *Ethics, Place & Environment*, 9, 2, (2006): 173–186.

[97] Quoted in Roger J. H. King (op. cit.).

interactions and responses of organisms and systems from different perspectives. Warwick Fox illustrates this capacity when he discusses "weak" versus "strong" anthropocentrism.[98] We cannot leave the context of being human, but this does not mean we cannot consider the systems from various perspectives of their enmeshment.[99] Indeed, the evolutionary drive that allowed the development of imagination and curiosity is at the root of this capacity to explore the workings of systems quite outside our own immediate experience.

A further difficulty pointed out by King is Taylor's division of the biosphere into three (moral) realms which, King maintains, creates an "ethical gap between the domesticated and the wild landscape, the landscape altered by the human presence and the one left unmodified by human beings".[100] King is right: this kind of division is untenable if we imagine ourselves as human systems enmeshed within systems that impact upon one another intimately and inseparably. So is the third division that Taylor considers relevant, that between "wild" nature and domesticated nature (what he calls, "the bioculture"). Just because humans have had intense and relatively permanent impacts on systems that they have used to their gain, from golf courses to chimpanzees in laboratories, from farm animals to forestry plantations, dealing with these systems as though they were immune from consideration using the same idea of "the good" of systems is unjustified. All the systems we are enmeshed in feed back into one another and therefore there is no realm that we can consider entirely independently of any other.

Ross Wolfe suggests that human cultural systems require that we bring the whole of nature within the realm of human culture.[101] In a sense, the human project has necessarily carved out an imperative to increase the

---

[98] Warwick Fox, "Forms of Harm and Our Obligations to Humans and Other Animals" (op. cit.); see also "It need not be guilty of anthropo*centrism*, but it remains inherently anthropo*genic*", in Simon P. James, "Human Virtues and Natural Values", (op. cit.).

[99] "...[what] Nagel calls the backward step – humans have, as he says, 'the special capacity to step back and survey themselves, and the lives to which they are committed, with that detached amazement which comes from watching an ant struggle up a heap of sand' in John Foster, "After Illusion: Realism, Philosophy and Hope in a Seriously Warming World." (presented at the SAP sponsored event: *Climate Change and Philosophy at the Tipping Point*, Lancaster University, 2011).

[100] Roger H. J. King in "Playing with Boundaries: Critical Reflections on Strategies for an Environmental Culture and the Promise of Civic Environmentalism". (op. cit.).

[101] Ross Wolfe, "Man and Nature", (op. cit).

flow of energy towards humans and we are inclined to feel entirely justified at this appropriation, from coal to oil to diamonds to land to forests to wild nature as a place to visit, on an expensive holiday, where we can "find ourselves". Our narratives reinforce our justification for this process of enculturation and we are somewhat trapped by the cultural conditions in how we view this process. However, to suggest that the human project dominates and absorbs all other systems is to ignore our dependence upon those systems for our own survival. To seek to justify our absorption of all other evolutionary processes into our own is to create a kind of ideological facism, with all the instability that such a system implies. Instead, we need to broaden our understanding of our condition and that includes the realisation that what is good for us is what we normally consider the background, but that actually makes up, and contains, what we are.

We are in the Anthropocene, and it is inevitable that our species alters and adjusts the energetic flow, as all do. We are enmeshed within events and therefore perceptually transient. The systems that maintain us are more sophisticated, more unfathomable but also broader than Wolfe's narrative implies. The Anthropocene, and indeed human perception, has and will shape the directional flow of events within these peripheral spheres we inhabit, but it requires an effort of focus to see and, in the narrow sense available, choose, (or rather, allow choices to arise to decide) how we interact. Our only agency is in our capacity to realise, to elicit, and attune to, an attitude of compassion. This has more to do with consciously stepping back to see ourselves as perceptual, active, enmeshed organisms, than with directing the show.

When I talked about human systems and naturalism earlier, what I wanted to bring to light was the idea that human capacities for realisation are not exercised without effort. There are strong similarities between the effort required to pay attention to our enmeshment, and therefore to exercise agency as realisation, and Dōgen s call for effortful focus.

Contemporary human artefacts have been synthesised within a narrative that paints agency as dualistic, a process that is imposed from some realm of "mind" or "will". The idea of agency as realisation offers the potential to reimagine synthesising artefacts that allow the graduation of energetic dissipation. By allowing cultural systems and artefacts to function as participants, and not as segregated items, we may be able to realise that the interactions can be as good for the systems that maintain us as they can be for us, as humans within the mesh. In Confucianism, the agent is also the observer and her actions are not at her own discretion. The idea of agency as realisation closely echoes this. Actions are called for by a realisation of the relationship between the perceiver and the situation. This involves paying close attention to what is going in order to see what options arise when compassion is elicited. It is not as though we elicit compassion in ourselves. Rather, it is as though what is of value to us, as systems within systems, is compassion, or love (often tough love) which is our version of (aggressive) symbiosis. Similarly, cooperation (with a healthy measure of competition) is what is of value to other systems that dissipate energy through a graduated flow, that is, all living systems on the planet. When we attune to the latent pattern of "the good" of systems, by paying attention, options arise for action that otherwise remain hidden.

Lovelock has asserted, plausibly, that the human species has come to this unsustainable relationship with the ecosphere as a matter of blind course, not because we set out to create systems that would eventually damage our own flourishing.[102] If we make an effort to become aware of the situation of our enmeshment, then we also develop the capacity to exercise the system of realisation as agency, in particular in how we relate to the ecological emergency.

The practice of this kind of agency is the subject of the next chapter. Morton's suggestion that we see our situation as ironic is useful since it highlights our ability to detach ourselves from the perspective from which, perforce, we view the situation.[103] The danger of irony is that it can become cynical and limiting unless it is tempered by compassion. The metaphorical idea of a flow of energy in dissipative whirlpools fits with the idea of attitudes that facilitate this flow, so compassion as a facilitator for enlarging our sphere of consideration, rather than fear, anger, hatred or cynicism, all of which tend to cause the limits of consideration to shrink, is a better attitude for facilitation of this flow.

Likewise, in this metaphorical sense, patterns of judgment and resentment are as non-participatory as patterns of molecular synthesis that do not allow for information exchange. Since this is metaphorical language in any case, it is easy to see how one might talk of states that do not allow participation or dialogue to be energetic "traps", while states that allow for transience and dynamism to flow can be seen as allowing more energetic dissipation to take place. What I am suggesting, therefore,

---

[102] James Lovelock, The Revenge of Gaia: Earth's Climate Crisis and the Fate of Humanity, (op. cit.).

[103] Timothy Morton in discussion at "My Talk to the Rice Faculty" (Feb 2014) which is available at https://ecologywithoutnature.blogspot.com/2014/02/my-talk-to-rice-faculty-in-mid-feb.html.

is that this imaginary extends the metaphorical implications of energetic flow, since realisation as agency works like any other structurally real system, creating possibilities for information exchange and, teleologically, seeking its own state of entropy.

In this chapter, I have sought to revise Taylor's idea of moral agency in the context of a systems-based, physicalist understanding of how humans fit. In the next chapter, I want to explore the practical implications of this revised theory: how could it reform our approach to the ecological emergency? What might we be able to do differently, if we take this approach, and how realistic is it to advocate such a radical shift in perspective in an area that is dominated by, alternatively, pragmatic and ideologically-driven considerations?

Chapter Four

The practice of responding
to the ecological emergency

Introduction

This chapter explores the practical implications of realisation as agency, and realising "the good" of systems, in the context of the ecological emergency. To make it easier to understand how this revised idea of human responsibility, and "the good" of systems, might be translated into practice, I have divided the practical implications into three areas.

There is the practice of clarifying what the ecological emergency consists in, and, since this is primarily what we withdraw our attention from, the process of exposing or uncovering those relationships that exacerbate the emergency. This involves both a review and revision of our use of language and metaphor, as well as a focus on the effort required to explore our relationships to the biophysical and human processes that sustain us. This shifts how we relate to context, which then elicits different options in our awareness.[1]

The second area is how we respond. The idea of being able to see ourselves as enmeshed does not liberate us from context, but it allows us

---

[1] John Foster expressed his difficulty with a systems-based approach to me like this: "An interaction must be between two distinct things. If humans constitute one of these things, they can't also be "inside" the relation between them… Underneath the confusion, however, I take there to be a deep truth: we can't help framing ourselves explicitly as distinct from the empirical (natural) world, while we can't but know implicitly that this framing misrepresents our living status." (Personal communication, March 2014). I am grateful to him for pointing this out. It is a deep problem that we are in the context, but that we feel as though we are independent from it, and the section on "independence" in the last chapter, as well as this first section, is my attempt to address this.

to pay attention, and this elicits an attitude. When we attune to our own response, we find that compassion is elicited by the act of reflection on context. This, in turn, opens up an array of possibilities for how we respond that we were hitherto unaware of. Responses that are more compassionate facilitate the "graduated flow" of energy, which is the rate of flow our own system requires for survival, in the context of the survival of the systems that support and sustain us. I will use examples to show how our awareness opens us into, and connects us to, the idea of a graduated "flow" of energy that I discussed in the last chapter, and to "the good" of systems. Secondarily, because this kind of awareness creates a focus on our own attitude and how it shifts in the light of compassionate attunement, opportunities to address attitudinal divergence and entrenchment arise as areas for our engagement: how we approach an issue dictates how it unfolds. To put it crudely, we are only responsible for our own attitude, but that is much.

Some of the opportunities that emerge from clarifying our relationship to the ecological emergency will include opportunities to discuss this relationship with others. If we can maintain an attitude of compassionate attunement in our engagement, they, too, may begin to explore how they relate to their enmeshment. There is clear evidence that our views shift and are influenced by the people we admire. Therefore both our relationship with ourselves, as one that becomes more compassionate through reflection, and the way we influence others through becoming more attuned to compassion, shift the field from automatic reactivity to conscious responsibility.

The kind of shift in interrelationship with context that we need to create, in order to respond to the ecological emergency, depends on paying attention to our enmeshment and allowing, and deliberately cultivating compassionate attunement as an attitude, and as a practice. Any broader discussion of what possibilities and opportunities for altering our relationship to context as a species arises as a direct result of this initial focus. Paradoxically, the urge to shift others' approaches often closes off compassionate attunement as we create a "them" and "us" scenario in our minds.

As I said in the last chapter, many people identify with their beliefs and values, which contain the narratives they use to make sense of the world, and themselves. It is hard to imagine that they could question what they rely on for a sense of identity without raising concerns that this will undermine their sense of themselves. Many organisations are heavily invested in these narratives and to disentangle from them raises fears of a threat to their very existence. To explore this, I will use two examples.

Being able to experience our context as an explicit web of relationships gives us the opportunity to focus on the relationships, including how we practice (our manner, the language we use, and so on) rather than on outcome.[2] Therefore, paradoxically, despite the urgent need for a comprehensive and radical change in our response, I will argue that we face the challenge of focusing only on the way in which we respond – our manner, the words we use, our attitude – rather than on any goal or end.

The third area relates to the second, and is central to how we practice. It is an exploration of what it means to exercise the attitudes of humility and compassion while we are realising our agency. I conclude that this practice contributes to mitigating the ecological emergency by helping us explore what we can do, given that our freedom to act, or agency, is neither independent of context, nor predicated on our evolutionary superiority. This does not imply that I am pessimistic about our outlook. Humility is the realisation that where we are is vastly a result of forces completely outside our control. When we allow this to elicit compassion, however, a whole network of possibilities opens to us. I conclude that, counter-intuitive as it might be, to work with attitude is the most powerful thing we can do in response to the ecological emergency. It offers us the only key that will release us from the juggernaut of externalised attributions of our fate which lock us on a trajectory of inevitable cause and effect, hurtling us towards our own doom. During the discussion of these areas of practice, I will explore and compare some ideas from the physicalist approach with those from the non-dualist traditions of Dōgen Zen and, to a lesser extent, but still importantly, non-dualistic traditions out of which Yoga arose (Kashmir Shaivism, Advaita Vedanta, Tantra), and Daoism.

Clarifying the context: all practice is personal

The first, and in fact, the only, area for practice, is personal (although since this influences all our interrelationships, including political and cultural ones, it does not stop with the intra-relationship). It is through reflecting on our own context that we clarify what the ecological emergency consists

---

[2] This calls to mind Robert Burns' famous poem when he observes we lack the gift "to see oursel's as ithers see us", Robert Burns, "To A Louse", *The Collected Poems of Robert Burns*, New edition, Ware: Wordsworth Editions Ltd, (1994). We can never achieve this, if we are enmeshed and unwilling to make the effort to see that enmeshment. However, taking the unconditioned view allows us to become aware of our enmeshment and that, paradoxically, is the opportunity to see ourselves from another view.

of, in terms of the relationships we are involved in ourselves. However, since we are involved in relationships at so many levels, it might be useful to begin by considering how clarification could take place, using the premise that we are biophysical systems. Therefore I will begin by exploring how we might clarify, to ourselves, the way that data and information on our biophysical status, and on the biological and physical status of the systems we are involved in, is interpreted at present. What can we do to reflect on this process, if we understand our agency to lie in our capacity to understand and experience context, and then to allow this to elicit compassion for and within this context, opening to the possibilities this creates? I will then illustrate how personal practice might manifest itself in two example situations.

Firstly, I want to reiterate, briefly, what I said in the last chapter, to clarify the relationship between natural laws as probabilities, the flow of energy, and "the good" of systems. I take it that we can agree to accept basic physical laws as probabilistic descriptions of the activity in the universe, and among these is the second law of thermodynamics. Biophysical systems can be described according to these laws. They involve a structural relationship between the predominant form of energy for the planet (solar energy, although of course there are subsidiary forms of energy available) and the capacity that biophysical systems have to dissipate that energy (maintaining and regenerating themselves in the process). Biophysical systems absorb and circulate (mainly) solar energy, and dissipate it as effectively as possible (thus obeying the second law). This process means that the solar flow of energy is *graduated* through the activity of biophysical processes. Another way of putting this might be to say that the sun's energy is filtered through biophysical systems at just the rate needed to allow complexity, like ours, to flourish, in the context of the current complex ecosystems that have created and continue to sustain us.

The more complex the biophysical structural relationships are, qualitatively (in terms of complex organisation in organisms and ecosystems) and quantitatively (in terms of numbers, including of micro-organisms), the more graduated the flow of energy can be. I do not agree with those theorists who say that biophysical systems are progressing towards complexity: this is, I think, one of the errors that has arisen as a result of our hierarchical thinking, and tendency to see humans, as complex organisms, at the top of the evolutionary pile. Instead, it is worth thinking of biodiversity as progressing through time (and thus the relationships between different organisms becoming more complex) but not necessarily leading to more complexity in individual organisms or species. Evolution progresses, in the sense that it branches out along different exploratory paths, but it does not necessarily improve, or get better, at evolving, because the process is blind and unguided.[3]

Processes that interfere with the graduated flow of energy are those that steepen the energetic gradient. If there is less biodiverse complexity, or vast destruction of ecosystems through agriculture, monocultures, mining, and so on, the gradient will be steepened, and the process of energy dissipation will become more unstable, less graduated. Alternatively, if there is obstruction to the process (through introducing synthesised artefacts (plastics), for instance, or through the production of radioactive isotopes that cannot break down or become part of the energetic cycle) then the informational energy (for instance, electron exchanges in molecules) that is locked into these artifices cannot participate in this graduated flow. This steepening, or obstruction, of the graduated dissipation of energy is "bad for" biophysical systems.[4] The converse – the increase in biodiversity and complex interrelations between biodiverse systems – is "good for" these systems. If human agency as realisation can respond to this knowledge (and understanding this *is* a response) then we have a way of adjudicating what activity to pay attention to, and what to disengage from, to the extent that disengagement is possible. What we pay attention to, in this sense, could include, for instance, recycling wastewater through systems that release energy and purify water in the process, while withdrawing our engagement from, for instance, single-use water systems that are both polluting and resource hungry.[5]

Paying attention to imagery and imagination

The predominant authorities amassing data on the ecological emergency belong to the scientific community.[6] Summaries of this data are

---

[3] It may be that complexity is inherent in the universe. This is the contention defended in Stuart Kauffman's book, *At Home in the Universe*, OUP, (1995), which gives an excellent defense of the notion that complexity and self-organisation arise inevitably, given the probabalistic laws that structure universal reality.

[4] One could see cancerous growths in the same vein: the "flow" of energy is speeded up to a pathological degree, eventually sequestering energy from the rest of the organism at its own expense, to the point where the organism dies.

[5] https://www.tcd.ie/news_events/articles/trinity-researchers-showcase-pollinator-and-sustainability-friendly-gardens-at-bloom/

[6] The IPCC predominantly collects and assesses scientific papers summarising data on climate change, for instance. However, its panel also includes a number of economists and even a moral philosopher (Professor John Broome), so there is some recognition that values are inherent in the conceptual models and need to be

interpreted through conceptual models, since conceptual models precede and shape scientific ones.[7] Scientific language still regularly relies on mechanistic metaphors and a quantitative reductionism, and this indicates a dependency on conceptual frameworks that no longer reflect more accurate explanations of the conditions we find ourselves in.[8] The claim that scientific data, and in particular, how that data is presented, is ideologically neutral, is false, then, unless we can also become aware of, and make explicit, the values and beliefs that underlie the various scientific interpretations of data.[9]

---

identified. The Brundtland Report on sustainable development in the context of environmental systems also questioned whether or not a natural scientific approach to the issue of population growth, economic and social development and environmental impact could be worked out in quantitative terms, without implying that some sort of value judgements have been made about how to weigh up the various interests involved.

[7] This point is raised at various points in discussions on the Azimuth project blog, particularly more recently:
http://johncarlosbaez.wordpress.com/2014/04/07/what-does-the-new-ipcc-report-say-about-climate-change-part-1/.

[8] See David Bolinsky talking about his creation of the film *Visualizing the Wonder of a Living Cell* <http://www.ted.com/talks/david_bolinsky_animates_a_cell.html> :
"these micromachines power how a cell moves.. they power our hearts, they power our minds..." [3.55m ff
http://www.youtube.com/watch?v=wJyUtbnOO5Y&feature=youtube_gdata_player].
The idea that any position, even the most rigorously scientific, is shaped by a set of foundational beliefs that cannot be proved, is the basis of the important philosophical concept of scepticism. Karl Popper illustrated this when he pointed out that for a hypothesis to be considered, it needed to accord with observational evidence, be the simplest possible explanation, explain a wide range of phenomena, be predictive, and, most pertinently from the sceptic's view, be falsifiable. Culminating in the radical scepticism of Descartes (1596-1650), the term "scepticism" is used to justify much of the denialism of anthropogenic impact, particularly on climate. As Friedrich Nietzsche famously proclaimed, "... facts are precisely what is lacking, all that exists consists of interpretations." in Frederick Nietzsche, *Will to Power*, (1906) trans. Walter Kaufmann, New York, Viking, (1967); 481. However, some interpretations resonate well with the feedback we get from the world, while others, like the interpretation that 2+2=6, do not.

[9] For a detailed analysis of the implications of a barely examined set of principles being used to guide the strategies and policies shaping funding and research decisions, see, for instance, Martha Nussbaum, *Not for Profit: Why Democracy Needs the Humanities*, Princeton, Princeton University Press, (2010).

Questioning, through language and metaphor, how we talk about our interrelationship within systems, deliberately choosing and creating metaphors that allow us to envisage systems as organic, dynamic, and probabilistic rather than predictable, isolated and mechanistic, alters how we interact. We can do this through questioning and offering alternative terminology in discussion and debate, in both scientific and in political or even activist circles. We can look at the imagery of nuance, of spectrum rather than black and white thinking, given that the quest for an unimpeachable consensus has slowed the response to the impact our species is having. We can also do this through the use of artistic and literary responses, through education and the opening up of more channels of communication between humanities and the disciplines of mathematics, economics and the sciences.

We can question some of the paradigms used in the fields of agriculture, fisheries, business and politics, opening the stage for a broader debate about the terminology used to conceptualise the relationships we have with the systems that sustain us, and the systems we create to exploit them. This is one way of paying attention to, and discovering other possible responses to, these relationships. Some human systems have drawn (and continue to draw) attention away from these interconnections that imply violence within systems.[10] Therefore the act of bringing our attention back to the language we use to describe our interactions includes highlighting this avoidance, and developing ways of describing our relationships in language that is consistent with a clearer appraisal of what is going on. An obvious example of this is the use, in the military world, of terminology like, "collateral damage" to describe the extraneous, accidental or by-effect killing of non-military people by bombs or gunfire. In industries where there is the opportunity to make enormous profits by exploiting natural resources, particularly in the petrochemical industry, drawing attention to the use of terminology that distracts from or disguises non-compliance with corporate responsibility indices, for example, can open up the possibilities for articulating an insight into how these processes of avoidance allow violence to thrive.[11]

---

[10] Timothy Morton, *The Ecological Thought* (op. cit.); Morton talks to Cary Wolfe about how attention is directed away from what is "behind" our phones and coffee cups: http://www.youtube.com/watch?v=iaoQwgt_Bfw; Morton and Wolfe also discuss the "violence" inherent in the production of food, the provision of transport, clothing, and so on.

[11]For an example of a petrochemical industry's self-presentation distracting from and disguising non-compliance, see http://www.shell.com/global/environment-

Much work has already been done to reframe the ecological emergency as an issue that was caused by, but that now envelops, us. Morton's metaphorical descriptions are particularly creative in this respect, from the use of the idea of hyper-objects, to links he makes between consumerism and the nineteenth-century notion of consumption (the disease, as well as the act of devouring).[12] His work challenges us to reinvent how we think and speak about our relationships within the mesh, and this confirms that realisation arises as a meta-system we can elicit through juxtapositions that question, rather than cement, our existing belief systems. Developing a clear picture of how energy is dissipated, and linking this with how living systems support and maintain themselves, is likely to enhance any efforts made from a philosophical perspective on legitimising a process of mitigation of the effects of the Anthropocene, both for ourselves and for the planetary systems in the future.[13]

Our ability to interpret data is further distorted by the tendency to conceptualise an ideal "other" state, a state of perfect relationship with the world. This creates a gap between the reality and the ideal. This kind of ethical dichotomy is, as I have attempted to illustrate already in the last chapter, problematic. It is implicitly impossible (or unverifiable) to achieve an ideal relationship, whether in the specific case of Taylor's

---

society/performance/indices.html. A detailed look at this page reveals that, while the name of the page is "Sustainability Rankings" and at the top of the page is the claim, "we continue to be included in a number of leading indices" [of corporate social and environmental responsibility], all of the quoted indices exclude this company from their rankings. This exclusion is excused with statements like "...while we continued to score well, we were not included in the CDLI [Carbon Disclosure Leadership Index]" and "we were again not included based on DJSI's [Dow Jones Sustainability Index's] view of the operations of Shell companies in Nigeria, although our score was above the threshold for inclusion."

[12] For an interesting discussion of Morton and Harman's use of language and metaphor, see Jane Bennett, "Systems and Things: A Response to Graham Harman and Timothy Morton", *New Literary History*, 43 (2012), 225–233 http://dx.doi.org/10.1353/nlh.2012.0020.

[13] As I mentioned earlier, John Baez set up The Azimuth Forum with the specific aim of identifying features of physical and biological systems and seeking to understand their interactions with human impacts and systems in order to better conceive of how human systems might have to alter or adjust to become more integrated within larger systems. Steven Pacala worked on the idea of "wedges" of impacts that would have to be tackled if a comprehensive approach to the ecological emergency was to be managed. Many other scientists have also worked in this area but few make a concerted effort to frame their work within or appeal to the disciplinary fields of the Humanities or the Arts. See www.johncarlosbaez.com.

aspirational ideal for a harmonious relationship between humans and wild nature (that he recognised cannot be realised) or in the broader tendency of religious, political or social ideologies to aspire to a utopia, or an ideal, here, or in a future life. Dōgen uses the metaphor of walking in his "Mountains and Waters Sutra" and Brian Schroeder reminds us that walking is a great metaphor for being in a state of almost-constant falling, of destabilising and restabilising. Perhaps if we conceive of our human relationships in this sense of being in a state of flux, of a momentary stability, or consensus, followed by the instability of new information, or having to restate something to better the chance of being understood, then we would be less prone to sitting only with the tight-knit groups with whom we have never, so far, disagreed.

Almost anything can be justified in the name of a better future. Hitler justified the murder of millions on the basis that he was protecting the identity and values of a particular culture and people. The ideal future he foresaw had that at its core. Religious ideologues like Sunni fundamentalists or various homophobic interpreters of the Bible believe strongly that their actions, however brutal or violent, are "the will of God", and will bring about, here or in heaven, a brighter future (at least for other believers). These may be extreme examples (although, unfortunately, they are rather more prevalent than we might like to acknowledge) but more moderate versions of ideological narratives underpin much of the interpretative work on scientific data.

Here, then, we have an opportunity to exercise our agency in the way that I described in the last chapter. This involves, first, seeing the context and conditions of our own interpretive frameworks. We can reflect that we are inseparable from, and yet that we can bring to conscious awareness, the conditions, and the context, that both frames and creates our awareness. This process deepens our understanding of our context and this, in turn, elicits an attitude. I have called this attitude compassion, but the name is immaterial. It is the deep sense of appreciation that we are entirely enmeshed, that we have not created the conditions for our enmeshment, that we are not unlike anything else in the universe in this respect, but that we have the capacity for self-reflection, for realisation, which is also the capacity to step back, and into which can flow the compassion that realisation elicits. This, then, creates opportunities for alternative responses to arise. The opportunities that arise do so in the light, as it were, of this compassionate attitude, and it is through this arising that a shift in our response capacity occurs. Such a shift may well better allow energy to flow or matter to cycle through the context.

This may sound paradoxical, since we are both within the context, and with the capacity to observe the context. In a trivial sense, we exercise this kind of capacity all the time, from the moment we question the values and beliefs of those who have educated us in what to believe. Agency as realisation is a more comprehensive exercise of this capacity. We are not so much questioning, as bringing to conscious awareness, the conceptual frameworks through which we are interpreting information. In a sense, this allows us to "step back" from the interpretations and see what has framed them (and, therefore, whether or not they are open to other kinds of interpretation).

Data is bound to be interpreted one way or another. *Facta* are, by definition, "made", or created through the frameworks of interpretation. However, some interpretive frameworks rely more heavily on ideological commitments than others do. Those that are most rigorously collated in accordance with the scientific method are likely to give more accurate results than those research projects designed to fit some pre-existing ideological commitment.[14] We must also, of course, explicitly understand that every scientist, economist or politician brings their own conceptual framework to the interpretation of data, just as we do. This is the first step we can take: we can recognise our context, recognise how our own interpretations arise as a consequence of this context, find out, and take into account the interpretive framework used to read off the data, and then decide what the data means. An example or two might help.

First, then, let us consider our interpretation of data relating to climate change. Much of the data is contradictory or confusing, yet the overwhelming consensus is that there is a serious impact, through military, agricultural, domestic and industrial emissions, on the global atmosphere, causing climatic changes. If our agency consists in our capacity to reflect on this (rather than in our capacity to make a mental determination, and translate that into physical action), then all we can do (although I hope to demonstrate that this is potentially a great deal) is consider our own framework, and the framework through which the data has been interpreted. Only then are we in a position to decide whether or not to accept the body of evidence. After this, we can see how

---

[14] I could be accused, in maintaining that humans are biophysical systems, of being ideologically committed myself. The difference between believing in biophysical systems and believing in fairies, or heaven, or perfect social harmony, is that my beliefs can be tested, empirically. Perhaps perfect social harmony can be tested for (it has never been found; neither have fairies) but Heaven does not even have a definable realm for testing.

incorporating this understanding shifts our own perceptual framework. We might become more aware of our personal activity, and of how this contributes to this global phenomenon. This might include bringing our attention to our work and lifestyle habits, to the interrelationships that these depend on, to leisure, travel and even eating habits. We may well find that many of these are tightly bound up with our identity, in which case, we can begin to uncover some of the narratives that lie beneath our convictions that we must eat meat, fly to Malta, or work for Shell in order to live a happy, fulfilled life. By uncovering - and discussing - our convictions, and the narratives that underlie them, we shift allegiance, make new connections, develop communities and networks that have common, or at least overlapping interests, either in the virtual world of the internet and social media, or through actual group forming. This uncovering therefore allows us to interact differently, to grow communities and thus to shift how we, and others, interact.[15]

The process is hard work, in the sense that this level of reflection requires that we pay close attention to context, and to uncovering our tacit acceptance of relationships that, on reflection we can see are not "good" for systems. The effort required is sometimes overwhelming, and, because so little appears, on the surface, to change when all we do is become aware, this approach feels counter-intuitive. It can also seem grindingly slow as a response: unpicking our attachment to narratives that adhere us to particular habits, addictions, or ways of living is time-consuming. Whether we do this in formal meditation sessions, or simply while taking time to reflect, it is hard to believe that what we are doing is shifting the entire mesh. However, because we are acting within a system, the impact of even a moment's reflection is profound and far-reaching.

Our enmeshment is absolute: we are never outside the mesh. Yet our capacity to realise this is exactly what creates our agency, our ability to effect change within the mesh. What we alter is our relationship to ourselves. Our realisation includes recognising being interdependent with the system within which we arise. This involves developing the practice of realisation, of allowing compassion to arise more often as we reflect upon our enmeshment, and noticing the opportunities this brings to light.

---

[15] Building virtual communities on social media platforms has been almost entirely dominated by the concepts of marketing and profitability. However, all the tools exist to build communities that are driven by common purposes, of, for instance, developing research databases or building effective lobbying strategies by networks of individuals with common interests.

Those opportunities become evident precisely because we develop the capacity to elicit compassion, for ourselves, and, by extension, for "the good" of the systems within which we are enmeshed.[16]

One clear conceptual frame of reference is the idea we have of a separable "self". In shifting our frame of reference to the structural relationships of our enmeshment, we begin to see the identity that we normally consider "the self" to be open to dissolution, a fluid experience within the context. When we are responding in the way I have just described (reflecting, for instance, on our historical and social context) we are identifying less with the reference points that create a particular view of our conditions, and more with the creativity and understanding that realisation brings.

It is as though we are watching ourselves, and in doing so, another layer of possibilities emerges. As we reflect on our actions, and where they come from, we begin to see how inevitable our reactivity is, how only by reflecting with compassion do we create the microspace within which alternative possibilities for action arise.

One thing that becomes clear in reflecting upon our experience in this way is that we tend to withdraw our attention from aspects of our experience, largely as a result of the historical and social context, and, as I have mentioned before, the narratives that underpin how we frame this context. Partly, perhaps, this withdrawal is an understandable reaction to the difficulty with facing our own imminent annihilation. The threat to identity is based on the narrative that identity is fixed, and this in turn creates desires and cravings to fill the space behind the boundary. The hunger for consumption further fuels and generates this illusion, and even the frames we use to describe the competitive drive are designed to justify the process of sucking in as much energy as possible in order to strengthen one identity, at the cost of another.[17] And yet this narrative,

---

[16] "Human nature can be seen as both great and wretched regardless of time and place; it is the manner of dealing with one another that determines greatness or wretchedness". Hee-Jin Kim, *Eihei Dōgen: Mystical Realist*, Boston: Wisdom Publications, (2004): 17.

[17] Michael Stone, yogi and visionary, is one of many thinkers who recognised that a hollow sense of self, or intolerable emotions, or a combination of both, created conditions for addictive behaviours, leading to massive overconsumption of food (and associated eating disorders and obesity, with all the ills that implies), drugs and alcohol, and the urge to fill the void with unnecessary material belongings. See Michael Stone, *Awake in the World: Teachings from Yoga and Buddhism for Living an Engaged Life*, Shambala Publications, (2011).

and the framework it filters interpretations through, is muddying. In practice, Graham Parkes says, "it's possible to become aware of this distortion [created by our desires and cravings] and clarify our experience."[18]

Experiencing ourselves as fuelled by systems that create and sustain our identity, we can see that any urge to become more authentically ourselves by consuming more is going to reflect more on what is consumed than on the creation of a more authentic self.[19] Our identity depends not on any inherent separable self but on the myriad combination of conditions that have gone into shaping our existence. Instead of being interested only in the protection of a single self, or even of our own community, or of our own species, we realise that we, like them, are the culmination of impermanent forces that develop and dissipate. We therefore become more inclined to show an interest in, and explore the possible options that arise from focusing on those forces that create and sustain us, rather than being caught up in the illusion that stoking a fire secures it as a solid, individuated, identity.

Realisation and Dōgen Zen

In the Dōgen Zen tradition of thought, the practice of realisation is itself the embodiment of "buddha nature".[20] A moment of realisation brings into being the manifestation of the Buddha, of an awake and compassionate understanding of the interdependence of this awakening with all else, and of the capacity to release the bondage of suffering which is also the bondage of attachment, or conditioning.

As I have said before, recognising systematic enmeshment at the cultural, biological and physical level elicits a sense of compassion and humility. However, compassion and humility are elicited only if we make an effort also to recognise that our awareness is an emergent capacity, arising from what we are enmeshed in, and never free of it.

There are more differences between the physicalist and the Asian tradition approaches than there are parallels so it pays to tread carefully when attempting integration. Texts that describe the practices and experience of non-dualism from the point of view of the Dōgen Zen

---

[18] Graham Parkes, "Kūkai and Dōgen as Exemplars of Ecological Engagement", *Journal of Japanese Philosophy*, 1 (2013): 85–110.

[19] Parkes (Ibid.).

[20] Described, for instance, in Hee-Jin Kim, *Eihei Dōgen: Mystical Realist* (op. cit.): 37.

tradition developed out of a soteriological approach and there is, inevitably, a religious, mystical, and faith-based aspect to this that is absent from the secular, scientific approach. Yet, as I have just described, the physicalist approach itself elicits compassion as a response to the realisation of enmeshment, and it does so in a way that is remarkably consistent with the ideas and imagery of Dōgen's Zen. To focus in this way requires effort, but not an effort of the mental, willed kind. Paying attention is not an attempt to direct the action, but a commitment to reflect on what the action is. This is expressed in Zen literature using the imagery of "pointing at the moon", or to the illusions of relative movement between external objects and ourselves, when really movement is much more complex and dynamic and includes and involves our own changes in perception.

This relates to our view of the ecological emergency as a process of emergence that is not external to us, but includes and involves the illusion that we can direct and influence the world from without, without it fundamentally altering ourselves. It relates to the other illusions that the ecological emergency is nothing to do with us, or that it is everything to do with us but that there is nothing we can do about it. In exploring and understanding our deep involvement, both because we are intertwined, and because we have relied on narratives and imagery in which we are superior and independent, we can stop identifying with those narratives. This, too, strongly parallels the Zen process of disentangling from the idea we have of a separate "self".[21]

From the perspective of Dōgen's *Bendowa*, the self as a perspective is examined in great detail.[22] The view of Seneka, the traditional view that gave us the narrative of Atman, contrasts with the shifting, relational anatman or "no self" of Dōgen. Dōgen's no self is never one thing, in one place.[23] It has no atomistic identity whatsoever, but is, instead, entirely

---

[21] See, for instance, "Fukan Zazen" Appendix 1 in Dōgen, *Shōbōgenzō* (op. cit.); The Time Being *Uji* (facsicile12 in Dōgen, *Shōbōgenzō*, (op. cit.).

[22] Jason M. Wirth,"Dōgen and the Unknown Knowns", *Environmental Philosophy*, 10, (2013): 39–61.

[23] See Jason M. Wirth, "Shikantaza during the Sixth Great Extinction", *www.ecobuddhism.org*, n/d; Jason M. Wirth, "Painting Mountains and Rivers: Gary Snyder, Dōgen, and the Elemental Sutra of the Wild", in *Wild Times with Gary Snyder*, presented at the The Elemental, Hawai'i, hosted by The University of Hawai'i Philosophy Dept, (2012); Jason M. Wirth, "Dōgen and the Unknown Knowns", (2013), (op. cit.).

made up of the conditions that come into being. The human capacity for self-reflection is one of these conditions but it, too, is temporarily bound, shifting and impermanent. This alternative view is described by Jason Wirth when talking of Dōgen:

> The Buddha famously dismantles Sāti's adherence to a fixed self by exposing all of the relations co-dependently working together that underlie the self. Pratītyasamutpāda, dependent co-origination, demonstrates that the independent, free standing self is nothing but abstraction that if taken to heart causes turmoil.[24]

We can see that the image points to the condition itself, a condition that depends entirely on the practical effort we make as individuals to maintain ourselves in a state of awareness of our context. Realising our context is a recognition that we are not separable from that context, but that we have the capacity to develop a sense of compassion, first and foremost towards ourselves as fluid, and dissolving elements that emerge out of, and will be reabsorbed by, the mesh that has created and sustained (and will destroy) them. This elicitation of compassion gives us an attitudinal stance from which to acknowledge that there are conditions that remain "good for" the biophysical systems from which we emerge, regardless of our particular situation, and that these, while we remain, will remain good for us, and when we are gone, will remain good for other emerging and dissolving selves like us.

Beyond the self: how we practice

Practicing realisation and understanding it as the sole source of our agency, or ability to exercise any influence over the mesh, makes us less inclined to depend, for our identity, on a commitment to a particular set of ideological beliefs or values. Although it takes a huge effort, it is possible to step back from our cultural bias and individual intuitions. Jonathan Haidt talks of the potential to do this through engaging with those on the other side of cultural or intuitive divides by discovering "a shared sense of fate", suppressing "freeriders" and amplifying our similarities. He admits this does not mean that we can create a utopian state where everyone is included and loved, but this situation would be far preferable to the

---

[24] Wirth, "Dōgen and the Unknown Knowns" (op. cit.): 49.

fragmentation and polarisation that threaten to increase as the ecological emergency proceeds.[25]

We tend to fit our experiences into narratives, memories and concepts with which we are already familiar, only allowing the nature of the new experience (person, relationship, thing) to poke its way through the "perceptual envelope", to paraphrase Aldous Huxley, when there is no longer any coherence in containing it. Realising in this way is an experiment with shifting focus between the coherent state of individuals, groups, species or even systems, and what we think of as the "self", until we become fully engaged in paying attention. This includes paying attention to how we ask questions, to what phraseology we use to speak to people, even to how we move and breathe. In the context of the ecological emergency, another example might be useful here.

In exercising our agency as realisation in this way, we can find that opportunities arise to consider the relationships we have (with work, food, energy, and in particular with other people, and how we create community, since this can further influence our relationships with work, food, and energy). Reflecting on what work we do, and who for, and what systems that supports, on what we eat, and on what our attitude is to travel, requires not just an enormous effort, but the determination to remain compassionate, since the options that arise as a result of such reflections are demanding. If we reflect, we can see how heavily our enmeshment requires us to rely on energy systems that destroy and exploit the irreplaceable systems on which we depend.[26] Acknowledging this means acknowledging that the compassionate attunement we open to turns our attention to exploring possibilities for developing energy and other systems that mitigate our impact, or allow us to restore damage or destruction. This does not avoid, but rather embraces the fact of our involvement and enmeshment but it alters the framework of our discussion. We can come to question, individually and in communities, why certain elements of our enmeshment make us complicit in this exploitative sequestering of energy from other systems. We can begin to lobby for a different kind of relationship, to shift the context of our enmeshment to a more graduated flow.

If we raise these issues without an awareness of our own enmeshment, we will find ourselves and any other interlocutor locked into divergent

---

[25] See Jonathan Haidt (op. cit): 284.

[26] See John Baez on climate change responses at www.johncarlosbaez.wordpress.com (op. cit.)

positions. However, by raising issues as relationships that we can pay attention to, rather than by making pejorative statements, we can find ourselves able to "step back" from the evaluative, judgemental, self, and into a state where we are able to allow response to arise from the values that stand beyond us, but that come to light through our holding our reactivity in abeyance.

There is no doubt that to shift in this way is, at least initially, a ferociously difficult task. Practicing the shift from reactivity to compassionate attunement is as problematic as "seeing" the alternative in an ambiguous image for the first time: duck, or rabbit? Vase, or face? Decision, or openness to allowing compassionate attunement to work into the space I create by not reacting, until a response presents itself? Yet it is only through exploring this holding of ourselves open to compassionate attunement that the alternative options in our relationships and in the relationships of those we befriend arise.

In a broader, less personal context, we may find paying close attention alters how we ask about, or point out, gaps in the focus of research, or in the underlying narratives that obstruct the possibilities for a research culture that explores what is "good for" systems, regardless of any obvious or immediate financial benefit. In this way, we can highlight the manner in which data is gathered (considering the impacts of dredging the ocean floor, rather than diving, to collect research material, for instance), or what models are used (considering the difference between data gathered from dead organisms, and that gathered from living organisms in habitats where they evolved). Yet this will only be effective if the manner of our approach becomes the focus, rather than any end or goal.

In structural realist terms, this practice of realising as agency is fundamentally egalitarian: anyone can express this facility of paying attention, or realising, through their manner of commentary and observation. Adopting this manner is not exclusive to a few expert practitioners and it does not necessarily require special training (although the intellectual exegesis of this approach requires careful exposition that does need to be taught).

It is sometimes inevitable, and unavoidable, that conflicts emerge, and even that these evolve into violence, or between societies and communities, into war. Compassionate attunement meets such confrontation with the space into which response options arise. This is the ultimate "keeping a cool head" since the facts of the situation can be observed and emotional reaction, evaluation and judgment left to one side. None of this implies that we are unable to react immediately in a crisis. In an emergency, instant defense or avoidance (walking away) may still be necessary. Yet we can allow the cyclical nature of conflict to dissolve using this practice, since a conflict can always be recognised for what it is: a singular event that need not imply generations of subsequent cycles of conflict.

Since confrontation and conflict is wasteful of resources, completing any defense must be as swift, and efficient, as possible. The Daoist principle is useful here. While we need to make every effort to avoid war and its "terrible waste of energies", dealing with conflict as effectively as possible requires consideration: "A successful campaign would have the enemy overextend himself. With his energies exhausted, his armies would collapse."[27]

Again, it is important to recognise that there is, from an impartial point of view, nothing "righteous" about our anger or other emotional reactions: we experience things the way we do for a multiplicity of reasons, including genome, background history, and current circumstances. This does not put us on the side of right, though we can exercise compassion towards ourselves most effectively on the occasions when we feel most frustrated or overwhelmed at the intractable nature of determined and malicious harms. We are not "right" in the sense of being morally superior. We may well still be better attuned, and more sensitive to "the good" of systems, but our agency lies in our capacity to realise, understand, and thus create a meta-system for eliciting alternative responses.

We are just as much a part of systems as everyone and everything else, including those who are exploiting it for short-term gain, and no doubt justifying their actions in the same way that we do, as righteous. However difficult it may be to accept that others with different ideologies believe in their being right as firmly as we do, we must take this step to understand the partiality of our own views before we can hope to address the situation it leaves us in. In a sense, the very ideologies that confront us from those we deem our "enemies" are precisely that part of the system that we must understand and, in a sense, incorporate (or at least sense what their embodiment might mean) if we are to dissolve their power over us as alternative truths. In this broader understanding of identity, this conclusion is unavoidable.

Acknowledging it engenders a more realistic sense of ourselves: we include even the relationships that create the ecological emergency. This acknowledgement elicits humility and avoids the stink of smug self-

---

[27] Hans Georg Moeller, *The Moral Fool* (op. cit.): 53ff.

satisfaction that can arise in those who consider themselves "enlightened".[28] We may then be in a position to disentangle our reactivity from what is actually going on. When this happens, an enormous shift in how we understand, and therefore in how we engage, with the context emerges.

A physicalist approach allows us to acknowledge the directionality, and therefore the "good", of systems. The ability to distinguish what is good for systems in this way allows us to see what obstructs them or causes their collapse.[29]

One such set of systems that could be a focus of our practical response is the interrelationship between micro-organisms and macro-organisms. Our knowledge of this interrelationship is still in its infancy. Research into human systems is reasonably well established, but research into how micro-organisms relate to one another, and how these systems relate to macro-systems, is still a relatively new field within which new discoveries, including the discovery of new species, is still possible. Developing connections between this field of research and humanities-based studies of how human systems operate would benefit our understanding of enmeshment and allow a more open debate about what we need to do to realise more fully, in the active, creative sense, the relationships between us as macro-organisms and us as hosts or co-identities with these communities of micro-organisms. It is in changing the narrative that we open to the possibility of changing how we relate to these systems, to how we see ourselves, as systems, and to where we acknowledge, and exercise, our agency.

Another, related, practice could involve the restoration and re-appreciation of systems that have been degraded, but that are still partially connected to their evolutionary history. We could invest less energy in the exploitation of those areas of the planet that remain relatively pristine, and more in understanding, through research, the possibility of generating

---

[28] Alan Watts used the phrase, "the stink of Zen" in his 1957 classic, *The Way of Zen*, New York: Vintage, (1999). Leonard Cohen used the same phrase in a recent interview (https://www.youtube.com/watch?v=FAoHYBpj8vY). Watts implies that focussing on books, teachings and rituals instead of moving beyond them to the experience creates "the stink"; Cohen implies that there is something smug about those who think they have found enlightenment, or who consider their way of living to be superior to other people.

[29] A very similar point is made in Roger J. H. King's, "Playing with Boundaries: Critical Reflections on Strategies for an Environmental Culture and the Promise of Civic Environmentalism", (op. cit.).

energy or products through emulating systems, through "biomimicry", for instance, and through "cradle to cradle" technologies.[30] In drawing attention to these possibilities, we need to realise that our agency is this capacity to continuously reflect upon, and to be a reflection of, context and perspective, and therefore, that we are not seeking to develop universalisable principles from these activities.[31]

To summarise this section: being able to move beyond a conditioned sense of self requires an effort to focus much more on how we participate in all the biophysical relationships we are involved in. This gives a context to understanding and exploring how human systems might thrive within and in conjunction with these other systems. Just as important is the understanding that the context includes a time when the human species has ceased to flourish, and when the conditions under which we thrive no longer exist. Understanding the "good" in this context means realising what we need to do to mitigate our impact, through creating less that is permanent and damaging to other systems, in direct contrast to the material consumerism we are currently enmeshed within.

We can pay attention to whether or not we are prepared to make the effort to realise in this way, individually or as a species. We can ask ourselves whether or not we are prepared to educate ourselves to the extent that we question the prioritisation of current profitable enterprises (like extraction and burning of fossil fuels) over the thriving of multiple systems that will increase the probability of benefits for human and other systems now and in the future. This is paying attention to the "good" of systems, to the narratives, analogies, metaphors and imagery used to defend the status quo, and where possible, to pointing out any tendency within these narratives to obfuscate, confuse or otherwise distract attention from features that obstruct the stochastic flow of energy through systems. This gives us grounds for responding to "the good" of systems through compassion. It is not the self-realisation in the manner talked of by Naess, Fox or Leopold. The "Self Realisation!" of Naess is of a transcendental self, a structure inherent in, but also hovering beyond, the physical universe. Realisation as agency is, by contrast, a biophysical

---

[30]Braungart, Michael, and William McDonough, *Cradle to Cradle*, London: Vintage, (2009).

[31] cf "The deep ecologists would do well to take a few other leaves out of the Daoist/Zen book—those emphasizing the importance of context and perspective and the problems that arise when one tries to universalize." Graham Parkes, "Voices of Mountains, Trees, and Rivers: Kūkai, Dōgen, and a Deeper Ecology", (op. cit.): 120.

system that is emergent, just as compassion is a value that exists within the universe, and does not transcend it. Realisation allows compassion to be elicited, and compassion has the peculiar property of a metasystem in that it interacts back through its enmeshment. Because it is dynamic and interactive, its importance lies in bringing systems in to focus, and that involves how we exercise this capacity for self-awareness.

Realisation as making real

In this sense, this physicalist approach is comparable with the approach described in the Dōgen Zen tradition of thought. Dōgen's descriptions of practice contain elements that parallel the physicalist approach. What we realise, while commenting on, or observing the areas we have withdrawn attention from, is both the actualisation of a system and the expression of a practice that is potentially available to all persons:

> Although this inconceivable dharma is abundant in each person, it is not actualized without practice, and it is not experienced without realisation. When you realise it, it fills your hand - how could it be limited to one or many?[32]

Dharma has many meanings, including both teaching, and working, but also practicing, or behaving, in accord with the way that the universe is already unfolding, interdependently. Observation and commentary are both ways of making explicit this unfolding (including any notable obstructions or interferences) but they are also implicit examples of this unfolding and therefore they co-create whatever is emerging.

The Dōgen Zen approach understands us to be the same context as all humans throughout the ages: the kinds of urgent problems and issues we face are entwined with our humanity. We are, and have always been, as humans, very much in an emergency situation that requires us to wake up to what we have to do. However, the ecological emergency has shifted the relationship between human systems and other evolved systems on the planet and so in a sense, the context is insisting on our attention in a completely different manner. If we can respond by becoming alive to the systematic distraction of our attention, and begin to practice focusing on what compassion would do, what alternatives to current production and consumption involve less suffering, for instance, we find we are back in

---

[32] Dōgen, Chapter One, *Bendowa*, "On the Endeavour of the Way", *Shōbōgenzō: Treasury of the True Dharma Eye* (op. cit.).

the tradition that has raised questions about how we are to live that have faced our species since it developed the capacity for self-reflection. The global scale of the impact of our avoidance of these issues is becoming apparent but our primary response has been demanded of us since we evolved the capacity for distraction.[33]

Where there is clear evidence that some directional flows are more beneficial than others, we can draw attention to this. However, the work of realisation is not to concern itself with the end, but to focus on the way in which we see and the way in which we respond, and therefore what matters much more than success or failure to achieve a final outcome is the process, or the way, of realisation, itself. Dōgen points up the relationship between how we understand, how we talk about, and how we respond to what creates our conditions:

> If you doubt mountains' walking, you do not know your own talking; it is not that you do not walk, but that you do not know or understand your own walking. Green mountains are neither sentient nor insentient. You are neither sentient nor insentient.[34]

Mountains are not apart from the systems, including the gaseous, climatic, weather systems, the solid soil-based, cellular, geological systems or the liquid, water, oil, and circulation systems that we inhabit and that sustain us. We are maintained by and contained in systems that are both much larger and much smaller than any idea of sentience could make sense of. To consider humans as exclusively sentient or other systems as exclusively insentient is inaccurate. Bringing more attention to the interconnected nature of human systems with systems upon which we rely, including undertaking and disseminating research into the relationships we have with macro-systems (the atmosphere, the climate) and micro-systems (soil, microbes) is fundamental to understanding and responding to "the good" of systems.

---

[33] See Wirth, "Painting Mountains and Rivers: Gary Snyder, Dōgen, and the Elemental Sutra of the Wild", (op. cit.).

[34] Dōgen, Chapter Fifteen, "Mountains and Waters as Sutra", *Sansuikyō, Shōbōgenzō: Treasury of the True Dharma Eye* (op. cit.): 155.

Parkes refutes the idea that the impermanence of existence excuses us from contributing to its destruction.[35] The opposite is true: recognising the impermanent, energy-dissipating nature of our own existence and of the existence we are enmeshed in gives us an idea of how to assess what is "good for" and what is "bad for" the systems we are enmeshed within. Creating more permanent structures is detrimental to impermanence: we require structures that can "walk" within the dissipating flow, a circular economy that moves energy through and towards the human but then feeds it back to be available to other patterned forms of existence.

The vast majority of biodiverse systems have evolved independently of human cultural systems. Yet Morton's point about our being enmeshed extends to biodiversity, which is enculturated, in the sense that we perceive it, through human systems that encompass our entire understanding of the universe. It is also enculturated in the sense that the impacts we have had on systems that sustain us, and even on wider sets of systems, will long outlive us.

However, our bio-physical enmeshment is also stranger, and in Morton's sense, wilder and more alien, than we can imagine. It is encultured only at the level of language, and our language still needs to adapt to the sense in which we are within reactions, and wider forces, that are beyond our capacity for acculturation. Human systems are within bio-physical systems, in the way a fish is within, and dependent upon, water. Dōgen's "Mountains and Waters as Sutra" (*Sansuikyo⁻*) provides a good analogy for this process of "seeing" the medium we exist within.[36] If we are to use our capacity as realising agents to any effect, then we must recognise,

---

[35]"If natural phenomena demonstrate the ideas of impermanence and interdependence – in broad terms, the lessons of contemporary ecological science – what is the non-biodegradable plastic ... telling us? [It is] disrupting the fabric of interdependence on which our own existence depends. Plutonium waste teaches a more extreme version of the same lesson ..." Graham Parkes, "Kûkai and Dōgen as Exemplars of Ecological Engagement", (op. cit.): 106.

[36] Parkes points out that Dōgen "introduces water as evading all dualistic categories" (Graham Parkes, "Body-Mind and Buddha-nature: Dōgen's Deeper Ecology", in *Frontiers of Japanese Philosophy: Classical Japanese Philosophy*, J.W. Heisig and R. Raud. Nagoya (eds): Nanzan Institute for Religion and Culture, (2010) 122-47: 136). We can extend this to the idea that the separation between subject and object dissolves even as it is realised, in the same way that realising that the shape and content of our lungs relies entirely on the medium (or, in space or underwater, a crucial pocket) of local air, allows us to understand that we are contained within, but also contain, the medium of our survival.

acknowledge, appreciate, and thus become motivated to realise this understanding, including practicing keeping focused on the urgency of our response:

> You should be resolved not to waste time and refrain from doing meaningless things. You should spend your time carrying out what is worth doing. Among the things you should do, what is the most important?[37]

"What is important" is what is "good for" the systems we are enmeshed within, and resolving what to do involves being able to keep focused on how we are relating within those systems. By-products of consumerism parallel by-products of unrealised action: when we stop watching, we become involved in interactions that fuel the emergency.

Poles apart

Zimmerman points out that Continental philosophers in the phenomenological tradition developed their responses to the growing awareness of anthropogenic impact from quite different contexts to philosophers from the analytic tradition of Anglo-American philosophy.[38] The former were likely to experience ecosystems as, for instance, parklands, or even as well cropped trees in Parisian boulevards, while environmental ethicists raised in the pioneering traditions in Australia, New Zealand and the United States came up with a very different picture of how ecosystems and human systems interact. Carole Pateman in her work on "The Settler Contract" makes it clear that intimacy with place among Aboriginal people in Australia was completely obscured and ignored by laws, including the notorious terra nullius ("empty land") laws

---

[37] Quoted in Graham Parkes, "Nuclear Power After Fukushima 2011: Buddhist and Promethean Perspectives", *Buddhist-Christian Studies*, 32, (2012): 99. From *Shōbōgenzō-Zuimonki*, trans. Shohaku Okumura, Kyoto: Kyoto Sōtō Zen Center, (1987): 97.

[38] Robert Zimmerman, "What Can Continental Philosophy Contribute to Environmentalism?" *Rethinking Nature: essays in environmental philosophy*, Robert Frodeman (ed.), Bloomington, IN: Indiana University Press, (2004) 207–229. Zimmerman recognised, as do I, the difficulties with this kind of generalisation. Yet it is still worth noting that the ideas that shaped philosophers associated with these two traditions do in fact fall largely into these two groupings. Arne Naess is an exception.

that British colonisers used to justify their ownership claims (and other acts of violence to the people).[39]

This may appear to be an extreme example of not being able to see from another perspective, and yet in the context of debates on the ecological emergency (whether from the point of view of sceptics, or between different groups and individuals who consider that we are in some level of emergency) the adherence to a particular perspective is just as fierce. Just as Zimmerman points out that it was hard for the two groups he mentions even to understand one another, so we can extend this to the difficulties faced by those committed to different views on this debate.[40]

The disparateness of views, the lack of understanding that exists in debates on the ecological emergency, tends to emerge from conflicts in the prioritisation of different sets of values. The continental philosophers tend (according to Zimmerman) to prioritise social over ecological interests, while the Anglo-American tradition tends to prioritise, or at least lend its focus to, the Wild, wilderness, or the Natural over the consideration of human interests.[41]

---

[39] Carole Pateman, "The Settler Contract", Chapter Two in Carole Pateman and Charles Wade Mills, *Contract and Domination*, (op. cit.).

[40] Zimmerman, (op. cit.): 5. The difficulties faced by French philosophers trying to understand Anglo-American environmental ethics are laid out in Luc Ferry, *The New Ecological Order*, 2nd edition Chicago: University of Chicago Press, (1995): 12. Ferry's criticisms of Anglo-American moral extensionism and radical environmentalism (including deep ecology and ecofeminism) reveal only a partial understanding of these varieties of environmental philosophy.

[41] Bjørn Lomborg, *Cool It: The Skeptical Environmentalist's Guide to Global Warming*, (op. cit.). His scientific credentials made him a poster-boy for the "sceptics", but recently he began to shift position to a stance that is rather akin to Pinker: instead of his earlier view that the science behind the attempts to put the ecological emergency on the political agenda was "bad science", he began to turn his attention away from this debate and argue, instead, that social interests (poverty, rights, access to infrastructure and jobs) trump ecological interests. See, for instance, Lomborg's debate with Eamon Ryan on

http://www.rte.ie/radio1/today-with-sean-o-

rourke/programmes/2013/1202/490406-today-with-sean-o-rourke-monday-2-

december-2013. See, too, Mirjam de Groot, Martin Drenthen, and Wouter T. de Groot, "Public Visions of the Human/Nature Relationship and Their Implications for Environmental Ethics", *Environmental Ethics*, 33, (2011): 25–44. This paper is an attempt to debunk the myth that anthropocentric perspectives dominate in Europe, by showing that respondents had predominantly a partnership or stewardship view of their relationship with the ecological systems they were involved with. It does not

Realising our agency does not involve disentangling ourselves from context. It involves recognising that biophysical systems shift under the (biophysical) process of self-observation, that how these shifts happen depends entirely on the manner of observation, including the attitude with which observation takes place. We can either realise, and thus potentially graduate, the dissipation of energy through systems, or our attention, or more likely our lack of it, can obstruct or (damagingly) increase the flow.

Elucidating a process of graduated informational exchange implies paying attention so that, when the tendency for divergence increases, we can see how our own contribution exacerbates or mitigates the process. Watching how interactions fuel or block existing attachments reveals what interests are being maintained and what narratives are being reiterated. It becomes possible to pay attention to what is behind the narrative and, by drawing attention to this in the manner described above, to develop a neutral space through which our understanding can develop. Our narratives, we begin to see, are additional, and unnecessary for understanding what is going on. We need only look at what is being said, without the story, to find out if a connection with the other is possible.

In this process of paying attention to what is being said, we can see that even our own understanding wavers and is not consistently unconditioned. We cannot help, through being human, our capacity to be distracted, to fall back into patterns of reactivity, and therefore, neither can others. Knowing what to do is no guarantee that we or they will make the requisite effort. Holding our attention on our enmeshment requires practice, and certainly requires effort, even after years of practice. Conditions shift and sometimes bind us so tightly into reactivity that we fail to step back.[42] Sometimes our only recourse is irony: we would like to

---

actually refute the idea that an anthropocentric narrative prevails, however, because it still finds that there is a dualistic relationship between human and non-human interests, and this view is vastly prevalent in this paper's survey results.

[42] Compare, for instance, Jonathan Glover and M. J. Scott-Taggart, "It Makes No Difference Whether or Not I Do It", *Aristotelian Society Supplementary Volume*, 49 (1975) 171–209 where they argue, in similar vein, that we should attempt to do what is right even if there is no evidence to show that our actions will make a difference. This parallels recent arguments for divestment that are current and prevalent in university circles, since the debate around whether or not a small action, like divesting of a small number of shares in an oil company, can actually cause the oil company to alter its exploitative and destructive policies, is only part of the issue: the central issue is the authenticity of the project of universities that claim

act to realise "the good" of systems, but our enmeshment is such that we have failed to loosen the bonds of our reaction. Yet it is the manner of how we deal with each momentary realisation, and, eventually, to the practice of realisation that creates the potential for a larger, more established shift in perspective.

The capacity to realise obviously does not give us instant, miraculous power to control attitudinal divergence. Yet, the act of focussing attention in the way I have suggested allows participants in any discussion to bring to consciousness their own commitments, to examine possibilities for reflection, particularly on what is tacitly accepted as part of their own ideological context. This parallels two very different, but importantly related, ideas: Warwick Fox's account of "responsive cohesion" and Rawls's idea of "reflective equilibrium".[43] Following Fox's ideas in their earlier (1990) conception, the idea of agency as realisation is similar to "an expression of the spontaneous unfolding (development, maturing) of the self", although this idea goes beyond Fox's, since realisation creates a system of interconnections that other systems then respond to.[44]

Like Rawls' idea, the process of realisation reflects back on, and causes readjustments within, the belief systems (among other systems) that are reflected upon. Unlike Rawlsian "reflective equilibrium", there is no balance point to which to return, only a further unfolding of the compassionate attunement that emerges to reorientate the relationships, including divergent relationships within which it is enmeshed. Yet the same kind of effect takes place: by encompassing and adjusting to new informational exchanges, in each case, systems respond and a better

---

intellectual independence when they are substantially beholden to oil companies for research funding (see, for a discussion of this issue, Leferna, Alexandre Georges, "Betting on Climate Failure: The Ethics & Economics of Fossil Fuel Divestment" (unpublished: uploaded on www.academia.edu, 2014); for an amusing discussion of the (hypocritical) gap between expert theoretical understanding of moral issues and somewhat less expert practice, see Eric Schwitzgebel, "Do Ethicists Steal More Books?", *Philosophical Psychology*, 22, (2009): 711–725.

[43] Fox's theory of responsive cohesion is laid out most comprehensively in Warwick Fox, "Responsive Cohesion: Thinking in Context," *Resurgence*, 241,(March/April 2007); 22-25; and again in Fox, "Ethics, Architecture, Responsive Cohesion and the Transition to a More Habitable Future," Paper presented to the *Ethics and the Built Environment* conference, Nottingham University, (9-11 Sept 2009): John Rawls, *A Theory of Justice, Revised Edition* (op. cit.): 18ff.

[44] Warwick Fox, "Problem 14 in Human Relationships, Nature, and the Built Environment: Problems That Any General Ethics Must Be Able to Address", in *Sage Handbook of Environment and Society* (op. cit.).

"flow" of information between systems is established. Reflecting on narratives that propose a strict boundary between ourselves and the context within which we are enmeshed, and observing that these do not cohere well with the best accounts we have of our enmeshment, is central to the foundation of our responses.[45]

On practical terms, we could imagine a scenario where those with strongly divergent views on a particular issue related to the ecological emergency were asked to come to a meeting to discuss the possibilities for convergence in their views. A good example of this occurred in northwest Mayo, in Ireland, in which a local community came up against Shell, supported in its project by the state. The result was hugely divisive locally, included allegations of police brutality, and resulted in the jailing of five members of the community.[46] Problems since the project's inception have seen a glaring lack of investigation into impacts on local human and ecological health when there have been malfunctions during its operation so far. [47]

As with more relational issues, a more productive approach would have been to have acknowledged, and listened to the particular community and personal histories and experiences. This would have formed a backdrop to any individual's attitude, including, perhaps, the experience of intimidation or empowerment, marginalisation or inclusion, financial advantage or disadvantage, and so on. From the point of view of agency as realisation, the process of discussion could then have gone on to explore both the context of the proposed project, and a broad contextualisation of the ideological commitments of the discussants. During this stage, a clear effort at engaging in a personal way, at reaching out for common, neutral areas for discussion would need to be made.

There would then have to be some agreement to step back from the ideological commitments, to see them as intuitions that are a part of the fabric of a particular individual, and to note that each set of commitments is, in fact, unique, because each enmeshment is unique. There could then be an illustration of how stepping back from one's own particular

---

[45] I use this term in the way that Warwick Fox proposes: in a broad sense, we are all anthropocentric, given that the context of our perspective is necessarily human; in a narrow sense, however, anthropocentrism is not a viable perspective, given the systems-based approach I have described earlier.

[46] For a detailed review of this controversy, see, for instance, Liam Leonard, *The Environmental Movement in Ireland,* Springer, (2007).

[47] "The report does not make any reference to the impact of this flaring on local residents living around the refinery." Siggins, Lorna, *Irish Times*, (1 Aug 2018).

situation allows one to see oneself in context. This would give a more impartial context, and into this, one could introduce any further areas for consideration, including, perhaps, the "good" of systems affected by the project itself. This discussion would then take place with the acknowledgement of existing commitments, but using techniques to allow the participants to recognise, acknowledge, and create an observational distance between those commitments and the current area of consideration.[48] There could have been proposals and an acceptance to include mitigating strategies, including wildlife restoration and rewilding projects in the area, pilot research schemes to investigate alternative, low-carbon energy projects, and ways to create coherence and support for more marginalised individuals and groups within the local and wider affected community.

Rather than what is "good" for systems simply replacing or over-riding existing commitments, this technique provides a way of making much clearer how convergence between existing commitments and the "good" of systems can take place, even between those who are committed to opposing ideologies. This differs from many current political negotiating strategies that recommend a great deal of secrecy: this technique is an opportunity to be clear and open about one's commitments and experience. It differs from ethical approaches since it has no aim or end in mind: it is an opportunity to practice how to engage in discussion, rather than a search for a solution. Considering the "good" of systems may imply a focus on an end to this process, but in recognising that systems themselves are dynamic, unpredictable and impermanent, there is far less focus on achieving a "harmonious" outcome, and far more on exploring a better understanding of the systems involved. The "good" of systems is also not separate from personal as well as interpersonal and other non-human activity, as the process shows.

This process can jolt us out of an acceptance that others are responsible for negotiations and decision-making on our behalf. It could mean allowing policy- and strategy-makers to have less control over individual

---

[48] This is very much in line with Haidt's conclusions in *The Righteous Mind*. Of course, as I have said earlier, there is no ideal conclusion, no utopia in which harmoniously, all views coalesce. Instead, we are in constant process. It is the manner of our engagement, therefore, that is at the crux of how engagement proceeds and, indeed, that is at the crux of any hope of a workable outcome, one that mitigates harm to the greatest degree, and one that allows that dynamic concept, the "good" of systems (which is also never ideal or fixed, but always falling towards another state) to be realised.

lives, since the facilitation of the kinds of discussion the above example represents need not take place in venues or under the sanction of any legitimising authorities. In a sense, therefore, the realisation of our agency is a radical, and gently anarchic, process. We come to understand the profundity of our own responsibility. Even a moment of realisation has resonant effects, and taking responsibility for where, and how, we direct attention, has cumulative effects.

Changing our attitude towards our enmeshment includes shifting focus from "overcoming" or "balancing" with nature, but also with one another, including with the authorities that make decisions in our names. It involves seeing human systems and individuals as being within these larger systems but also as being able to respond within them using this powerful technique.[49] Paying attention in this way is an extension of the Buddhist idea of "waking up" to our experience, or of Lovelock's metaphor that we become aware of what we have done only by paying close attention to what we could have done differently, and so to what we could do differently now.[50]

There is a marked contrast between this paying attention as a practice in response, and the justification for more robust activism that is advocated for by a cohort of ecophilosophers coming at the issue from a dualistic, "them" versus "us" perspective.[51] The practice of paying attention is

---

[49] Zimmerman talks of the "we can overcome" attitude that was deemed appropriate to the attempts to "conquer" America; Botkin talks of the misconstruction that has led to our imagining that natural systems reach harmoniousness or arrangements of stability: this is not to deny that homeostasis does exist as a feedback process within systems (and this is precisely the kind of feedback loop that allows the graduation of flows of energy that maintain systems for long enough that we, as humans within these systems, can exist at all, and benefit from the graduated dissipation of energy through systems within which we are enmeshed). But it is to question the problematic idealism that has led ecological thinkers to advocate for "harmony" with nature, an impossible dream and one that distracts from the issue and polarises those on either side of the debate.

[50] I have already mentioned Lovelock's deep pessimism at humanity's prospects. We have the capacity to think things through, but we will not exercise this capacity as long as it is easier not to, and by the time we have to, it will be too late.

[51] See, most obviously, David Foreman of *Earth First!* in David Keller, ed., *Environmental Ethics: The Big Questions*, (op. cit.): 327. But also interesting on this topic is the argument put forward by Zimmerman concerning the partiality of "environmental activists". See, for instance, Robert Zimmerman, "What Can Continental Philosophy Contribute to Environmentalism?"(op. cit.): esp note 48: "...one could argue that environmentalists, far from being righteous champions of

essential in combating this tendency to simply mirror the very attitude and conditions that have created the problems in the first place. Indulging in a power-struggle of ideas only feeds into the very systems we have been attempting to ease ourselves out of.

There are situations in which a consensus view develops as a result of independently and objectively assessed data collection. We can clearly see that accepting the validity of such a consensus is an appropriate response. However, even such recognition does not legitimise or justify confrontational activism or a sense of moral superiority at having "got it right".

The imagery of a practice-based response to attitude divergence through paying attention to the manner of our response has strong parallels among Asian traditions of thought. However, these ideas resist penetration by analytical approaches. If they are to offer an alternative to current habits of thought and guide us from the precipitous threat to the graduated flows we rely on, there needs to be extensive work on drawing out what a physicalist approach can learn from them.

Where we can usefully engage with Asian traditions of thought is in looking at relationships from angles that are non-standard and that resist the "domineering norm".[52] Some of the non-standard perspectives presented by Dōgen give rise to a more profound consideration of relationships than the dominant conventions of the global North. "Study not only that you become a mother when your child is born, but also that you become a child", Dōgen observes.[53] The point of separation between mother and child is not clear but is better conceived of as both a continuum and a relationship that creates its mirror image: "At the moment of giving birth to a child, is the mother separate from the child?"[54] In the same vein, we are not entirely separable from the polarised opposing view. Our resistance maintains it. It only dissolves when we manage to avoid responding in mirror fashion.

---

nature, are motivated by power-interests of their own. Environmentalists make truth claims about this eco-calamity or that scientific fact, but such truth claims must be regarded with suspicion, since they are power enhancing perspectives. In effect, environmentalists are the mirror image of industrialists."

[52] Robert Zimmerman (Ibid.): 213.

[53] Dōgen, Chapter Fifteen, "Mountains and Waters as Sutra", *Sansuikyō, Shōbōgenzō: Treasury of the True Dharma Eye*, (op. cit.): 155.

[54] (Ibid.): 156.

Non-dualist Asian traditions of thought also recognise that a particular situation is neither right nor wrong. The standpoint of the observer, the particular conditions of their enmeshment, will dictate how they see the situation, but more than this, the capacity to encompass observations in a broader awareness will release them from the obligations of responding with evaluative judgements. Moeller describes a passage from the Zhuangzi in which he illustrates this:

> ...if assuming a standpoint from which it is right you see it as right, not one of the myriad things is not right; if assuming a standpoint from which it is wrong you see it as wrong, not one of the myriad things is not wrong.[55]

From the Asian tradition of thought, it is not the individual "I" but the situation that "wakes up to" or "realises" itself through our coming to observe it and this is central as a practice:

> When even for a moment you sit upright in samadhi expressing the buddha mudra in the three activities (body, speech and thought), the whole world of phenomena becomes the buddha mudra and the entire sky turns into enlightenment.[56]

It is difficult to imagine awareness without a locus, yet being aware of one's involvement connects the physicalist's idea of enmeshment with the Zen idea of awareness that brings itself to light through an individual's efforts. This individual is able to see themselves and their awareness as having the same kind of impermanence as that implicit interconnectedness within which they are enmeshed. This is a further link between the physicalist approach and that of the Asian non-dualist tradition.

Watching brings to light obstructions to the flow of impermanence.[57] Among these obstructions are rigid sets of dogma that are accepted unreflectively. Adopting a sceptic's questioning attitude to any ethical corpus allows us to disengage from blind acceptance, to be open to the possibility that the codes we inherit may require adaption or even dissolution in the face of the changing conditions that are emerging. Some

---

[55] Hans-Georg Moeller, *The Moral Fool* (op. cit.): 31.

[56] Dōgen, "On the Endeavour of the Way" , *Bendowa* Chapter One, *Shōbōgenzō: Treasury of the True Dharma Eye*, (op. cit.).

[57] Graham Parkes, "Nuclear Power After Fukushima 2011: Buddhist and Promethean Perspectives", (op. cit.).

Asian traditions of thought, particularly those of the Sōtō Zen school, and the Daoists, allow this to be the case. Dōgen's approach, in particular, reminds us that, rather than being concerned with how our acts fit into an overarching set of principles, "our every action can be (is already) its own end."[58] Instead of the dualistic idea, represented in Christianity by the schism between Martha, the humble domestic practitioner, and Mary, the spiritually aware listener, Dōgen calls for a recognition that "preparing food, washing clothes, and so forth" are not "mere chores, necessary evils to be tolerated or passed on to someone else".[59] Rather, they are "the supreme activities of the buddhas and patriarchs."[60]

Rather than this implying that we respect and practice the rites and traditions of non-dualistic approaches, this is an opportunity to engage mindfully at every moment. Rites that formalise mindful awareness of practice reflect a respect for tradition, a linking back to lineages that are culturally and intellectually significant. However, the practice of realisation as agency is a way of stepping back, and observing that what is important in these rites and rituals is the development of awareness in all somatic engagement.

"Just sitting" as "sitting with"

Our focus must switch to the way in which we, as energetic dissipation systems, graduate the flow, rather than to any outcome or endpoint for the process.[61] For a few, the idea of stepping back might suggest a retreat from the norms and conventions of mainstream society (through, for instance, a withdrawal to an abode in the mountains). Yet this privilege is not an option for most practitioners, and Dōgen is quite clear that, just as realisation is expressed in the practice of the everyday, so it is experienced

---

[58] Graham Parkes, "Body-Mind and Buddha-nature". (op. cit.): 124.

[59] (Ibid.): 124.

[60] (Ibid.): 124.

[61] This is one theory but it is a plausible explanation for biodiversity maximisation and accords, surprisingly, with the Maximum Entropy theory (the theory that living systems obey the laws of thermodynamics by maximising entropy, using up solar energy in as many disparate ways as possible, but that this has the unexpected effect of broadening and making more shallow the gradient drop in solar energy dissipation). For more work on this, see John Baez's work, and notes on a conference he organised on the topic at
www.johncarlosbaez.wordpress.com/2013/11/02/entropy-and-information-in-biological-systems/.

in the relationships, intimate or reluctant, we are currently enmeshed in. The capacity to open to realisation has to take place in the context of cold calls, current family duties and demands, storm surges, and drought. Realisation as agency recognises that these systems, too, bind our perspective unless we make the effort to mentally step back and observe our engagement. Unexercised agency sharpens the gradient of dissipation.

The practice of stepping back, particularly in the context of divergence in attitudes where it is most damaging, is very challenging. The practice, however, is straightforward. Taking a step back and seeing what realisation might mean in the relationship with the systems we are involved in includes maintaining detachment while bringing attention to, discussing, and negotiating all aspects of systems. This means a comprehensive appreciation, from the technological (the relationships between resource extraction, labour, pollution, transport and energy use) to the biodiverse (land use, agricultural systems, food and consumer choices).

Stepping back also means realising that mountains exist with integrity and rivers follow their courses, not randomly, but as an expression of myriad forces. We can learn much more by minimising unnecessary interference, and developing our capacity to observe, and learn, than we can by imposing mechanised solutions that purport to be "good for" us, but usually only serve certain interests.[62]

To address attitude divergence, it is necessary to agree to a set of rules of engagement that need not be ethical, but will include a strong incentive to comply. These could include some detail of the manner of engagement. The only sanction to the constant breaking of the rules would be the withdrawal of engagement of those who were keeping the rules and the defence of any activity that had been agreed by those who kept the rules.[63]

Any imposition, however benign, cannot allow informational exchanges that give space for eliciting a response. Therefore any rules would have to be agreed on through discussion and negotiation under agreed conditions

---

[62] Unnecessary interference serves, for instance, interests that funnel energy through narrower and narrower channels. Where interference can be graduated so that any sharp increase in the energy gradient is mitigated, compensated for, or otherwise reduced for "the good" of systems, it may be justifiable. However, as I have attempted to illustrate throughout this dissertation, generalisations are rarely useful in formulating our responses and sensitivity to the details of each case is a better approach.

[63] See Moeller (op. cit) for details of this idea that game rules and laws are sufficient for organising social action.

and would include the idea that no ideological argument would count as a valid ground for persuasion. Only attention to scientific findings, to research into processes that are "good for" systems, and to practices that allow a greater participation in the informational exchanges, or in the practice of paying close attention, would do.

This practice of setting aside is central to the practice of agency as realisation, just as it is central to Dōgen's practice of "just sitting" or "practice-realisation". Dōgen uses the paradoxical idea that walking backward should not obstruct walking forward.[64] This idea that we can step back from the situation as a practical response, and this will allow the situation to continue in its directional flow, is a clear illustration of how the possibility of reorientating the relationship both with one another, and with wider systems, arises. Instead of viewing the other as something involving an opposing view, we can begin to see how we create the relationships within which we are enmeshed. This opens us to choice, to the opportunity to commit ourselves, not to action, but to the practice of realisation.[65]

Agency as realisation is precisely the practice of drawing attention to the hidden or obscured obstructions within systems, without creating more tension through the manner in which these observations are framed. We can engender discussion among political and business individuals to elicit a realisation in relation to their own attitudes and beliefs, and offer opportunities to them to practice realisation themselves in a broader context. We can be pessimistic about the prospects for a solution to the problems as an antidote to the blind optimism, wishful or even magical thinking and spin that are so prevalent in cultural narratives. We can challenge situations of radical ignorance, particularly among the most privileged citizens on the planet. Science deniers are part of this group but so are so many who do nothing even though they accept the science.

Reviewing ideas of graduated dissipation within human economic systems includes recognising the obstructions and vulnerability to collapse within (relatively) unfettered capitalist systems. The notion of constrained dissipation applies to this area too. Incomes or resource equivalence of \$40,000 per annum per capita, for instance, could allow a comfortable income in all countries and reduce the insupportable impact

---

[64] Dōgen, Chapter Fifteen, "Mountains and Waters as Sutra", *Sansuikyō*, *Shōbōgenzō: Treasury of the True Dharma Eye*, (op. cit.): 155.

[65] Hee-Jin Kim, *Eihei Dōgen: Mystical Realist* (op. cit.): 173.

of high earners on ecosystems.[66] The problems with imposing limitations on income, or indeed on providing everyone with a basic income, are many and well discussed elsewhere, but they have some interesting implications that are relevant to, and connected with, the ideas of graduating the flow of energy through systems.[67]

We can raise, and raise again, the problems with the massive subsidies for carbon-based fuels. We can point out that the relative cost of energy only favours carbon because of these massive subsidies. We can discuss the potential that shifting subsidies to new infrastructure would actually create jobs and profit. But we are likely to meet a brick wall if those we are talking with have vested interests in the status quo. Discussion, and continuing attempts to elicit an empirical response to the realisation that we really are in the midst of an ecological emergency, is the only slim hope we have for avoiding the steepening gradient.

It is difficult to imagine anyone wanting to swap their lifestyle voluntarily for one that puts them lower on the income scale than they are at the moment. This can be particularly true of people who have recently, within their own or their parents' living memory, experienced "want". Yet we are living within systems that have become more violent in response to our violence. This very much echoes the idea that "Green mountains are always walking, and Eastern mountains travel on waters", that systems are always moving and will always more in relation to other systems, including the systems within which we are enmeshed, and the systems move more quickly now, by our not paying attention, or when we ignore our interdependence with them, than when we realise this.

Compassion for moving mountains

Compassion, according to the OED, is "the feeling or emotion, when a person is moved by the suffering or distress of another." It is not pity, which is the recognition of another's suffering without the complete empathetic appreciation that compassion implies. The compassion that

---

[66] Shoibal Chakravarty, Steven Pacala, et al. "Sharing Global CO2 Emission Reductions Among One Billioon High Emitters", *Proceedings of the National Academy of Sciences*, (2009).

[67] See, for instance, Catriona McKinnon, among many other notable scholars, who has made extensive and comprehensive explorations into the idea that a universal basic income could be operable, should a consensus emerge. For one example, see Catriona McKinnon, "Basic Income, Self-Respect and Reciprocity", *Journal of Applied Philosophy*, 20 (2003): 143-58.

develops as a result of being able to see the entanglement of systems, including ourselves, arises as much out of an intuitive sense of appreciation of our capacity to perceive, and experience that perception, as it does in empathetic response. Appreciation, of course, is neither negative nor positive, neither joyful nor sad: it is simply the deep awareness of a set of conditions, but that ought not be underestimated as an experience.

The development in our cultural narrative of deliberate ignorance of our interdependence has meant we have voyaged blindly into the steepening gradients that now urgently demand our attention. If we can accept that there is no intentionality within the systems, then we can accept that none of us either mean, nor do we not mean, to create this emergence. Agency as realisation contains the prospects for an attitude of compassion to develop out of this understanding of our enmeshment. This indicates that we have a basis for extending this compassion so that we can meet any tendency to be overcome by the flood of eloquence from one quarter, or stymied into paralysis by another. The demands of this level of thinking are almost overwhelming and we must certainly realise that there is a tendency to withdraw from such a process simply because it threatens to absorb the entire capacity for thought and action.[68] T. S. Eliot's famous line, "humankind cannot bear very much reality" says much the same thing. Yet realisation as agency indicates that we have a basis for extending this compassion so that we can meet any tendency to be overcome by the flood of eloquence from one quarter, or stymied into paralysis by another.[69]

---

[68] H. P. Lovecraft in "The Call of Cthulhu", quoted in Ben Woodward, points this out: "The most merciful thing in the world, I think, is the inability of the human mind to correlate all its contents. We live on a placid island of ignorance in the midst of black seas of infinity, and it was not meant that we should voyage far." Ben Woodward, "Thinking Against Nature Nature, Ideation, and Realism: Between Lovecraft and Shelling", in Paul Ennis, (ed.), *Speculations I: A Journal of Speculative Realism*. Publisher Unknown. (2010).

[69] The argument that conditions are improving, or that a focus on human social development will mitigate further ecological degradation, ignores two important factors: the first is that improving social conditions for humans rarely ends there Consumerism as a system accompanying democratising or economic benefits has had a globally negative (even if sometimes locally positive) impact on biodiverse systems and, in the context of this discussion, therefore on "the good" of systematic flows. Even if there is less deforestation locally, for instance, the total amount of energy use increases, perhaps to oil energy for fuel and transport rather than local timber energy for fuel. There are exceptions but this, so far, has been the rule. When

Developing a narrative that acknowledges and appreciates the correlational impacts of our activities is vital, since we can ill afford to rest under the illusion that we will manage continuing anthropogenic impact using narratives of human superiority and independence, nor will the emergency spontaneously decrease or self-correct. Yet agency as realisation is a frail and fragile capacity, dependent on our ability to hold our attention steadily at points we have a tendency to avoid, and necessarily always in process, never complete or perfected. Therefore the focus must be on the practice itself, personally and publicly, as both a particular way of doing, and continuous effort at developing skill.

However, when we return to Dōgen and even to the Daoist texts, we can draw some comfort from their recognition that we are only ever in the process of realisation, never at a point of completion. Dōgen wrote most memorably about this when he wrote instructions for monks on the intimate activities of eating, cooking, brushing teeth or defecating.[70] None of these activities go away. The realities of living and dying are the focus of attention, not some escape to a utopia where we are spiritually and physically purified.

Our focus is on finding a place for each activity we are involved in and then settling it in its place so that it is neither dominant nor dormant, indulged, nor ignored. This measured approach to action is a good analogy for the process of solar energy dissipation, during which the solar gradient is reduced through complex systems that neither trap nor block informational exchanges, nor send them spiralling into chaos.

Many of the systems within which we are enmeshed are violent precisely because dominant narratives restrict what is included in compassionate consideration. Extending compassion towards those systems is a recognition of our appreciation not just of sentience, but of some degree

---

these human populations increase their spending power (usually at an increasingly uneven rate), there is increasing global pressure to exploit natural systems (like oil fields) on the justification that more energy is needed to support an increasingly complex infrastructure. Since this development of infrastructure (itself highly energetically expensive) can, and often does, lead to land conflicts, even the benefits of increased wealth are quickly swallowed up if populations are forced to migrate from their lands and swell the ranks of the disenfranchised.

[70] See, for instance, Dōgen, Chapter Seven "On Cleansing", *Senjō* and Chapter Eight "On Washing the Face" *Semmen* in *Shōbōgenzō: Treasury of the True Dharma Eye*, (op. cit.). This focus is also referred to in Graham Parkes, "Body-Mind and Buddha-nature: Dōgen's Deeper Ecology", (op. cit.).

of organisation.[71] Appreciation for the tendency of systems that graduate energetic dissipation most effectively (highly complex ecosystems, as well as well-ordered and well integrated human systems that "fit" into their contexts) is an extension of this intuitive sense. Since more highly organised systems rely more heavily on symbiotic relationships than on competitive ones (although both are present) there may be an argument for suggesting that we are inclined, as evolved organisms, to appreciate these kinds of systems more. This is one area where further empirical research would benefit our understanding.

One approach to anthropogenic impact from scientists and mathematicians interested in energy theory has been to consider how exergy, "the maximum amount of work that can be obtained from a stream of matter, heat or work as it comes to equilibrium with a reference environment", could be used as a measure of the efficiency of human systems.[72] This is a highly practical way of applying the idea of a systems-based approach, with realisation that attention can be paid to those aspects of the systems that are usually lost in consideration (exergy is more than efficiency). In the same paper, Rosen and Dincer raise the issue of what is effectively an intuitive response by humans to more organised versus less organised systems. They tentatively suggest that, "perhaps human values are related to exergy and order".[73] If they are correct, we have an intuitive sense of the graduated flow as more aesthetically satisfying than chaotic systems. This closely parallels the idea of the Dao, or flow, of energy, as something that resonates with what we are.

One other relevant passage from this paper refers to the idea that systems can "block" informational exchanges if the conditions are not right for such exchanges to take place. Some latent energy exchanges are almost always present in systems on Earth because the conditions are such that "many chemical reactions in the natural environment are blocked because the transport mechanisms necessary to reach equilibrium are too slow at ambient conditions".[74] However, the authors

---

[71] Marc A. Rosen and Ibrahim Dincer, "On Exergy and Environmental Impact", *International Journal of Energy Research*, 21 (1997), 643–54. This issue is also explored in Ibrahim Dincer, "Thermodynamics, Exergy and Environmental Impact", *Energy Sources*, 22 (2000): 723–32.

[72] Marc A. Rosen and Ibrahim Dincer, "On Exergy and Environmental Impact", (op. cit.): 647.

[73] (Ibid.): 648.

[74] (Ibid.): 647.

also point out that there is a difference between constrained and unconstrained exergy: exergy in the form of resources is "good for" systems, because it is constrained by not being able to dissipate energy through systems willy-nilly. Unconstrained exergy - for instance, sulphur pumped into the atmosphere from stack gases - has negative value because it does not allow other systems to participate in the graduated dissipation of energy. This parallels what Parkes and others have noted in relation to the dissipation of energy and the blockage of energy dissipation in systems that create synthesised artifices like radioactive isotopes (particularly when these are unconstrained emissions, as in the heating that took place and continues in the Fukushima Dai ichi plant in Japan) and plastics (from the unconstrained emissions involved in extracting the resources to the blocks in systems as a result of their creation).

The elicitation of compassion increases and deepens our understanding and appreciation of the systems that facilitate graduated energetic dissipation. Oceans, mountains, and even air can be seen as dynamic systems of interaction with the ecosystems that depend upon them, and that depend upon one another, including us. In practical terms, this means questioning any social programme that cuts off human contact from these systems. This includes the process of urbanisation (a global phenomenon) that requires humans to live in ways that can make it more difficult to access minimally "produced", clean water, minimally polluted clean air, and access to ecosystems whose evolutionary history has not been significantly impacted by deliberate anthropogenic lack of attention. It means, in practical terms, considering ways of creating more access to, and more awareness of, even more protection and restoration of, the ecosystems and species that evolved and are evolving in what have become urban surroundings.

Compassionate attunement elicits a practice that could include the restoration of biodiverse ecosystems more broadly.[75] The regeneration of these systems is giving space to the system, refraining from or minimising

---

[75] See, for instance, Robert Elliot, *Faking Nature: The Ethics of Environmental Restoration* (op. cit.). Elliot makes it clear that there is something deeply inauthentic about the process of attempting to emulate what was there before intervention since the evolutionary trajectory has been interrupted by anthropogenic impact both at the destructive, and at the restorative stages. Restoration of systems may imply that systems that emerge are very different from those that would have emerged without such an impact. This, of course, brings us back to the respect in which we can regard human interference as "natural" and, in the argument I am presenting, back to the idea of mindful versus mindless human impact.

pollution and exploitation, and not by proactive engineering, so that these systems are able to regenerate.[76]

Compassion, like love, is holding a person or a thing in attentive awareness of their fragility, their impermanence. Dōgen uses the stronger idea of love in his "Mountains and Waters as Sutra" fascicle. Awareness of the fragile impermanence of enmeshment evokes a sense of compassion. The perceiver identifies with what she is perceiving. Identification with what is being realised is essential to the idea of interdependence, and that is also at the heart of what Francis Cook describes in his essay on "The Jewel Net of Indra", a realisation that interconnectedness generates an attitude of attentive awareness:

> One of the most important implications of such a view [of interconnectedness] is that every single thing in the universe comes to have an important place in the scheme of things.[77]

Relationships are characterised by the manner of their interaction, so we can conclude that how we act, in every single instance of every single relationship, is important as a manifestation of realising our enmeshment. Compassion is called a virtue in much of the literature on Buddhism, but compassion is also simply the felt response to the realisation of being:

> In the home of all, including human civilization, as well as the many other forms congregating and being in packs that pulsate through life, one comes to see that even rocks are alive, that they too have their own songs, songs particular to their own living geology.[78]

The work of realisation is to appreciate, completely, the resonances of every relationship so that we hold them in attentive awareness, neither succumbing to, nor seeking to screen out, this reverberation. In terms of interactions within human cultural systems, the same approach holds: attentive awareness and the manner of engagement will create a context for a response that allows for the "good" of systems, in interchange of

---

[76] Dōgen Chapter Fifteen, "Mountains and Waters as Sutra", *Sansuikyō, Shōbōgenzō: Treasury of the True Dharma Eye*, (op. cit.): 156.

[77] Francis Cook, "The Jewel Net of Indra", in Nature in Asian Traditions of Thought: Essays in Environmental Philosophy , SUNY Press, (1989): 225.

[78] Jason M. Wirth.,"Dōgen and the Unknown Knowns", (op. cit.): 52.

information between the perceiver and the relationship, whatever the nature of the exchange.

Such a compassionate approach risks its own destruction. We are told that the manner of perpetuation of ideas is through the development and replication of "memes", ideas that breed, as it were.[79] This stance takes a different approach: there is nothing to imitate, no way of describing how to practice, other than by practicing. There can be no follower, no leader in an approach such as this. Realisation as agency and the compassionate attunement it elicits has no purpose, in the sense of no aim, or goal, since it is not focused on any end state. The focus is on the manner of our action at each moment, and it is through this focus that any mitigation takes place. Each time we perceive ourselves as systems in dynamic interaction, and other systems as interactive also, we can draw the focus back to the process of engagement. Again, Dōgen's insights into how easily we become entangled in trains of thought, replicating existing ideas or identifying ourselves with current trends, accurately portrays our tendencies:

> You ceaselessly chase things and make them into the self, and you chase the self and make it into things. When emotions arise, wisdom is pushed aside.[80]

The narrative that by acting with compassionate awareness as perceivers, we can shift the relationships with those with whom we come into contact, is much more useful than the myth that we can use force to impose our views on others. Such radical pacifism is unlikely to convince those who maintain that human violence is inevitable. Yet in the same way that recognition is a reflection, and so a disassociative process, so realisation is key to freeing ourselves from the inevitability of the reaction with violence to violence.

This practice is not a practice of altered awareness. It is a process of "sitting into" the realisation that encompasses, and also allows space for, the concerns, interests and issues of whatever we pay attention to. Like

---

[79] "Examples of memes are tunes, ideas, catch-phrases, clothes, fashions, ways of making pots or building arches. Just as genes propagate themselves in the gene pool by leaping from body to body via sperm or eggs, so memes propagate themselves in the meme pool by leaping from brain to brain via a process which, in the broad sense, can be called imitation". Richard Dawkins, *The Selfish Gene*, OUP, (1976): 192.

[80] Dōgen, Chapter Four, "One Bright Pearl", *Ikka Myōju, Shōbōgenzō: Treasury of the True Dharma Eye*, (op. cit.): 26.

watching a drop of water disappear into an ocean, we can see that the individual set of concerns is part of a much larger set.

Realising that we are involved in systems of violence, particularly when these systems threaten to annihilate us, is a good reason to pay attention to them, if paying attention allows us to mitigate the violence to any degree. This may mean, as part of the feedback process, that we develop strategies to respond by defending ourselves and the cultural and other systems we inhabit, and also that we use strategies for evasion so that any aggressor becomes exhausted, uses up energy excessively, and is reduced to having to return to discussion and negotiation for resolution. Meeting aggression with aggression implies the competition of two ideas on the same trajectory and realisation as agency being an "anti-meme", an idea that cannot be imposed, is not competitive in this way. In a sense, then, this approach cannot "solve" the ecological crisis, just as it cannot "win" in any battle of ideas. We will never "solve" the ecological emergency: all we can do is understand that it is a part of the way that we manifest our experience and that, individually and collectively, our attention shifts this.

This is a situation that must be acknowledged and appreciated in all its monstrous scale if we are to mitigate its effects even to the most meagre degree. The emergency is not happening independent of the perceiver. The practice of agency as realisation, very like the practice of zazen, is also a practice of preparation for, and an acknowledgement of, our non-being, or death. In accepting a situation that will, undoubtedly, kill us, we can move through the stages of grief that such a confrontation demands.

Coming to terms with chaos

No condition can be perfect in the physical, structurally relational, sense, because each state is dynamic, in flux, and as long as informational exchanges are taking place, there is rebalancing and only transitory harmony.[81] This implies that any effort is not aspirational, but pragmatic. All we can do is what we can do at each moment, regardless of any final outcome. This is deeply challenging to the mindset and narratives of the global North but it is vital to understand if we are to practice exercising what agency we have.

Inherent stability is not "good" for systems. The idea that natural systems have an inherent stability is as false as the idea that there is a goal

---

[81] Daniel Botkin, *Discordant Harmonies: A New Ecology for the Twenty-First Century* (op. cit.)

to this process. Biological, and indeed physical, systems are never in a steady state. The most common confusion is the belief that there are only two possibilities for a system: "complete stability and complete chaos in the Greek sense of without form or pattern. This is incorrect," as Botkin writes. "There are many kinds of non-steady-state systems" that, nevertheless, maintain and recreate patterns of interchanges that reduce the solar gradient.[82] It is these we need to realise.

Conclusion

Dōgen talks of the "fear that the days and nights are passing quickly" and it is precisely this fear that we must confront in the context of the ecological emergency. Doom-laden statements about our predicament are not conducive to better relationships. We should certainly practice paying attention with a sense of deep urgency, since this is the only capacity we have to influence the situation even if the process itself only involves minute shifts in perception.[83] Realising that what we are enmeshed in, we cannot escape, except through death, we can come back to a moment to moment awareness that is free and pure and fulfilled.[84] Instead of feeling overwhelmed, we can recall that each moment of realisation contains the capacity to open and release obstructions throughout the system, and so to shift our attitude in each act.[85]

Likewise, the realisation of our own death, and of the dynamism of systems, reveals that this death is taking place at every moment. The only element of agency we have in regard to it, as to the emergency that is its mirror, is to pay attention, to watch it, to watch our reaction to it, and to step back from each engagement that clings and blocks the graduation of its dissipation.[86]

In experiencing realisation as agency, we come to recognise that we are more profoundly, more intimately, more enormously interdependent than

---

[82] Daniel Botkin: personal communication (Feb 2014).

[83] Dōgen, "Points to Watch in Practicing the Way" *Gakudō-yojinshū*, in *Dōgen Zen*, trans. Shohaku Okumura (Kyoto: Kyoto Sōtō Zen Center, 1988):1; *Shōbōgenzō-zuimonki*, trans. Shohaku Okumura (Kyoto: Kyoto Sōtō Zen Center, 1987): 97.

[84] Hee-Jin Kim, *Eihei Dōgen: Mystical Realist* (op. cit.): 221.

[85] Hee-Jin Kim, (Ibid.): 219.

[86] The point about death arising in living at every moment is made by Parkes, with reference to Dōgen, in "Voices of Mountains, Trees, and Rivers: Kūkai, Dōgen, and a Deeper Ecology", (op. cit).

we could have realised at any other time in human history. One way we can make this less repugnant is to remind ourselves that the experience of living with attention brings its own rewards, and particularly through the elicitation of an attitude of compassion to the awareness.

Human realisation is the only intervention over which we can exercise any control. Systems transformed without awareness have devastated "the good" of wider and wider systems in a way that systems transformed with awareness have not. The humility with which we approach this task is based on the knowledge that there is very little we can do, now, given the kind of agency we have, and even this little may prove too much for us:

> The realness and resistance of the world, the difficulty of labor, call us towards a modesty with respect to our practices, deriving from a sober and even chastened recognition of the inevitable limits of planning and the essentially unpredictable consequences of our actions.[87]

We can also, through this realisation, generate responses to this enmeshment, through paying more attention to conditions that are "good for" systematic flow (in particular states) and through paying more attention to those aspects of our systematic enmeshment that human cultural systems have distracted us from, or ignored (the links between consumption and violence, for instance). Finally, we can see the importance of discernment in how we act, so that the way we act becomes the focus or our awareness of how we are graduating the dissipation of energy through our own actions.

---

[87] Steven Vogel, quoted in Robert Zimmerman, "What Can Continental Philosophy Contribute to Environmentalism?" (op. cit.): 217.

Chapter Five

Slaying the dragon and areas
for further research

Introduction

The work of philosophers has often been characterised as that of clearing away assumptions and faulty narratives or beliefs.[1] Such clearing sometimes reveals underlying structures that are fundamental to how we relate to the context. "Agency as realisation" is one such structure. Recognising (and responding, in a particular manner) to the "good" of systems is another. In seeing ourselves as somatic practitioners rather than as theorists, the full implications of our enmeshed identity come to light: it is only through this practice that we can realise our responsibility, and respond effectively, to the ecological emergency.

What this book has attempted to show is that it is possible to make a coherent case for revising what we understand as our agency from a rationalist perspective. That is, when we follow the theory of evolution to its logical conclusion, we find that our freedom to choose what to do, and our moral agency in the sense in which we are free to choose to do good, or evil (that is, to mitigate, or inflict, suffering, or deliberate harm or destruction), are illusory by traditional moral or ethical standards. Instead, it is through the process of realisation that we become reflective enough to create a space between the impact of our enmeshment, and our response.

---

[1] See, for instance, John Locke's "Epistle to the Reader", as the preface to *An Essay Concerning Human Understanding*. Oxford, Clarendon Press, (1979). Other definitions of the work of philosophy include, of course, Descartes' famous statement on the need to clear away all that can be doubted in order to reveal what remains.

This revision is comparable with the "practice realisation" that Zen masters have been pointing us to for many centuries. The act of realisation in this manner, and the options that a compassionate attitude elicits, are the only viable keys to how to respond to, and take responsibility for, the ecological emergency. All the tools for such a response lie within our grasp: we can make this shift in our awareness and "see ourselves in context" at any time, and the compassion this elicits opens us to options for action which otherwise remain latent.

Our context is both broader and more intimate than we have hitherto imagined. There are, objectively and without human valuing, conditions which are "good" for systems. How widely we can apply this is open to discussion, but certainly within the realm of our own planetary existence, from rainforests to rainbow trout, the graduated dissipation of energy allows complex relationships to emerge, and these mean that the patterns within which systems exist can be maintained.

The attitudes of humility, forgiveness and compassion arise out of a rational reflection on our systematic interdependence. Values like these are inherent in the universe, because they represent nothing less than a human interpretation of the graduated flow of energy that maintains and creates the patterns and vortexes of biodiverse life within which we evolved and exist. Complex systems operate within a complicated dynamic of cooperation which includes, but is not overwhelmed by, competition. If competition outstrips cooperation, the graduated dissipation of energy is either obstructed, or the gradient steepens towards collapse.

The practice of realisation is not complicated. The adjustments to how we respond in practice arise as we attune to compassion. The efficacy of this system is in its cumulative impact. In doing what we can, we already mitigate the obstructions and steepening gradients that are at the heart of suffering. Each act of realisation shifts the entire mesh, minisculely.

There is no "one size fits all". If someone meditates once a week and drives off in their SUV to work for a chemical explosives factory, they are not "off the hook". However, their degree of reflection can only deepen with practice, and judgement or blame cannot create more impetus to change. If this way of practicing is embraced, practitioners will become sensitive and self-responsible enough to assess and adjust their own activity. This process is really a process of exercising our full capacity for autonomy and responsibility as a result of the exercise of the agency we actually have: realisation of compassion.

There are still a few issues to clarify and criticisms that may remain problematic. I will attempt to address these in this chapter. I will also consider what areas could be explored further, and the fuller implications of the results of this research.

Explicit realisation of implicit context

On the one hand, we are entirely enmeshed and contextualised by the conditions and relationships that create and entwine us, and on the other, we have the capacity to somehow stand outside and observe the very processes that create and sustain us. In proposing that agency is exercised through realisation, I am defending the idea that the realisation that this generates is itself a system, arising out of, and yet interdependent with, existing systems. This claim looks paradoxical: if conscious awareness is no more than the result of physical, evolved processes, how can it bring into being another layer of interactions within the mesh? Additionally, how can we both be aware of, and be apart enough to realise we are a part of, the system?

In a sense, the first claim is no more extraordinary than the claim that complex systems have characteristics and aspects that are absent in simpler systems and for some critics, that sort of defence will suffice. However, some philosophers, following a biological lead, suggest there is no flexibility in our (physiological and therefore physical) Pleistocene inheritance. If we are physiological organisms, then we are also genetically driven to desire more goods, to push back limits, to maximise our capacity to exploit "resources", and so on, and no matter what degree of attention we pay to our activity, the rail tracks of our DNA will dictate our direction.[2] If these critics are right, then being able to recognise our enmeshment is no more than an accidental evolutionary hiccup, and a tragic one at that, since it allows us to watch the uncontrollable acceleration of our demise while strapped to the engine that is driving it.[3]

Yet recognition of our enmeshment is more than just waking up to the condition we are in. To be agents through our capacity for realisation is to exercise a capacity for self-awareness that, while being subject to natural laws and processes, nevertheless allows for the interactions to open to increasing possibilities in reaction and response. The act of awareness

---

[2] Holmes Rolston III, "The Future of Environmental Ethics", (op. cit.): 566.

[3] This point is also made by Callicott and Ames in the "Preface" to *Nature in Asian Traditions of Thought* (op. cit.).

alters how other interactions take place, and there is modest, but significant, evidence to support this.

While there is also plenty of scope for further investigation, there is considerable research into related fields. Neurophysiology, studies of the physiological impact of meditation techniques, and of the impact of acting with compassion, for instance, do indeed show a strong correlation between these states and better relaxation, more resilience in the face of traumatic impacts, better psychological and physiological health, and so on.[4] All of which implies that compassion is a beneficial attitudinal stance to adapt as one mitigating effect on the impact of the ecological emergency, where increasing stressors are inevitable for individuals and societies. Studies into the impact of these and related techniques on human to human relationships is fairly well established, with research into the impact on systems beyond the human less evident, although it is certainly becoming clearer that in the "other direction", the ecological context is vital to human health and well-being.[5]

---

[4] The focus of studies into the impact of mindfulness practice has generally been on those with cognitive disorders: see David A. Silbersweig David R. Vago, "Self-Awareness, Self-Regulation, and Self-Transcendence (S-ART): A Framework for Understanding the Neurobiological Mechanisms of Mindfulness", *Frontiers in Human Neuroscience*, 6, (2012). Among the more recent studies into the effects of different kinds of mindfulness training are the interesting divergences between mindfulness as heightened self awareness and mindfulness as a process within which the self becomes less and less significant: see Yair Dor-Ziderman and others, "Mindfulness-Induced Selflessness: A MEG Neurophenomenological Study", *Frontiers in Human Neuroscience*, 7, (2013).

[5] See, for instance, Richard J. Davidson and Antoine Lutz, "Buddha's Brain: Neuroplasticity and Meditation", (op. cit.); J. W. Carson and others, "Mindfulness-Based Relationship Enhancement", *Behavior Therapy*, 35 (2004), 471–94; S. Barnes and others, "The Role of Mindfulness in Romantic Relationship Satisfaction and Responses to Relationship Stress", *Journal of Marital and Family Therapy*, 33 (2007), 482–50; A. E. Beddoe and S. O. Murphy, "Does Mindfulness Decrease Stress and Foster Empathy among Nursing Students?", *Journal of Nursing Education*, 43 (2004), 305–12; Nirbhay Singh and others, "Mindful Parenting Decreases Aggression and Increases Social Behavior in Children with Developmental Disabiltiies.", *Behavior Modification*, 31, 749–71. In terms of research into nature as therapeutic practice, there have been a plethora of recent studies into the benefits of, for instance, shinrin yoku (forest bathing), ocean therapy (see, for instance, Easkey Britton et al., "Blue Care: A Systematic Review of Blue Space Interventions for Health and well-being," *Health Promotion International*, accessed January 23, 2019, (https://doi.org/10.1093/heapro/day103).

This research is, of course, beyond the realm of philosophy.[6] For the purposes of answering the criticism that an awareness of the conditions we are enmeshed in makes no difference, what empirical evidence we have suggests that it has no foundation. There is clear evidence that our state of awareness has an impact on our physical, physiological experience and relationships. This is most clear when the relationship is intimate (the physiological relationships in the brain and on biochemical reactions in the body are the clearest) but there is good reason to suppose that physiological changes within one organism will affect responses throughout the systems it is engaged in, including the kinds of responses that an organism makes when engaging with other organisms.

In other words, a much more global (although more difficult to measure) effect is likely to occur as a result of these local effects. It is possible to imagine studies that could demonstrate the impact of realising agency on the wider systems of our enmeshment, and in particular on those systems that are most affected by human activity (including ecosystems, species and habitats).[7] I will speculate on what this might mean for future research in the conclusion to this chapter.

The second claim – that there is a difficulty in both viewing oneself as within, but also as having a relatively objective, explicit perspective upon, the interactions of systems – is hard to reconcile without acknowledging some level of dualism. We may be able to forget the self, and we may even be able to shift our relationship with the systems we are enmeshed within, but this still implies that someone is doing the forgetting or the shifting. We cannot escape the fact that there is a distinct locus with particular conditions that must exist before "I" can forget itself.

I want to reiterate here that Warwick Fox's approach is a useful response to this criticism. Fox answers the criticism that we cannot be anything other than anthropocentric by pointing out that, while true, this is a "trivial" charge and there are enough parallels to merit transposing his response to this criticism. Fox's critics maintain that it is impossible to escape anthropocentrism since all our views are necessarily human

---

[6]Although there has been some work on linking Zen meditation, from a philosophical perspective, with physiological changes in the brain. See, particularly, James H. Austin, *Zen and the Brain: Toward an Understanding of Meditation and Consciousness.* 2nd edition., MIT, (1999).

[7] See, for instance, Rachel Lilley, Mark Whitehead et al., *Mindfulness, Behaviour Change and Engagement in Environmental Policy,* Aberystwyth University, (2016).

views.[8] Realisation as agency is the idea that we can, with effort, step back and take an "unconditioned" view, but this is still, necessarily, conditional on being human. Fox identifies the anthropocentrism charge as weakly, or trivially true: we cannot escape taking a human view, because that is necessarily where we are looking from. However, Fox argues that it is not this weak sense of anthropocentrism that matters and in the context of our being conditioned, it is only trivially true that we cannot escape being conditioned by our outlook and situation.

In the weak and tautological sense that we are human "I"s and can only necessarily see from the particular place we are in, it is true that "I" am inescapably an identifiable individual with a particular perspective. But it is palpably untrue that "I" cannot see beyond what is immediately relevant only to me. Fox points out that when we characterise a position as anthropocentric, we mean it in an "informative, substantive sense" and he gives the instance that, in this sense, anthropocentrists necessarily exhibit "unwarranted differential treatment of other beings on the basis of the fact that they are not human".[9] In the case of the charge that we cannot take an "unconditioned view", it is similarly true that we can never take a view that is "nowhere". But we undoubtedly have the capacity both to view our own experience objectively by becoming aware of it, and to imagine what is important from other perspectives. In fact, being human, and having the associated capacities for imagination, and for the conditional, the "what if?" cognitive experiment that took us from the African savannah to all other parts of the globe, we are primed to explore other perspectives in a way no other creature, as far as we know, is. Therefore, we may not be able to take a view from "nowhere" in the sense that we, as organisms, do not disappear during realisation, but we can take the view that is "now, here", that is empty of any specific reference to the ego except, perhaps, as just another context (like the weather).[10]

---

[8] Warwick Fox, *Toward a Transpersonal Ecology: Developing New Foundations for Environmentalism* (Albany, NY: State University of New York Press, 1995): 20.

[9] Fox, (Ibid.): 21.

[10] This play with words was first pointed out to me by Holmes Rolston III, who generously responded to a request for comments on my work. It is more than a play with words, however: realisation of being "now, here" is realisation both that no such time or place exists, since this is necessarily an inaccurate way to consider ourselves and the picture that contains us, but it is also the realisation that arises moment by moment, and therefore out of now, here, and if we are considering the ecological emergency without this awareness, we cannot hope to address it. Lawrence Buell points out that this problem arises in particular in the context of our

Relative awareness

One response to the criticism that we cannot have a sense of what to value without a valuer, referred to in King's paper, is given by Karen Warren: it is relevant and appropriate to consider not the atomistic positions of different viewpoints, but our awareness of the relationships between them. This systems-based approach recognises that certain kinds of relationships are "good for", while others are harmful to, the flow of information within systems. What is of value is not located in any entity within the system but systems, including those we are intimately enmeshed in (biologically, socially, and so on) have conditions that allow them to proceed with the graduated dissipation of energy (as "information"), or that obstruct this process.

By bringing our attention to this process, we are much more able to realise where these informational exchanges are being obstructed, and therefore keep our attention and focus on the possibilities (that self generate through the elicitation of compassion) for disengaging from such obstruction. The more aware we become of how we bring our attention, either during a reflective moment (in meditation) or more generally in how we practice during our days, to the social, biological, material relationships that enmesh us, the more we alter our sense of responsibility for these interactions. We can see that this is comparable with ideas in the Asian tradition, where these lay out practices to "see through" the "ego-generated anthropomorphic projections", to consider the relationships even with inanimate objects, like knives, or a rice bowl, to be as essential to the way of engagement as human to human relationships.[11] The way of realisation is in the manner of our actions.

---

contemplation of ecological systems, and our attempts to understand our relationships with them, particularly in literatures: "Here arises the paradox that nature writing–as well as nature poetry that pursues the same end of instilling awakened consciousness–is in principle both intractably I-centered and intractably dedicated to the overcoming of an I-centered mentality." Lawrence Buell, "Ecological Contemplation as Spiritual Practice: The Case of Henry David Thoreau", presented at the Buddhist Ecology and Environmental Studies, Cambridge, MA: Center for the Study of World Religions, Harvard Divinity School, (2005): 9.

[11] See Graham Parkes, "Human/Nature in Nietzsche and Taoism" in J. Baird Callicott and Roger T. Ames, *Nature in Asian Traditions of Thought: Essays in Environmental Philosophy* (SUNY Press, 1989); see also Dōgen, Chapter Eighty-Two, "Instructions on Kitchen Work", *Ji Kuin Mon*, Dōgen, *Shōbōgenzō: Treasury of the True Dharma Eye* (op. cit.).

Each time we bring to awareness the manner of our engagement, it alters. Each time we become aware of the relationships we are engaged in, whether socially, politically, materially or ecologically, we see how violent, aggressive or even neglected aspects of these relationships arise. By giving these relationships due observation and regard, we can disentangle, to whatever extent possible, from an unthinking acceptance of our Pleistocene inheritance. We can, indeed, rein in our impulse to consume unreflectively, not through the agency we have mistakenly attributed to ourselves, but through the capacity we have to see ourselves seeing. Alongside this, we can also rein in our impulse to blame or deride others who consume unreflectively. It requires effort (particularly at first) to maintain attention, and it requires practice, but this is the kind of shift that is required to reorientate our relationship with the systems we are enmeshed in.

Inimitable realisation as an anti-meme

The ecological emergency is a system of dissipation that is increasing in gradient and intensifying precisely because our traditional conception of agency allows a failure to pay attention, to realise. It could be said that the narrative that has encompassed our thinking is a meme. Meme theory suggests that ideas compete for survival, like genes. This idea of the kind of entities we are, and therefore of how agency operates (the Cartesian picture of the (mental) homunculus conducting physical action) has dominated our understanding of our interactions.

Agency as realisation is the antithesis of a meme. It is experiential, and inimitable. Each realisation is unique. Critics might say that such an approach is bound to fail since the very nature of evolution shows that only those elements survive that out-compete, dominate and reproduce themselves: that recreate an entity.

If agency as realisation is an anti-meme, but better describes our freedom to choose than the traditional view, then there are two responses to the criticism that a meme is the only means of transferring information. The first is to imagine human understanding developing not by replication of ideas (and the "chance mutations" that come about in the course of such replication, but better fit the facts), but through individual investigation of ideas that "point to" and demand, further questioning. The scientific method is actually the method of putting a theory to the falsification test. Ideas and narratives are more like migrating geese than competitive runners. The evolutionary push for survival acts like the polar orientation to a flock in flight. We have an inherent drive to align with what is good for us, which is to get a more accurate picture of where we are, so we can move away from what threatens to annihilate us. Realisation as agency moves us away from reactivity and this space points to, and opens the question to, others, which they then must answer for themselves.

The second response to the "meme" criticism is that the "language of nature" is, of course, the language of scientific neutrality, but this is also the language of systems, of the "long broad tongue" of rivers and mountains.[12] We can see what creates and maintains the graduated flow of energy through systems and we can see which human activities interact with and obstruct these flows. In this sense, we can maintain awareness not by receiving or replicating an idea from another source, but by becoming our own "buddha", by being awake to what is going on around us.

Therefore if we have a model of the transfer of information as memetic, the reproductive force of ideas predominating as our conceptual model, then we fail to take into account other means of informational transfer, means that leave no trace. For instance, in the transfer of information between "packets" of energy at subatomic level, the only trace of the exchange is in any release of energy as structural relationships alter. Biological systems are physical systems primarily, even if they are highly complex. Therefore the idea that we must work to regenerate or reproduce an idea only follows one conceptual model of evolutionary progress and does not take into account other explanations for how information is exchanged.[13]

"Speaking the language of nature" could mean reassessing the narrative or conceptual framework that we use to describe evolutionary "progress". Progress itself is not hierarchical, necessarily: to progress can mean merely to go onward, rather than to increase in complexity or sophistication. Realising that we are not, therefore, at the apex of some evolutionary journey, but entirely a party to the unfolding evolutionary project in all its manifestations and directions is an important shift in how we couch our understanding. Realisation as agency could generate sufficient potency to shift the human trajectory if we realise the potential for humans to listen

---

[12] "Did we have to wait for the ecological catastrophe to hear the long, broad tongue of the Buddha?" Jason M. Wirth, "Painting Mountains and Rivers: Gary Snyder, Dōgen, and the Elemental Sutra of the Wild", in *Wild Times with Gary Snyder* (op. cit.).

[13] Another analogy that might provide illumination on this approach is that of the difference between horizontal, and vertical, gene transfer: the former can sometimes "leave no trace", and yet be highly influential in any subsequent evolutionary trajectory, while the latter always leaves a clear lineage.

to the language and metaphors of their own systems, and to recognise how these echo other evolved conditions. This is the teaching that is available in natural systems, of which we are a part. This is not learning by transfer of ideas:

> When the finger points to the moon, will we quibble over it after we have hypostasized it yet another dogmatic doctrine vying for universal validity?[14]

Instead of considering ourselves from within the mechanistic model of replicator machines, and our ideas as having similar kinds of methodological structure, we can consider ourselves as relational systems, eluding atomistic categorisation, and likewise, we can understand the transfer of ideas as relational, dependent on context rather than on mechanistic reproduction. We can be open to signs within the context, realising that our agency lies in attentive relationship with the context, while at the same time becoming aware that this reflective capacity is context also. We take place in the world not just as organisms but as realisations that arise out of the context and then reflect back on it. This is very like the realisation that our agency is just the way of freeing up obstructions to the graduated flow, or dissipation of energy, or Dao:

> But what happens if we "turn it the other way"? What is the wild to the wild? Animals become "free agents, each with its own endowments, living within natural systems … the wild "comes very close to being how the Chinese define the term Dao, the way of Great Nature…"[15]

Realisation as agency is a non-replicable method of acquiring understanding, but this does not discount the validity of this system of acquiring understanding. Realisation is not emulation, or the reproduction of a thought. It is an increasing sensitivity to the conditions in which awareness develops. Eliciting compassion does not imply having to experience what another has experienced: it implies having had an experience that sensitises one to the process of interdependent relationship:

---

[14] Jason M. Wirth, "Dōgen and the Unknown Knowns", *Environmental Philosophy*, 10 (2013), 39–61: 44.

[15] Jason M. Wirth, "Painting Mountains and Rivers: Gary Snyder, Dōgen, and the Elemental Sutra of the Wild", (op. cit.): 12.

> Solidarity is not discovered by reflection, but created. It is
> created by increasing our sensitivity to the particular details of
> the pain and humiliation of other, unfamiliar sorts of people.[16]

It is not just people that we can become sensitive to in this way. Indeed, in drawing the circle of consideration in the past, we have had a historical tendency to close off what we include.[17] Ideas do not have to be replicated as the factory-like metaphorical narratives of neo-Darwinism might have us believe. They can arise and subside and leave no trace and yet the interchange of information, the way that they are realised, is just this graduated flow. We are in the difficult situation of bringing to awareness an understanding of our condition that can only be experienced, that cannot compete as an ideology or an alternative to existing commitments.

While I have attempted to address some of the criticisms that arise from a consideration of the inimitable experience of realisation, there is still a problem with how to elicit an incomparable experience without misrepresentation. Perhaps the best we can hope to do is to speak in fullest possible awareness that the inescapability of our human condition is only partly true. The very fact of being human contains the capacity to increase our sensitivity to our situation from any number of viewpoints, or even from an unconditioned view. Agency as realisation is not communicated through reasoning or even through language but through pointing towards an experience which must then itself be experienced. This is very like what Jason Wirth describes in his paper "Dōgen and the Unknown Knowns":

> One can only see what has been shown by the Buddha's eye
> with one's own Buddha eye ... One does not communicate from
> person to person but from enlightened mind to enlightened
> mind ... communication is the possibility of two or more people
> speaking the language of nature.[18]

The second thing we can do is clarify the difference between describing the idea of the experience and the experience itself. We quite often

---

[16] Thomas M. Alexander, "John Dewey and the Moral Imagination: Beyond Putnam and Rorty Toward a Postmodern Ethics", *Transactions of the Charles S. Peirce Society*, 29 (1993), 369–400: 379.

[17] A point made by Thomas M. Birch, "Moral Considerability and Universal Consideration", *Environmental Ethics*, 15 (1993), 313–32.

[18] Wirth, "Dōgen and the Unknown Knowns", (op. cit.): 47.

describe ideas and phenomena that, when experienced by others, remain necessarily obscure (colours, perhaps, or other sensory phenomena). Our understanding of, or describing, realisation is not itself realisation. To summarise, I suggest that even an idea that cannot be replicated, like the idea of realisation, because it arises out of a specific context each time, and because it operates as an antithesis to a meme, nevertheless can be pointed towards. It is more powerful as a result of this because it is not so vulnerable to mutation, unlike ideological memes (religions being the prime examples) that metamorphose, gathering errors even as they adapt to different circumstances.

The very fragility of the act of realisation is its strength. It is indefinable, yet even a child can have the experience. It does not matter that it is indescribable because it is possible for us to talk around it and indeed, since language is both a game and entirely metaphorically dependent, all we need to understand it are some basic guidelines for practices that lead us to the act of realisation.

Quietism, passivity, fatalism

The charges that Zen, and other Asian philosophies, are unable to offer a response to the ecological emergency that could in any way be meaningful stem from two roots.[19] The first arises from the argument that, regardless of the validity of Asian traditions of thought, the practical impact of these traditions has been just as devastating environmentally (and continues to be so) or at least has failed to mitigate the devastation to any significant degree, as any western practice.[20] The second is the idea that, as Lawrence Buell puts it, the "crude binary thinking" that persists in contrasting western and eastern cultures relies on a supposition that "westerners are active and aggressive whereas Asians are unassertive and contemplative".[21]

To begin dealing with these charges, it is worth noting, first, that Asian cultural traditions of thought, in the form, most notably, of Buddhism, Daoism and Confucianism, did indeed represent a relational understanding of context that could have led to the kind of reflective, reciprocal understanding of ecological systems and human systems I think we need, and realisation as agency gives us. The problem was that

[19] See Lawrence Buell (op. cit.): 3.

[20] See Lawrence Buell (op. cit.), though this point is made widely in relation, particularly, to the environmental impact on East Asian species and habitats, of philosophies that should have mitigated the impact.

the rulers were never Daoists or Buddhists, and they tended to enact legalism rather than Confucianism.[22]

Viewing the world as a pre-ordained set of structures that will remain the way they are or change, regardless of any human action, implies a willingness to keep quiet, to remain disengaged from every process. The practice of detachment implies a willingness to tolerate any process, no matter how destructive or harmful, that nothing can be altered, and therefore that everything must be endured.[23] These charges are levelled at non-dualist approaches, and could, by extension, be levelled at the idea of agency as realisation. Such an approach is bound, not only to be ineffectual, but actually to encourage exploitative and self-interested acts and attitudes among those who ridicule such an approach.

Hargrove goes further: non-dualistic philosophers are not only beguiling, but ineffectual: they are insidious insofar as they undermine the gains made by the technical advances underpinned by the analytic, scientific approach that has achieved so much for western civilisation and democracy. Yet, as Hargrove himself counters, we can learn, as we have already learnt, much from the aesthetic appreciation for "nature" that emerges from Asian traditions. He maintains that it was really only through the Asian tradition that Europeans learnt to see the beauty of naturally evolved landscapes.[24] I would temper this somewhat by suggesting that there were more immediate contextual reasons (the western agrarian and then industrial revolutions) that radically altered the relationship between Europeans and the world they inhabited.[25] Part of the quantitative success of the human evolutionary project has been its

---

[21] Lawrence Buell (op cit): 3.

[22] Personal communication, Graham Parkes, (June 2014).

[23] Eugene Hargrove, "Introduction", *Nature in Asian Traditions of Thought* (op. cit.): xvii.

[24] "At the very least, we can say that the simple fact that seventeenth and eighteenth-century Europeans knew that people in other parts of the world aesthetically enjoyed nature paved the way for similar values to emerge in Europe". Eugene Hargrove, Preface to ... (op. cit.): xviii-xix.

[25] This brings to mind a related criticism that I will tackle later on: that it requires a certain amount of material security, or what Jason Brennan calls "independence", to be able to appreciate the aestheticism that non-human ecosystems provide. Jason Brennan, "Dominating Nature" (op. cit.):523.

capacity for aggressive exploitation.[26] However, this material success has been at the price of an inherent cultural appreciation of the aesthetic, and empathy for those beyond a narrowly self-selected troupe.[27] These tendencies to narrow focus have been aggravated by cultural and belief systems that Asian traditions could do much to counter.

Cultural understanding of humans as entirely separable from nature estranged Europeans from their sense of connectedness to, and therefore, perhaps, from their sense of aesthetic appreciation of, nature, in a much more fundamental way than Asian traditions did. This resulted in the widespread use of mechanistic metaphors and narratives in describing natural processes. More recent research into ecosystems, evolutionary progression, ethology, and so on, have allowed us to appreciate as beautiful what we might once have rejected as unappealing and this is directly as a result of being able to conceive of organisms and ecosystems in non-mechanistic terms, as well as challenging the idea that in order to be beautiful, a situation must exhibit signs of human "cultivation". "Beauty" lies, not in the "eye of the beholder", but in the relationship between a trained observer and a system that is fully functioning in evolutionary integrity:

> One person's idea of a "beautiful" landscape can be an ecologist's idea of a "disaster area" ... similarly, one person's idea of an ugly or uninteresting landscape – like a "swamp" – can be an ecologist's idea of a precious "wetland."[28]

---

[26] A point dwelt on extensively in the context of evolution and gene transfer in Frank Ryan's *Virolution* (op. cit.). Ryan points out that other organism-systems, organelles, and microbial systems, have relied for species longevity on a process he calls "aggressive symbiosis", a conceptual model that could prove very useful in envisaging the kind of relationship that might allow our species to thrive more successfully, and for longer, than the current exploitative approach will allow.

[27] Robert Burns is one example among many pre-industrial poets of the global North whose work demonstrates that there was a deep sensitivity to the connectedness of natural systems and an accompanying realisation that their sensitivities were under threat and being eroded by projects of mass movements of peoples off the land for social "improvement", an exclusive and increasingly powerful elite of landowners, and the undermining and subjugation even of the vernacular language that allowed an expression of more nuanced understandings of earth and seasons.

[28] Warwick Fox, Toward a Transpersonal Ecology: Developing New Foundations for Environmentalism (op. cit.): 118.

The second charge, that the practices that arise from Asian traditions of thought are ineffective, is one we might frame in terms of passivity. Agency as realisation is not a passive process, however. There may not be clarity over the degree to which realisation can influence enmeshment. Certainly, some aspects are inescapable, and different individuals' circumstance will render them more or less entrapped by their enmeshment. Financial, social, geographical conditions can all contribute to how deeply one is bound by circumstances.

Yet the process of realisation as agency shifts the balance from attempting the impossible task of altering these larger conditions to seeing more clearly, and thereby shifting, some of the relationships within them. As a practice, realisation brings to light gaps that reveal themselves within, or obstructions to, the flow. If the context of one's enmeshment allows it, this can lead to engagement in the political process. For Dōgen, and for realising agents, it is imperative to raise questions, for instance, on factory farm practices, or on subsidies for oil and gas projects. This is the practice of directing the attention back to where it has been deflected from, through distractions that have sprung up to obscure are divert attention. In this, as in all areas where agency as realisation applies, the manner of engagement is critically important and as much attention to the manner as to the observation itself is a necessary part of the engagement.

Agency as realisation is not Zen

To some degree at least, realisation as agency will fail to capture the richness and depth of the Zen, cherrypicking only those elements that suit a secularist approach. Yet this is not a fundamental charge. To begin with, taking this pragmatic route in dealing with the ecological emergency may mean that any practitioner is naturally drawn deeper into exploring meditative traditions. Zen is often seen as the most "stripped back" of meditative traditions, so realisation as agency is simply extending the implications of this by reducing it to the essential practice of realisation.

Secondly, understanding philosophy as a practice, rather than as a theoretical field, means that every aspect of one's life is open to scrutiny, and this kind of personalised practice does not require a label to further complicate the experience. In reviewing how to live, each moment becomes an opportunity to see what allows itself to drop away, to begin to find voluntary simplicity a more peaceful way of interacting, to depend less on the opinions of others and more on the authentic sense of integrity that arises through the consistent reflection of activity.

The Buddha himself pointed out that "beliefs themselves are the origins of war". In positing the idea that agency is realisation, I have attempted to avoid aggravating the existing fray between ideologies. Instead, in delineating the linkages between these two very different ways of thinking about the human condition, I have worked to show how we can step back from ideological commitments and find a way of responding that is not conditioned by, because is open to and aware of, its conditioning.[29]

Many of the images and ideas of the *Shōbōgenzō* describe the relationship between practicing realisation and the impact of such a practice on the observer and on the relationships themselves. Yet Buddhism has shown itself, tragically, to be as vulnerable to interpretation for exploitation and self-interest as any dualist religion. Our relationship to what active participation we have becomes clearer through the teachings of Zen but it does not depend on them. Other traditions have recognised this connection too, and therefore there is no need to advocate for one tradition over another.

The idea of "buddha dharma", or interdependent arising through awareness, is prevalent within formal traditions of Dōgen Zen. Yet we can learn from, and experience, this sense of "buddha dharma" through the practice of realisation as agency, outside its formal transmission, What we now know of how energetic systems interrelate and proceed, combines with the Zen imagery of co-creation and somatic practice. This is an aspect of Zen practice that can usefully be experienced within the physicalist context.

Viewing this approach as ethically neutral liberates it: realisation is the practice of compassionate observation that arises out of understanding that we, like all else, are inseparable from context (and that elicits, therefore, a sense of empathy with other systems, particularly sentient systems). However, this practice does not require belief in any faith tradition. Such a belief could accompany realisation but it is not essential to it, since realisation is simply openness to and engagement in a state of consciousness and awareness of our condition.

One of the most cogent and instructive images that agency as realisation can elicit echoes a key insight, not of Zen, but of Daoism: that *wu-wei*, or the tendency to "just sit there" rather than "doing something", is the prime manner of engagement. Much of the activity of realising involves

---

[29] I think it is important to reiterate here that there is no inherent contradiction between holding an ideological commitment and taking this "step back" and

becoming increasingly aware of both conditions and conditioning, but this act of turning attention to interdependence is most effective when there are fewer distractions. This means that, while agency as realisation is not passive, or fatalist, or quietist, it is disinclined to engage in the narrative of a "top-down" response. We can respond more effectively if we are inclined to wait for what is elicited by the context, and this can come about through watching, for a moment.

Our agency is, in this sense, more like the process of *wu wei* than the confrontational forcefulness of *Earth First!*ers. The linguistic turn with which we focus matters too. In focusing on the narrative, we can become aware of the kind of language we and others use in engagement, making us more likely to take care in choosing how to express our response. This further supports the idea that the manner of engagement is key to our response.

Good in the universe

It is still highly contentious to suggest that any kind of "good", even in the ethically neutral sense of a directional flow in systems, exists for us to pay attention to, or ignore, beyond the human "good". Yet, there are precedents, even in traditions of thought of the global North. Lawrence Vogel, for example, argues that nature (that is, non-human organisms, communities and processes) have biological teleology, ends that they "pursue", regardless of the human project.[30] The revised idea that I have suggested of seeing these ends not as biological only, but also within the wider context, as physical processes, expands and extends the potential for what to include, but also overcomes the difficulty with partiality in deciding how to assess what is "good".

By coming at what is "good for" systems from a physicalist perspective, it is easier to see how common ground might be reached in understanding how to assess human impacts. No longer dependent on arguments for a "locus" of value, we can consider the relationships within systems, and how various human impacts affect these. It is the process, rather than the entities, that we need to pay attention to.

In seeking to show that the dissolution of the boundary between what is "good for" an individual and what is "good for" systems in general (or at

---

reflection upon, through realisation, on the conditions that create that commitment.

[30] Lawrence Vogel, "Does Environmental Ethics Need a Metaphysical Grounding?" (op. cit.).

least those systems that maintain us), there remain many circumstances where we see a potential conflict arising. As the ecological emergency evolves, these are likely to become more, not less, frequent. I will use just one example to illustrate this problem, and a potential solution.

If we take the largest possible view of mitigation of human impact, for instance, we may end up feeling as though we have to approve policies that most people would find at least repugnant, policies that demand restrictions or restraints, that seem, therefore, to close up the weave of our enmeshment and give us less opportunity to step back. If we are to mitigate the impact of humans on biodiverse systems, for example, then this might mean setting aside and therefore strongly restricting access to relatively unaffected ecosystems.

There may be those who are still allowed to visit these places, scientists, for instance, but that involves reducing the potential for the vast majority to experience the aesthetic joy of wild places and that is a huge imposition to make, and further disconnects people from any sense of responsibility towards the richest, most biodiverse systems. Again, general principles cannot arise from a "realisation as agency" approach, but one way of addressing this kind of issue might be to both ensure that biodiverse systems are supported in microcosms in communities, whether that means in spaces in cities, or in suburban enclaves, or even as designated areas in rural regions. It could also mean that there is proportionate access to wild places for all, and that access has to be equitable, particularly perhaps for indigenous groups and others who have a cultural connection with the place, but also for those whose access to wild places is generally restricted by poverty or disadvantage.

Being able to get access to wild places in ways that are least damaging is essential to maintaining a realisation of interconnectedness and therefore this has to be a focus in considering how the good of systems is to be realised. Tigers and lions are cited in cases in India and Africa in competition with humans for food and resources but this too can be addressed by deepening the understanding of systems and maintaining or allowing natural prey to regenerate so that large predators are not looking for food in villages. This, too, demands that villagers have enough access to fuel and food so that they are not foraging in areas where they are likely to be preyed upon. These are simplistic responses, but they indicate that there are broader solutions to the issues of conflict than might first appear, that tackling ecological issues cannot be separated from tackling social issues and that both occur within the context of belief systems that must be explicitly realised in order to be appreciated and, perhaps, disengaged from.

Establishing that there can be a common sense of the "good" that is somehow objectively discoverable is a further criticism of this approach. It could be argued that we cannot know that our understanding of what is "good for" systems is objective, that we could easily be advocating what is "good for" systems by focussing on conditions that are proximal and ignoring others' perspectives, and then this is a kind of obstruction of their "good".

This criticism is really only an echo of current bias, however. So-called peripheral interests like ecological systems or species that are not seen as central to the survival of the human species (wetlands, waders, deep oceans, invertebrates, and so on) or the integrity of evolved systems that can be impacted with no obvious or immediate effects on human life, are largely discounted as having any weight in discussions. It does not matter what is "good for" those systems, in the dominant narrative. Yet realising that these systems – microbial and soil systems, watercourses and their ecosystems, and so on – are fundamental to the circulation and dissipation of energy through all peripheral systems (including our own) is a strong argument for paying much more attention to how these systems work, and how human systems can better accord with them.

Even if humans have already done too much to impair systems so that the graduation of flows is critically affected, it is still important that we respond by recognising that "the good" of systems will go on, regardless of whether or not we survive. And therefore it is still important to realise the "good" of systems, can be discovered impartially, through scientific and rational methodologies, whether or not we benefit as a species. Realisation as agency shifts the narrative.

A further criticism, from this perspective, is that the effectiveness of realisation of the importance of systems lends no weight to any call for altering human interaction. It is a recognition that may have implications for individuals but is impotent in the face of calls for human expansion. The response to this kind of criticism follows the same line as the response that many philosophers give to the criticism that anything we do, individually, has so little impact on global circumstances that there is no onus on any individual to do what he or she can. That response, translated into this context, is that every individual action matters precisely because small acts are cumulative. In the terms of agency as realisation, this is even more robust as a response, since we are not just affecting a single relationship, but shifting our attitude to, and therefore our interactions within, all our relationships.

Realising what we are and how we relate is our only agency, and therefore forms the basis of whatever response we make, and whatever responsibility we are able to take, for the impact we have had on systems. However minimal the effect of this response, if it mitigates our impact at all (and it does), then that is what we must do (as a reasonable response). Even if the human project fails or at least falters, realising our enmeshment is a recognition that the entire complex of systems we are enmeshed within dissipate energy, whether we, humans, are within the mesh or not. What is significant about what we do now is what mitigates suffering (seen as a process of attachment, or obstruction of the "flow" in the dissipation of energy), in whatever way possible, however minimally. When we understand this, we see that exercising any ability we have to respond to this understanding is a mitigation of some potentially obstructive impact.

Of course, we cannot know that what we do now will actually mitigate obstructions in the future, and therefore the attitude with which we come to this realisation is very much one of humility.[31] For the same reason, the focus is very much on the action now, and not some future consequence. When it is too late for mitigation, systems will adapt or collapse. The scale of human impact makes collapse more likely than adaptation, but this means that we must take every opportunity we can to bring our attention back to our interactions now, here, since the manner of our engagement is amplified by time.

Agency as realisation is paying attention to the manner of our engagement now. The act of realising how dependent we are on other systems is also, ultimately, a self-protective strategy, but this is not why it is important to exercise this function. The importance of realisation as agency is that it is the exercise of a capacity that exists for humans, but is often latent. Allowing it to remain latent has caused problems. Using our capacity to realise means we pay attention to issues we have ignored, and that have created the ecological emergency.

By realising our agency, we avoid creating the (often hypocritical) gaps that open up between principle and practice among those whose actions stem from ethical commitments. Yet this elicits the criticism than an ethical response has been barely adequate so far, so one that claims to be ethically

---

[31] This point is made in Lawrence Vogel's paper: "And given scientists' uncertain ability to predict the long-term effects of our technological incursions into nature, Jonas"s ethical axiom yields a "pragmatic rule": that we be cautious and only pursue modest goals, paying heed to prophets of doom before being seduced by prophets of bliss." "Does Environmental Ethics Need a Metaphysical Grounding?" (op. cit.): 35.

neutral can only lead us deeper into a moral vacuum.[32] In responding to this criticism, I must point again, to the biophysical nature of systems that make up our being and that are incremental, constantly in flux. If we are going towards anything, it is the deep chaos of entropy, where information is too distal to be interchanged. The systems that maintain us are in the process of levelling off, even if on the way, the gradient is becoming steeper. What we exist within, what biophysical systems in general exist within, is the persistence of this gradient at a level that is not too steep to sustain it, the "golden mean", the Goldilocks syndrome. This is what we have to respond to, regardless of any ethical call of duty.

This is not to say there are not "bumps in the ride"; it is the unpredictability of the systems that make it easy for sceptics and deniers to undermine any attempt to characterise what we are involved in as a condition requiring our attention. Energy interchanges are not mechanisms, and the organic nature of the process means that it waxes and wanes. But within the parameters of this dissipation of energy lies our survival range. It is these parameters that exploitation and self-interest undermine.

Paying attention to this process is not passive inaction. It requires absolute attention, and activism, in the sense of seeing what is required by relationships for energy to be conducted through us as systems and processes in the least disruptive way. It can be very unsettling to keep before ourselves an understanding that there is no ultimate meaning, nothing that this can end with but annihilation:

> If nature presents us with no ethical norms, then no effort to change our own nature in the name of perfection, convenience or experimentation could count as a transgression of essential limits or a violation of a natural standard of goodness. "[33]

This is the crisis, the challenge of our capacity to create chains of reactivity that extort nature's energy. Why care about the future when it does not directly affect us? Yet it is, eventually, no more paralysing to realise that one is within a system that has no inherent meaning than it is to realise that one is mortal. The process of acceptance is extremely challenging. However, the most appropriate response is an intense awareness of current existence, and a sense of compassion for the condition of oneself and one's relationships.

---

[32] (Ibid.): 30.

[33] (Ibid.): 30.

The limits of convergence

Drawing attention back to the areas we have distracted ourselves from could include pointing out when beliefs are expressed based on an unreflective acceptance of questionable facts. However, the manner of approach is central: the way we point out any obstruction to interaction (like an unreflectively adhered to the belief that is then used to defend a position that creates further polarisation) will directly affect the chances of engaging and opening up for discussion the unreflective view. If I exercise my awareness during interactions that are potentially polarising, this has a potential effect, small but significant, on others reacting with less polarity, and more moderation, in response. The individual effect may be tiny but the cumulative potential is great.

It might be argued that exploring possibilities for continuing engagement is feeding into the existing exploitative tendencies since unless these tendencies are resisted, they will simply quash any alternative view. Yet the success of polarising campaigns is highly contentious. Rather than focussing on the very thing that is arousing opposition, like "No Fracking Gas!" it requires more effort, but is far more likely to result in discussion and a shift in attitude, if we develop a relationship based on common interests, and come with clear idea of a positive strategy that is less obstructive, or damaging, to systems. This might imply negotiation. It might well imply that much more effort is put into a clear discussion of different positive alternatives than on emotionally fraught protest, and that as wide an array of scenarios as possible is considered for each area under consideration, including recognising that we come with different intuitive commitments which we do well to uncover before evaluating "the other's wrongs".

Acting to de-escalate conflict through shared recognition of our humanity, along with paying attention to any tendency for fragmentation to increase, or entrenchment in attitudes to deepen, bridges the deepening divides that threaten to open up. The more people become entrenched in divergent positions, the more unstable and potentially violent situations become and conversely, the more we are able to step back from our particular commitments, the more chance we have of creating conditions for changes in behaviour among others to arise.

The final defence for exercising agency as realisation in a situation where attitudes are becoming increasingly divergent is that we personally suffer less as a result of careful attention to engagement. In coming to appreciate the nature of the divergence, we begin to recognise our own role, and our own desire to disengage from or disown the conflict. When, instead, we see the external tension interpreted through our own fears and aversions, we can simply accept it as an inevitable feature of the interchanges between systems, and this defuses much of the tension. It also gives us an opportunity to "sit with" the tensions that arise. Doing this with an attitude of compassion at the realisation that all biophysical systems, like ours, are attempts to graduate the interchange of energy, but that we have the capacity to recognise this, creates less tension in our observation. Humility comes from the knowledge that this capacity is all there is to our agency. A less obstructed, less violent, graduated interchange of energy is just as beneficial for the realising agency as it is for every other system. The boundary, in this sense, between what is "good for" the situation, and what is "good for" the realising agency, dissolves.

However, Johnathan Glover raises another important issue in the context of action or inaction, and we can apply it here. It is the idea that when one acts with realisation, one might nevertheless have to admit that others, in their enmeshment, are not going to make that kind of effort. This argument is widespread: being unable to control others' exercise of realisation means that they can continue to obstruct systematic flows. It is much easier to continue not paying attention, and the chances are that this is what most people will do, and would do, even if they were told the benefits of realisation. One individual's mindfulness is, therefore, not going to change the trajectory of human progress and yet it requires an extra effort of attention to live mindfully.

This argument is particularly pertinent when it comes to employment, for instance, or to our level of material security. Glover uses the example of research into chemical warfare.[34] One could equally well point to the tar-sands industry, the fracking industry, the oil industry or even the agricultural, industrial or construction industries. In fact, with realisation comes the increasing awareness of how difficult it is to find work that does not contribute to the ongoing violence of the systems we are enmeshed in. The effort of realisation and the attempts to live with less dependence on the violent impacts of human activity can become overwhelming, particularly since no agency is independent and our networks are also affected by our actions.

As Jason Brennan, among others, observes, the kind of ecological awareness that realisation entails depends, at least to some extent, on having a certain level of material and physical security. It is certainly true that it is more difficult to realise one's condition in a broader sense when one is in pain, or financial difficulties, or experiencing addiction, or under threat of violence. Yet mindful awareness is possible under these

---

[34] Jonathan Glover and M. J. Scott-Taggart, (op. cit.).

circumstances and indeed this is an area where further research could be very fruitful. In prisons, hospitals and refugee camps, the impact of programmes to develop a meditative or realising state of awareness have had considerable success, even among those whose experiences have been of the most traumatic kind.

In spite of these admissible privations, and the challenges created by choosing to make the effort to realise one's agency, there is still considerable inherent reward in developing independence and resilience. Taking steps towards a less unsustainable, less violent way of being enmeshed are deeply enriching, not only for oneself but for the development of the resilience of others in one's network. Not being able to consume at the rate of those around one can be experienced as poverty but it can also be experienced as a test of one's creativity and resourcefulness. We are deeply enmeshed in networks that we can learn to educate ourselves from, resent or ignore. When we begin to see how widely the practices of resilient living are being exercised, ideas begin to be exchanged and to develop and the path becomes less isolating. Further research into how voluntary networks come into being as a result of a conscious effort to create relationships based on mutual support and local resilience would be useful to investigate this claim.

Even those who feel they have no choice may engage in discussion and this can lead, in some instances, to their beginning to view their own enmeshment in a different light. This is realisation as agency not as a meme, but as an elicitation of an experience. Taking the unconditioned view is, paradoxically, becoming completely aware of all the conditions of one's enmeshment. It is only through the context that one can see how realisation disengages, and then interacts with, the context.

A pragmatist's approach

In considering the effectiveness of the realisation as agency response, we can also find ourselves troubled by the question of the level of mitigation involved. There are clear parallels here with Peter Singer's work on alleviating poverty from a utilitarian perspective. Initially, Singer, it was suggested, asked people to go "too far" – to reduce themselves to a position barely less impoverished than those who have less than they have themselves.[35] Karann Durland criticised Taylor's approach using a similar argument: reducing ourselves to barely more than subsistence level on the

---

[35] Peter Singer, *Practical Ethics,* New York: Cambridge University Press, (2011).

basis that we can – just – survive – but maximally mitigate our impact is impractical and repugnant.[36]

However, reducing, for instance, our use of technological and chemical tools to kill other living organisms to a level far below the present level, to a level more proportionate to the requirements for survival, and less in line with whether or not we need bleached white towels to clean ourselves with, seems eminently sensible and accords with agency as realisation. If we assess each practical situation on a case by case basis, that will include measuring, all things considered, what it would mean to implement a particular strategy. Obviously, this is never going to be an exact science, but humanities research can complement and support scientific research in this area.[37] Science is a social process, in many senses, and influenced by the general understanding of which conceptual models to found interpretations on. This means that sometimes we go on interpreting events according to models that have lost their explanatory power, when new evidence actually demands that we alter how we conceive of relationships. We can correct this lag by returning to our conceptual models frequently and this practice is inherent in realisation as agency where we are on a constant lookout for a deeper understanding of the conditions we are enmeshed in, including the conceptual conditions.

The human systems we are enmeshed in allow vast quantities of energy to dissipate needlessly, as food wasted, and treated water leaked, as plastics or clothes are discarded, unused, or destroyed unnecessarily while still serviceable, animals bred for domestic consumption slaughtered in order to artificially inflate prices, pets bred and killed because they are unwanted. The vast wastage in the energy industry, too, where sites are constructed and then left to decompose, where regeneration of natural systems is thereby blocked, or where basic housekeeping, cleaning out tailings ponds to allow regrowth of marshlands, is not undertaken even though it would add a small fraction to the total operational cost of the project.

Naturally evolved systems can appear to be equally wanton in their dissipation of vast amounts of energy. Yet the processes and interactions within naturally evolved systems ensure that matter continues to cycle and energy to flow in graduated dissipation where ecosystems are

---

[36] Karann Durland, "The Prospects of a Viable Biocentric Egalitarianism", (op. cit.).

[37] See, for instance, John Baez and The Azimuth Forum (www.johncarlosbaez.com)for a detailed critique of the Climate Change Catastrophe.

concerned. Apart from interventions from far beyond the system (the suspected asteroid that wiped out the dinosaurs, for instance), the collapse of systems and the extinction rates we now experience are unprecedented. By drawing our attention to our involvement in the current collapse, we can see where we might stitch systems back, so the flow is graduated again, or a further entropic drive by restraining our consumption.

Integrating realisation

Human rights, too, are integral to agency as realisation. Ensuring water courses are clean involves ensuring that naturally evolved filtering systems, from reed beds to forests, are allowed to regenerate, rather than segregating water, or envisaging it as a "product". Adding sterilisation tablets may be a vital solution to an acute emergency, but it is not one that resolves a chronic pollution problem. Exploitation, immigration issues, labour and excessive consumption are all impacts that involve us in chains of enmeshment from which we can disentangle ourselves if we keep our attention on them. It would be pathologically odd if we did not treat our immediate networks, and perhaps, humans in general, preferentially in considering the impact of the emergency. But it is essential to see any preferential treatment within the broader context of our interdependence and to keep returning our attention to that level of engagement as often as possible.

The criticism that we cannot be completely detached and therefore completely objective in our response to the ecological emergency is valid but I do not think it undermines the overall argument for this approach. After all, realisation moves us towards compassion, not just towards the human species but towards an awareness that the species, just as much as we, as individuals, is enmeshed. Taking an unconditioned view does not require that we leave, or are indifferent towards, our own perspective and conditions. It requires only that we recognise that we can see these in context. The rest is entirely up to us. What we do, how much we realise, depends on how unconditioned our view is but even a moment of realisation shifts our interactions significantly and this benefits all the systems we are enmeshed in, near and far.

Conclusion: faring forward

Is it possible to teach agency as realisation? This is a little like asking if it is possible to teach "wisdom" and a considerable number of the same objections apply.[38] As I have outlined it, I think the techniques for understanding agency as realisation, and for practicing, exist and can be shared. However, the only test for whether or not the techniques have been mastered and the practice incorporated is by seeing the results through any mitigation on the ecological emergency, and because we cannot have a "control" situation to compare this with, such a test is not possible. Nevertheless, we can consider ways of measuring the impact on individual lives, on situations where views conflict on how to respond to ecologically critical situations, and on the impact of this practice on communities. This is an area where more research could be fruitful. This idea of agency as realisation may be ethically neutral, but it is still a "practical necessity" in the sense that Bernard Williams uses the phrase.

A reconstructed practice of consideration requires, and is required by, a staying in the place of the origination of practical necessities. I state this point this way, in terms of practical necessities, in order to accommodate Bernard Williams' illuminating proposition that what lies at the bottom of morality and ethics (which he distinguishes as the broader notion) is "practical necessity":

> the conclusion not merely that one should do a certain thing, but that one must, and that one cannot do anything else. We may call this the conclusion of practical necessity... This is a "must" that is unconditional and goes all the way down.[39]

A major area where further research is necessary is in interdisciplinary, cross-cultural work. This includes quantitative and qualitative research collaborations between the humanities and other disciplines. An example of a quantitative approach might involve conducting brain scans on volunteers who had undertaken extensive zazen training, for instance, over a specific period, and to compare groups in retreat with those practitioners who also engaged actively with questioning how current systems operate, particularly where these engender violence.

It is more difficult to imagine quantitative research techniques that could capture a broader connection between realisation as agency, realising the "good" of systems, and responding to the ecological emergency. Elinor Ostrom's work provides some precedent, in the sense

---

[38] Nicholas Maxwell, "Can the World Learn Wisdom?", *Solidarity, Sustainability, and Non-Violence*, 3 (2007).

[39] Thomas H. Birch, "Moral Considerability and Universal Consideration", *Environmental Ethics*, 15 (op. cit.): 23.

that she collected data on the use of resources after discussions about "the commons", and her findings showed that participants responded to the insight this gave them by negotiating the use of common resources much more equitably. We might imagine some similar parameters on participants' habits when it came to energy use, activism (particularly the kind of activism engaged in, and the nature of their participation), recycling habits, and other measurable parameters.

However, external indicators are sometimes misleading and do not always give insight into attitudes, or other, more subtle, difficult to capture indicators of change. A qualitative approach involving, for example, questionnaires and the collection of oral testimonies might be more interesting. In conducting this kind of research, one would find that, as a researcher, one was both participant and observer in the process. It would be particularly interesting to do this kind of research in countries that have experienced war and other difficulties with establishing autonomy. While it is more obvious to conduct this kind of research in universities in the global North, the effects, both for the researcher, and for the participants, would potentially be more cumulative in a conflict zone. This might be particularly interesting research to conduct in a refugee camp, for instance, where people might have the opportunity to consider an outcome to their situation that involved developing and exercising autonomy and responsibility not just towards other groups of people who had been their "enemies", but to the species and ecosystems that had been affected by the conflict. This could provide a useful means of practicing reconciliation, and deepen awareness of what supports and systems are needed to bring autonomous systems back into place.

Ethical diversity

Paul Taylor wrote that, in an ideal world:

> ...the cultures' ways of regarding nonhuman living things and their views concerning the proper place of human life in the natural world ... again have great variation in what constitutes human civilisation in the ethical ideal. But this variation must always be consistent with an attitude of respect for nature.[40]

Taylor went on to say that there are a number of different positions (including various monotheistic or polytheistic stewardship approaches,

---

[40] Paul Taylor, *Respect for Nature* (op. cit.): 308.

and a Gaia-like religion that sees the Earth as sacred) that are consistent with respect for nature, as well as the "national and scientifically enlightened" approach he has taken to respect for nature. In a sense, all I am doing is taking one step further back, and agreeing with Hans-Georg Moeller that we do not need the extra paraphernalia of an ethic to agree on a set of rules on how to approach the ecological emergency.

I agree with Taylor that it is perfectly consistent with recognising the "good" of systems to take a stewardship or a Gaia-like Earth-worship approach, and many other positions are also consistent with what I would argue is the "rational and scientifically enlightened" approach of recognising the "good" of systems, and creating rules and policies that take this into account. I think we can excise the idea that we are aiming for an ideal relationship. Recognising our agency lies in our capacity to reflect on, rather than to take independent decisions separate from, context. Whatever we need to respond to sits alongside ethical approaches. Certainly, there will be those who resent this kind of approach and argue that it undermines any sense of volition. In a sense, they are right: agency as realisation is the idea of a biophysical feedback process that emerges, either by chance, or through the use of techniques like meditative or mindfulness practices, but it is not "free will". However, there is nothing inherently contradictory about taking an agency as realisation approach, and believing that the capacity to realise is god-given. It seems to me that this adds more than we can know, but at least it offers the possibility of consistency for those who want to argue for it.

Undoubtedly, there are religious and other ethical positions that are inconsistent with realisation as agency. Those whose ethical code justifies wholesale destruction of ecosystems or species on the basis that the world is a temporary resource to be disposed of by humanity do not have a position consistent with a rational and scientifically enlightened approach. Just as we have rules that override and constrain personal preferences that violate human integrity (female genital mutilation, slavery, and so on), so we can have rules of engagement that override and constrain preferences that violate systems integrity. These will not be "aspirational" towards an "ideal" or "harmonious" relationship, but a pragmatically worked out system of rules that accepts the possibilities that these rules may be violated, and considers the Daoist manner of defence (evasion, self-defence, techniques to ensure the "enemy overpowers himself" and the like) to be the most appropriate strategies (rather than attempts to overpower, attach, and confront).

This set of rules could be worked out at a global level, and at a regional level. Their effectiveness (a little like the effectiveness of human rights) would lie in the degree to which people were educated to understand and appreciate them, although, of course, like rules for a new game, there would be room for negotiation and debate in how they should be implemented, and there could well be regional variation.

At present, the general consensus is that some sort of global system is needed to police these rules, because people do not always act responsibly. Yet agency as realisation is ultimately the condition of complete self-responsibility. Therefore, rather than concerning myself with how this might roll out in political terms, I will limit myself to imagining that the act of exercising agency in this way has potentially cumulative effects. Individuals practicing agency as realisation can exercise this perspective to discover a method of realising the potential alternatives that arise from a consideration of the matter in its current, rather than in an ideal, context. They can practice identifying and questioning when arguments are made to persuade them on moral or ethical grounds (and these are often couched in emotional terms, so this would be an education in the language of propaganda). In terms of negotiations between groups with divergent positions, agency as realisation offers a way of engagement that has a potential for reducing conflict through bringing to light the context of beliefs, and through a focus on the manner of engagement.

Dancing with awareness

The main implications of what I have discovered through this research are that we can, and we must, change how we view our agency. This has, potentially, enormous and cumulative effects. Let us just indulge in idealism for a moment (in a purely hypothetical experiment). If people took full responsibility as a result of realising their agency, in the way that I have described, we would have no need for government, nor any need for a monetary system.

We would not see one another as separate individuals, and therefore, we would not focus on defending ourselves (physically, psychologically) against one another. We would not concern ourselves with being unable to understand others' views, or other ideologies, since we would realise that these emerge from context, and we could easily imagine that we, in a different set of conditions, might have arrived at these values. Nevertheless, given that we would be in the habit of discerning between narratives inherited as a result of a particular context, and the "good" of systems as seen from a rationally and scientifically enlightened approach, we would come to an overarching consensus on what kinds of activity to support and facilitate.

We would spend more of our time exploring freedom, ideas, and creativity, given the time and resources freed up from defence. We would concern ourselves with facilitating the lives of others and exploring how to develop deeper and more significant relationships, and less time contemplating how to pre-empt an attach from another. We would delve deeper into health indices (since the energy we would have available would allow us to spend more time on this kind of activity) and explore communication in far more creative ways.

Dealing with our impermanence would become a key feature of our world, and perhaps we could come to understand, and to live more fully, as we set out to embrace, the different stages of grief that a full realisation of death entails. We could come to relate to possessions and belongings in a completely different way, creating and sharing for the sake of well-being and self-expression, rather than for trade. We could, in summary, release ourselves from the repetitive cycles of suffering that characterise societies in so many ways. Being deeply aware and present to our own existence and its intimately relational nature would naturally lead to the end of wars, and of famines. It would end research for profitability, and create opportunities for research purely for the benefits of systems. Manipulation by advertising or propaganda would end: people would be far too secure in their own sense of themselves to feel the anxiety that advertising relies upon. A deep understanding that there is no "I" in "this body" separate from "you" in "that body" would change how we thought and experienced emotion. All talents would be expressed as gifts and available to benefit all. This would not imply that people could not, or would not want to, be alone: it would be perfectly normal and safe for individuals to spend as much time alone as with others. The pressure to conform to norms would be utterly eradicated. The full capacity of realisation would awaken everyone to the deeply enriching experience of being aware at each moment.

I am not an idealist, however, as I hope I have made clear during this book. Indulging in fantasies of a perfectly harmonious future is fun, but only in the way that fairy-tales are fun, and it reminds us of the conceptual frameworks that shape our experience. I offer the above as a poignant reminder that any idealisation creates a gap between the situation we are in, and an unknowable future. We do far better to focus our attention on what is going on at present than in dreaming of illusions, however pleasant that can be.

We are in a profoundly dangerous situation, yet we have the capacity, individually and collectively, to make the kind of adjustment to perspective, and therefore the responsibility that agency as realisation implies. It remains to be seen how many people, particularly among those who are in positions of power, and therefore social responsibility, at the moment, would be prepared to make this kind of adjustment in perspective. Thinking of our agency as something independent of us as biophysical systems, and as a capacity superior to the capacities of other organisms, is hugely insidious. The revision of agency that I have suggested is a subtle shift from the traditional view of agency, and it may be hard to communicate the subtlety more generally without risking misunderstanding, but it is worth the attempt.

After all, while environmental ethics has contributed hugely to our capacity for understanding the ecological emergency, in practical terms, the gap between what we need to do and what we are actually doing continues to widen. Any serious attempt to address this problem can only help to crystallise our thinking on this issue, and therefore, even if the approach I suggest is rejected outright, it may allow people to become clearer about their own approaches, which means it will not have been a wasted effort. I hope, however, that the idea of moral agency, and the idea of the "good" of systems, can be revised with useful effect.

Acting without a focus on reward may appear counter-intuitive, but the clear indications of those who have engaged in this practice are that it is deeply, viscerally, rewarding. Acting without hope of resolving or changing anything substantially may challenge our ideas of what it is possible to endure, given the current emphasis on positive thinking, and the bright optimism that assures us that humans will find a solution to the problem of the ecological emergency as soon as it becomes critical to do so. Embracing an acceptance of the enormity of our plight allows us to come to better terms with the inevitability of our demise, personally and collectively. We can focus, instead, on the manner with which we engage at every moment, using restraint not because it is personally of benefit (although, incidentally, it is), but because it is part of the process of graduating the flow of energy through systems, which is their "good".

In this understanding of our capacity for realisation, responsibility not just for our own enmeshment, but for the denial and violence inherent in the enmeshment, comes to light. Drawing our attention to the manner of our engagement with this awareness involves recognising our own responsibility for the condition we find ourselves in. We have to find ways to "sit with", in the sense of accept, and exercise compassion and forgiveness towards, these most challenging conditions, where the urge to consider ourselves as actors in the traditional sense is almost overwhelming. The important question, then, in mitigating the deeply divisive effects of the ecological emergency, is, what can we understand in common? Roger King asks:

> What should our shared conventions and background beliefs be? How should be write the rules for the language games governing our discourses about nature and our relationships to it?[41]

We can write the rules in the language of what we pay attention to, when we realise our enmeshment. If beliefs cause wars, and the risks of conflict are rising with this emergency and its accompanying character of divergent entrenchment, then we should, perhaps, learn to look at our beliefs as a part of the problem. If there is a way of stepping back and keeping our engagement in focus, even as we practice realising this engagement, then it is incumbent on us to take this backward step. The unconditioned view that this gives us, a view where we are both intensely and increasingly aware of our context, but also able to see ourselves within the experience of our context, from without, as it were, is the place of our agency. As the great poet, T.S. Eliot, might have said of this, too, "here, the dance is".

---

[41] Roger J. H. King, "Critical Reflections on Biocentric Environmental Ethics: Is It an Alternative to Anthropocentrism?" (op. cit.): 209.

Bibliography

Aitkenhead, Decca. '"Enjoy Life While You Can"' Interview with James Lovelock. *Guardian.* Section: Environment. 1 March 2008. http://www.theguardian.com/theguardian/2008/mar/01/scienceofclimatechange.climatechange.

———. '"Before the end of this century, robots will have taken over"'. Interview with James Lovelock. *Guardian* Section: Environment. 30 Sept 2016. https://www.theguardian.com/environment/2016/sep/30/james-lovelock-interview-by-end-of-century-robots-will-have-taken-over

Alexander, Thomas M. "John Dewey and the Moral Imagination: Beyond Putnam and Rorty Toward a Postmodern Ethics". *Transactions of the Charles S. Peirce Society* 29. 3. 1993: 369–400.

Anderson, James C. "Species Equality and the Foundations of Moral Theory". *Environmental Values.* 2. 4. 1 November 1993: 347–65. https://doi.org/10.3197/096327193776679837.

Attfield, Robin. "Biocentric Consequentialism and Value-Pluralism: A Response to Alan Carter". *Utilitas.* 17. 1. 2005: 85–92.

———. "Biocentric Consequentialism: Pluralism and the 'Minimax Implication': A Reply to Alan Carter". *Utilitas* .15. 1. 2003: 76–91.

———. "Biocentrism, Moral Standing, and Moral Significance". *Philosophica.* 39. 1. 1987: 47–58.

———. *Environmental Ethics: An Overview for the Twenty-First Century.* Cambridge, UK; Malden, MA: Polity Press. 2003.

———. 'Reconciling Individualist and Deeper Environmentalist Theories? An Exploration'. In *The Structural Links between Ecology, Evolution and Ethics,* edited by Donato Bergandi: 127–39. Boston Studies in the Philosophy and History of Science 296. Springer Netherlands. 2013. http://link.springer.com/chapter/10.1007/978-94-007-5067-8_9.

Austin, James H. *Zen and the Brain:Toward an Understanding of Meditation and Consciousness.* MIT Press. 1999.

Baez, John. 'Entropy and Information in Biological Systems'. In The Azimuth Forum (blog) . http://johncarlosbaez.wordpress.com/2013/11/02/entropy-and-information-in-biological-systems/.

———. *Creativity in the Face of Climate Change.* 2009. <http://www.youtube.com/watch?v=in5F3OfbtUA&feature=youtube_gdata_player>

———.The Azimuth Forum. www.johncarlosbaez.wordpress.com.

Barnes, S., K. W. Brown, E. Krusemark, W. K. Campbell, and R. D. Rogge. 'The Role of Mindfulness in Romantic Relationship Satisfaction and Responses to Relationship Stress". *Journal of Marital and Family Therapy*. 33. 2007: 482–500.

Bennett, Jane. 'Systems and Things: A Response to Graham Harman and Timothy Morton'. *New Literary History*. 43. 2. 2012: 225–33. https://doi.org/10.1353/nlh.2012.0020.

Berry, Wendell. *The Landscape of Harmony*. Hereford: Five Seasons. 1987.

———. *Home Economics*. San Fransisco: Northpoint. 1987.

Birch, Thomas M. "Moral Considerability and Universal Consideration". *Environmental Ethics*. 15 1993: 313–32.

Bolinsky, David. "Visualizing the Wonder of a Living Cell". TED Talk. March 2007. <http://www.ted.com/talks/david_bolinsky_animates_a_cell.html>.

Botkin, Daniel B. *Discordant Harmonies: A New Ecology for the Twenty-First Century*. New York, NY: Oxford University Press. 1990.

Braungart, Michael, and William McDonough. *Cradle to Cradle*. London: Vintage. 2009.

Brennan, Andrew. *Thinking about Nature*. University of Georgia Press, 1988.

Brennan, Jason. "Dominating Nature". *Environmental Values*. 16. 4.1 November 2007: 513–28.

Britton, Easkey, Gesche Kindermann, Christine Domegan, and Caitriona Carlin. "Blue Care: A Systematic Review of Blue Space Interventions for Health and well-being". *Health Promotion International*. https://doi.org/10.1093/heapro/day103.

Brockman, John (ed.). *What Is Your Dangerous Idea?: Today's Leading Thinkers on the Unthinkable*. New York: Harper Perennial. 2007.

Brown, Lester R., Christopher Flavin, and Sandra Postel. "Vision of a Sustainable World". In *The World Watch Reader on Global Environmental Issues*. New York: Norton. 1998: 299–315.

Buell, Lawrence. "Ecological Contemplation as Spiritual Practice: The Case of Henry David Thoreau". Cambridge, MA: Center for the Study of World Religions, Harvard Divinity School. 2005. http://www.hds.harvard.edu/cswr/resources/print/dongguk/buell.pdf.

Burns, Robert. *The Collected Poems of Robert Burns*. New edition. Ware: Wordsworth Editions Ltd. 1994.

Cahen, Harley. "Against the Moral Considerability of Ecosystems". *Environmental Ethics*. 10, 3. 1988: 195–216.

Callicott, J. Baird. *In Defense of the Land Ethic: Essays in Environmental Philosophy*. New York: SUNY Press, 1989.

———. 'Introductory Palinode'. J. Baird Callicott. http://jbcallicott.weebly.com/introductory-palinode.html.

———, and Roger T. Ames. *Nature in Asian Traditions of Thought: Essays in Environmental Philosophy*. New York: SUNY Press. 1989.

Case, Amber, "We Are All Cyborgs Now" TED Talk http://www.ted.com/talks/amber_case_we_are_all_cyborgs_now.html

Carson, J. W., K. M. Carson, K. M. Gil, and D. H. Baucom. 'Mindfulness-Based Relationship Enhancement'. *Behavior Therapy*. 35. 2004: 471–94.

Carson, Rachel. *Silent Spring*. London: Penguin, 1965.

Carter, Alan. "Inegalitarian Biocentric Consequentialism, the Minimax Implication and Multidimensional Value Theory: A Brief Proposal for a New Direction in Environmental Ethics". *Utilitas*. 17. 1. 2005: 62–84.

Carter, Neil H., Bhim Gurung, Andrés Viña, Henry Campa III, Jhamak B. Karki, and Jianguo Liu. "Assessing Spatiotemporal Changes in Tiger Habitat across Different Land Management Regimes". *Ecosphere*. 4. 10. 1 October 2013: art124. https://doi.org/10.1890/ES13-00191.1.

Chakravarty, Shoibal, Ananth Chikkatur, Heleen de Coninck, Stephen Pacala, Robert Socolow, and Massimo Tavoni. "Sharing Global CO2 Emission Reductions among One Billion High Emitters". *Proceedings of the National Academy of Sciences*, 6 July 2009. https://doi.org/10.1073/pnas.0905232106.

Chang, Raymond. *Chemistry*. 9th edition. Boston: McGraw-Hill. 2006.

Chitty, Andrew. "Ideology and Climate Change Convictions". Sussex University, 2013. http://www.associationforpoliticalthought.ac.uk/sussex-university-workshop-on-climate-change-and-the-humanities/.

Cockell, Charles S. "The Value of Microorganisms". *Environmental Ethics*. 27. 4. 2005: 375–390.

Cohen, Leonard. "Leonard Cohen on Depression and Relationships". YouTube Video. 13 Aug 2009. https://www.youtube.com/watch?v=FAoHYBpj8vY

Commoner, Barry. "How Poverty Breeds Overpopulation". In David Keller (ed). *Environmental Ethics: The Big Questions*. Chichester: Wiley-Blackwell. 2010: 443-446.

Cook, Francis. "The Jewel Net of Indra". In *Nature in Asian Traditions of Thought: Essays in Environmental Philosophy*. New York: SUNY Press. 1989: 213–29.

Cooper, GM. *The Cell: A Molecular Approach*. 2nd edition. Sinauer Associates; 2000. https://www.ncbi.nlm.nih.gov/books/NBK9841/.

Curry, Oliver. 'Who's Afraid of the Naturalistic Fallacy?' Evolutionary Psychology, no. 4 (2006): 234–47.

Davies, Chris, MEP, Personal Communication while at a meeting in the EU Commission (Fact Finding Mission with the Irish Environmental Network). Oct 2013.

Davidson, Richard J. and Antoine Lutz."'Buddha's Brain: Neuroplasticity and Meditation". *IEEE Signal Processing Magazine*, 1 January 2008: 176-174.

Dawkins, Richard. *The Selfish Gene*. Oxford: Oxford University Press, 1976.

DeGrazia, David. "On the Questions of Personhood Beyond Homo Sapiens", in Peter Singer (ed.) *In Defense of Animals*, Blackwell. 2004).

De Groot, Mirjam, Martin Drenthen, and Wouter T. de Groot, "Public Visions of the Human/Nature Relationship and Their Implications for Environmental Ethics". *Environmental Ethics*. 33. 2011: 25–44.

Diamond, Jared. *Collapse: How Societies Choose to Fail or Succeed.* New York: Viking, 2005.

Dincer, Ibrahim. "Energy and Environmental Impacts: Present and Future Perspectives". *Energy Sources.* 20. 4–5. May 1998: 427–53. https://doi.org/10.1080/00908319808970070.

———. "Thermodynamics, Exergy and Environmental Impact". *Energy Sources.* 22. 8. 1 September 2000: 723–32. https://doi.org/10.1080/00908310050120272.

Dōgen. *Shōbōgenzō: Treasury of the True Dharma Eye.* Edited by Kazuaki Tanahashi. Boston: Shambhala, 2010.

———. "Points to Watch in Practicing the Way" *Gakudō-yojinshū,* in *Dōgen Zen,* trans. Shohaku Okumura. Kyoto: Kyoto Sōtō Zen Center. 1988.

Dor-Ziderman Yair and others, "Mindfulness-Induced Selflessness: A MEG Neurophenomenological Study". *Frontiers in Human Neuroscience.* 7. 2013.

Duddy, Thomas. "Walking Respectfully Upon the Earth". In The '*From Ego to Eco' Conference.* NUIG. Galway. 2011. http://www.wix.com/nuigalway/from-ego-to-eco-conference.

Durland, Karann, "The Prospects of a Viable Biocentric Egalitarianism". *Environmental Ethics.* 30. 2008: 401–16.

Dworkin, Ronald. "What Is a Good Life?" *The New York Review of Books.* 10 February 2011. http://www.nybooks.com/articles/archives/2011/feb/10/what-good-life/.

Eliot, T. S. *Four Quartets.* England: Gramophone Co. 1950.

Elliot, Robert. *Faking Nature: The Ethics of Environmental Restoration.* Routledge. 1997.

——— and Center for Environmental Philosophy, The University of North Texas. "Instrumental Value in Nature as a Basis for the Intrinsic Value of Nature as a Whole". *Environmental Ethics.* 27. 1. 2005: 43–56. https://doi.org/10.5840/enviroethics200527140.

Emerson, Ralph Waldo. *Nature.* Boston : James Munroe and Company. 1836. http://archive.org/details/naturemunroe00emerrich.

Evans, Claude J. *With Respect for Nature: Living as Part of the Natural World,* New York: SUNY Press. 2005.

Feinberg, Joel. *Rights, Justice, and the Bounds of Liberty: Essays in Social Philosophy.* Princeton, N.J.: Princeton University Press. 1980.

———. "The Rights of Animals and Unborn Generations". In *Rights, Justice, and the Bounds of Liberty: Essays in Social Philosophy,* Chapter 8. Princeton University Press, 1980.

Ferry, Luc. *The New Ecological Order.* 2nd edition. Chicago: University of Chicago Press, 1995.

Filice, Carlo. 'Rawls and Non-Rational Beneficiaries'. *Between the Species* 13, no. 6. 2006.

Fodor, Jerry A, and Massimo Piattelli-Palmarini. *What Darwin Got Wrong.* New York: Picador/Farrar, Straus and Giroux. 2011.

Foreman, Dave ."Earth First!" In David Keller (ed.). *Environmental Ethics: The Big Questions*. Chichester: Wiley-Blackwell. 2010: 327-332.

Foster, John. "After Illusion: Realism, Philosophy and Hope in a Seriously Warming World". *Climate Change and Philosophy at the Tipping Point*. Conference.Lancaster University. March 2011.

———. Personal Communication via email, March 2014.

Fouke, Daniel C. "Humans and the Soil". *Environmental Ethics*. 2. 2011: 147–61. https://doi.org/10.5840/enviroethics201133218.

Fountain, Henry. "A Respite from Record Losses But Tropical Forests Are Still In Trouble". *New York Times*. 25 April 2019. https://www.nytimes.com/2019/04/25/climate/tropical-forest-deforestation.html.

Fox, Warwick. "Forms of Harm and Our Obligations to Humans and Other Animals". In Evangelos D Protopapadakis (ed.) *Animal Ethics: Past and Present Perspectives*. Berlin: Logos Verlag. 2012: 197–221.

———. "Problem 14 in Human Relationships, Nature, and the Built Environment: Problems That Any General Ethics Must Be Able to Address". In *Sage Handbook of Environment and Society*. London: Sage, 2007: 107–23.

———. *Toward a Transpersonal Ecology: Developing New Foundations for Environmentalism*. Albany, New York: SUNY Press. 1995.

———. "Responsive Cohesion: Thinking in Context," *Resurgence*. 241. March/April 2007: 22-25.

———. "Ethics, Architecture, Responsive Cohesion and the Transition to a More Habitable Future". Paper presented to the *Ethics and the Built Environment* conference. Nottingham University. 9-11 Sept 2009.

Glover, Jonathan, and M. J. Scott-Taggart. "It Makes No Difference Whether or Not I Do It". *Aristotelian Society Supplementary*. 49. 1975: 171–209.

Godfrey-Smith, Peter. *Other Minds : The Octopus, the Sea, and the Deep Origins of Consciousness*. Farrar, Straus and Giroux. 2016.

Gorman, James. "Aliens Inside Us: A (Mostly Friendly) Bacterial Nation". *The New York Times*. 1 April 2003. https://www.nytimes.com/2003/04/01/science/aliens-inside-us-a-mostly-friendly-bacterial-nation.html.

Goudie, Andrew S. *The Human Impact on the Natural Environment: Past, Present, and Future*. Chichester: Wiley-Blackwell. 2009.

Gruen, Lori, Dale Jamieson, and Christopher Schlottmann. *Reflecting on Nature: Readings in Environmental Ethics and Philosophy*. 2nd ed. New York: Oxford University Press. 2012.

Haidt, Jonathan. *The Righteous Mind: Why Good People Are Divided By Politics and Religion*. New York: Pantheon Books. 2012.

Hall, Matthew."Plant Autonomy and Human-Plant Ethics". *Environmental Ethics*. 31. 2. 2009: 169–181.

Hansen, James. *Storms of My Grandchildren*. London: Bloomsbury, 2011.

Hardin, Garrett. "Lifeboat Ethics: The Case Against Helping the Poor". *Psychology Today*. 1974: 800–812.

———. "The Tragedy of the Commons". *Science*. 162. 13 December 1968: 1243-1248.

———. 'Who Cares for Posterity?'. In Louis P Pojman and Paul Pojman (eds). *Environmental Ethics: Readings in Theory and Application*. Wiley-Blackwell. 2008: 350–57.

Hargrove, Eugene. "Editor's Response to The Monkeywrench Gang". In David Keller, (ed.) *Environmental Ethics: The Big Questions*. Chichester: Wiley-Blackwell. 2010: 336.

Harrell-Bond, Barbara E. *Imposing Aid: Emergency Assistance to Refugees*. Oxford University Press, Incorporated, 1986.

Harris, Samuel. *Free Will*. Free Press. 2012.

———. *The Moral Landscape: How Science Can Determine Human Values*. New York: Free Press, 2010.

———. Transcript of "Science Can Answer Moral Questions". Accessed 17 January 2019. https://www.ted.com/talks/sam_harris_science_can_show_what_s_right/transcript.

Hart, H. L. A. "Are There Any Natural Rights?" *Philosophical Review*. 64. 195: 175–91.

Hawkins, Ronnie. "Extending Plumwood's Critique of Rationalism Through Imagery and Metaphor". *Ethics and the Environment* 14, no. 2 (2009): 99–113.

———. "Introduction: Beyond Nature/Culture Dualism: Let's Try Co-Evolution Instead of 'Control'". *Ethics and the Environment*. 11. 2. 2006: 1–11.

Hickman, Leo. "James Lovelock: Humans Are Too Stupid to Prevent Climate Change". *The Guardian*, 29 March 2010, sec. Environment. http://www.theguardian.com/science/2010/mar/29/james-lovelock-climate-change.

Holden, N.J., F. Wright, K. MacKenzie, J. Marshall, S. Mitchell, A. Mahajan, R. Wheatley, and T.j. Daniell. "Prevalence and Diversity of Escherichia Coli Isolated from a Barley Trial Supplemented with Bulky Organic Soil Amendments: Green Compost and Bovine Slurry". *Letters in Applied Microbiology*. 58. 3. 1 March 2014: 205–12. https://doi.org/10.1111/lam.12180.

Hume, David. *A Treatise of Human Nature*. L.A. Selby-Bigge (ed.). Oxford: Clarendon Press. (1793). 1896. Available at Online Library of Liberty, http://oll.libertyfund.org/?option=com_staticxt&staticfile=show.php%3Ftitle=342.

James, Simon P. "Against Holism: Rethinking Buddhist Environmental Ethics". *Environmental Values*. 16. 4. 2007: 447–461.

———. "Buddhism and the Ethics of Species Conservation". *Environmental Values*. 15. 1. 2006: 85–97.

———. "Finding - and Failing to Find - Meaning in Nature". *Environmental Values*. 22. 5. 2013: 609–625.

———. "Human Virtues and Natural Values". *Environmental Ethics*. 28. 4. 2006: 339–353.

Jamieson, Dale. "Climate Change, Consequentialism, and the Road Ahead". *Chicago Journal of International Law*. 13. 2. Winter 2015: 440–68.

———. "Global Warming and the Ethics of Climate Change", http://www.youtube.com/watch?v=_pPnc-ocQOA

Kao, Ernest. "Air Pollution Is Killing 1 Million People and Costing Chinese Economy 267 Billion Yuan a Year, Research from CUHK Shows". *South China Morning Post*. 2 Oct 2018. https://www.scmp.com/news/china/science/article/2166542/air-pollution-killing-1-million-people-and-costing-chinese.

Kauffman, Stuart. *At Home in the Universe*. Oxford University Press. 1995.

Kalmanson, Leah. 'The Messiah and the Bodhisattva: Anti-Utopianism Re-Revisited". *Shofar: An Interdisciplinary Journal of Jewish Studies*. 30. 4. 2012: 113–25. https://doi.org/10.1353/sho.2012.0077.

Kawall, Jason. "On Behalf of Biocentric Individualism". *Environmental Ethics*. 30. Spring 2008: 69-88.

Keller, David. (ed.).*Environmental Ethics: The Big Questions*. Chichester: Wiley-Blackwell, 2010.

Kim, Hee-Jin. *Eihei Dōgen: Mystical Realist*. Boston: Wisdom Publications. 2004.

King, Roger J. H. "Critical Reflections on Biocentric Environmental Ethics: Is It an Alternative to Anthropocentrism?" In Andrew Light and Jonathan M. Smith (eds). *Space, Place and Environmental Ethics*. Rowman and Littlefield. 1996: 209–28.

———. "Playing with Boundaries: Critical Reflections on Strategies for an Environmental Culture and the Promise of Civic Environmentalism". *Ethics, Place and Environment*. 9. 2. 2006: 173–186.

Klarr, Lisa, Ryan Vu, and Gerry Canavan. *Ecology and Ideology*. Durham, N.C.: Duke University, 2010.

Korb, Judith. "Termite Mound Architecture, from Function to Construction". In David Edward Bignell and Yves Roisin (eds). *Biology of Termites: A Modern Synthesis*. 2nd Edition. Dordrecht, New York: Springer. 2010:349–73.

Kuiken, Todd. "A Prosthetic Arm That Feels?" TED Talk: https://www.ted.com/talks/todd_kuiken_a_prosthetic_arm_that_feels?language=en.

Knights, Paul. "Native Species, Human Communities and Cultural Relationships". *Environmental Values*. 17. 3. 2008: 353-373.

Ladyman, James. "What Is Structural Realism?" *Studies in History and Philosophy of Science Part A*. 29. 3. 1998: 409–424.

———, James Lambert, and Karoline Wiesner. "What Is a Complex System?" *European Journal for Philosophy of Science* 3. 1. 1 January 2013: 33–67. https://doi.org/10.1007/s13194-012-0056-8.

Lai, Karyn L. "Conceptual Foundations for Environmental Ethics: A Daoist Perspective". *Environmental Ethics* 25. 2003: 247–266.

Latour, Bruno. "'It's Development, Stupid !" or How to Modernize Modernization?' In *Postenvironmentalism,* edited by Jim Proctor. New York: Houghton Mifflin Company, 2007.

Leferna, Alexandre Georges, "Betting on Climate Failure: The Ethics & Economics of Fossil Fuel Divestment". Unpublished Paper. Uploaded on www.academia.edu. 2014.

Leiserowitz, A., Maibach, E., Roser-Renouf, C., Feinberg, G., & Rosenthal, S. "Climate change in the American mind: October, 2015". *Yale Program on Climate Change Communication.* Yale University and George Mason University. New Haven, CT: 2015.

Leonard, Liam. *The Environmental Movement in Ireland.* Springer, 2007.

Leopold, Aldo. *A Sand County Almanac: With Essays on Conservation from Round River.* New York: Ballantine Books. 1970.

Lilley, Rachel, Mark Whitehead, Rachel Howell, Rhys Jones, and Jessica Pykett. *Mindfulness, Behaviour Change and Engagement in Environmental Policy. Report of the MBCEEP Programme.* Unpublished. 2016. Available at https://changingbehaviours.files.wordpress.com/2016/01/mindfulnessr eportgapfinal.pdf.

Locke, John, and P. H. Nidditch. *An Essay Concerning Human Understanding.* Oxford: Clarendon Press. 1979.

Lomborg, Bjørn. *Cool It: The Skeptical Environmentalist's Guide to Global Warming.* New York: Alfred A. Knopf, 2007.

Lomborg's debate with Eamon Ryan on http://www.rte.ie/radio1/today-with-sean-o-rourke/programmes/2013/1202/490406-today-with-sean-o-rourke-monday-2-december-2013

Long, Todd R. "Moderate Reasons-Responsiveness, Moral Responsibility, and Manipulation". In Joseph Campbell, Michael O'Rourke, and David Shier (eds) *Freedom and Determinism.* MIT. 2004.

Lotto, Beau. "Optical Illusions Show How We See" YouTube. 2009. http://www.youtube.com/watch?v=mf5otGNbkuc&feature=youtube_gd ata_player.

Lovelock, James. *The Revenge of Gaia: Earth's Climate in Crisis and the Fate of Humanity.* New York: Basic Books. 2006.

Lucas, Caroline, and James Delinpole Debate. "Corby Wind Farm Ex-Candidate: 'I Won'". *BBC.* 1 November 2012. Section: UK Politics. http://www.bbc.co.uk/news/uk-politics-20168738.

Mackenzie, Fiona. "A common claim: Community land ownership in the Outer Hebrides, Scotland," *The Commons Journal.*1. 2010. Retrieved from http://www.thecommonsjournal.org/index.php/ijc/article/view/151/120.

Malthus, Thomas Robert *An Essay on the Principle of Population.* 1789. http://www.gutenberg.org/ebooks/4239

Margulis, Lynn. Endosymbiotic Theory described: https://lecerveau.mcgill.ca/flash/capsules/articles_pdf/endosymbiotic_ theory.pdf

Martin, Mike W. *Albert Schweitzer's Reverence for Life: Ethical Idealism and Self-Realization.* Aldershot, England: Ashgate, 2007.

Maxwell, Nicholas. "Can the World Learn Wisdom?" *Solidarity, Sustainability, and Non-Violence* 3. 4. 2007.

Mckinnon, Catriona. "Basic Income, Self-Respect and Reciprocity". *Journal of Applied Philosophy*. 20. 2. 2003: 143–158.

Moeller, Hans-Georg. *The Moral Fool: A Comparative Case for Amorality*. New York: Columbia University Press. 2009.

Moore, G. E. *Principia Ethica*. Cambridge University Press. 1993.

Moore, Patrick. "Dr. Patrick Moore". Accessed 26 January 2019. http://ecosense.me/.

Moore, Thomas Gale. 'Global Warming: A Boon to Humans and Other Animals'. *Hoover Institution Working Paper, Stanford*, 1995.

Morton, Timothy. "Don't Just Do Something, Sit There! Global Warming and Ideology". In Anne Sophie Witzke (ed.). Rethink: Contemporary Art and Climate Change. Copenhagen: Alexandra Institute. 2009: 49–52.

———. *Ecology without Nature: Rethinking Environmental Aesthetics*. Cambridge, Mass.: Harvard University Press. 2009.

———. "Environmentalism". In Nicholas Roe (ed). *Romanticism: An Oxford Guide*. Oxford: Oxford University Press. 2005: 696–707.

———. *Hyperobjects: Philosophy and Ecology after the End of the World*. University of Minnesota Press. 2013.

———. *The Ecological Thought*. Harvard University Press, 2010.

———. "Ecology without the Present". *Oxford Literary Review*. 34. 2012: 229–38.

———. "My Talk to the Rice Faculty". Feb 2014. Available at https://ecologywithoutnature.blogspot.com/2014/02/my-talk-to-rice-faculty-in-mid-feb.html.

———, and Cary Wolfe. "On Environmental Humanities". YouTube Video. March 2007. http://www.youtube.com/watch?v=iaoQwgt_Bfw

Moyers, William. *Wendell Berry: Poet & Prophet*, n.d. http://billmoyers.com/episode/full-show-wendell-berry-poet-prophet/.

Muir, John. *Travels in Alaska 1915*. Modern Library Inc. 2002.

Nagel, Thomas. "What Is It Like to Be a Bat?" *Philosophical Review*. 83. October 1974: 435–50.

Nietzsche, Frederick. *Will to Power*. Translated by Walter Kaufmann. 1967 1st ed. New York: Random House. 1906.

Nussbaum, Martha. *Not for Profit: Why Democracy Needs the Humanities*. Princeton, N.J.: Princeton University Press. 2010.

Olson, Eric. 'An Argument for Animalism'. In R. Martin and J. Barresi (eds). *Personal Identity*. Oxford: Blackwell. 2003: 318–34.

O'Neill, John. "The Varieties of Intrinsic Value". In David Keller (ed.) *Environmental Ethics: The Big Questions*. Chichester: Wiley-Blackwell. 2010: 120-129.

Ostrom, Elinor. *Governing the Commons: The Evolution of Institutions for Collective Action*. New York: Cambridge University Press, 1990.

Parfit, Derek. *Reasons and Persons*. Oxford: Clarendon Press, 1987.

Parkes, Graham. 'Kūkai and Dōgen as Exemplars of Ecological Engagement'. *Journal of Japanese Philosophy*. 1. 1. 1 June 2013: 85–110.

———. "Nuclear Power After Fukushima 2011: Buddhist and Promethean Perspectives". *Buddhist-Christian Studies*. 32. 1. 2012: 89–108.

———. "Body-Mind and Buddha-nature: Dōgen's Deeper Ecology", in J.W. Heisig and R. Raud. Nagoya (eds). *Frontiers of Japanese Philosophy: Classical Japanese Philosophy*. Nanzan Institute for Religion and Culture. 2010: 122-47.

———. "Voices of Mountains, Trees, and Rivers: Kūkai, Dōgen, and a Deeper Ecology". In Duncan Ryūken Williams and Mary Evelyn Tucker (eds). *Buddhism and Ecology: The Interconnection of Dharma and Deeds*. Cambridge, Mass.: Harvard University Center for the Study of World Religions. Distributed by Harvard University Press. 1997: 111–28.

Parsell, Mitch. 'Pernicious Virtual Communities: Identity, Polarisation and the Web 2.' *Ethics and Information Technology* 10. 1. 2008: 41–56.

Pateman, Carole, and Charles Wade Mills. *Contract and Domination*. Cambridge, UK; Malden, MA: Polity Press. 2007.

Piketty, Thomas, and Arthur Goldhammer. *Capital in the Twenty-First Century*. Cambridge, Massachusetts: The Belknap Press of Harvard University Press. 2014.

Pinker, Steven, *Enlightenment Now: The Case for Reason, Science, Humanism and Progress*, New York: Penguin Books. 2018.

Pollan, Michael. 'The Intelligent Plant'. *The New Yorker*. 23 December 2013. http://www.newyorker.com/reporting/2013/12/23/131223fa_fact_polla n?currentPage=all.

Rolston, Holmes III. 'Caring for Nature: From Fact to Value, from Respect to Reverence'. *Zygon®* 39, no. 2 (2004): 277–302. https://doi.org/10.1111/j.1467-9744.2004.00574.x.

———. "The Future of Environmental Ethics". In *Environmental Ethics: The Big Questions*. Chichester: Wiley-Blackwell. 2010: 561–74.

———. 'The Pasqueflower'. *Natural History* 88, no. 4 (April 1979): 6.

Rosen, Marc A., and Ibrahim Dincer. 'On Exergy and Environmental Impact'. *International Journal of Energy Research*. 21. 7. 1997: 643–654. https://doi.org/10.1002/(SICI)1099-114X(19970610)21:7<643::AID-ER284>3.0.CO;2-I.

Rowe, Richard. 'Tolerance'. *The Philosopher* VIII (1930).

Ryan, Frank. *Virolution*. London: Collins. 2009.

Sacks, Oliver, Tim Flannery, Caspar Henderson, H. Allen Orr, and Richard C. Lewontin. "The Mental Life of Plants and Worms, Among Others". *The New York Review of Books*. 24 April 2014. http://www.nybooks.com/articles/archives/2014/apr/24/mental-life-plants-and-worms-among-others/.

Salthe, Stanley. "Maximum Power and Maximum Entropy Production: Finalities in Nature". *Cosmos and History: The Journal of Natural and Social Philosophy*. 6. 1. 2010: 114–121.

———. "Purpose in Nature". *Ludus Vitalis: Journal of Philosophy of Life Sciences*. 16. 29. 2008: 49–58.

————, and Barbara M. Salthe. "Ecosystem Moral Considerability: A Reply to Cahen". *Environmental Ethics* 11, no. 4 (1989): 355–361.

Sampson, Scott. "The purpose of the universe is to disperse energy" in John Brockman (ed.). *What is your Dangerous Idea?* New York: Harper Perennial. 2007.

Schwitzgebel, Eric. "Do Ethicists Steal More Books?" *Philosophical Psychology* 22. 6. 2009: 711–25.
https://doi.org/10.1080/09515080903409952.

Sen, Amartya. "Population: Delusion and Reality". In David Keller (ed.). *Environmental Ethics: The Big Questions.* Chichester: Wiley-Blackwell. 2010.

Shell. "Sustainability Rankings". Web Page. Accessed Dec 2018.
http://www.shell.com/global/environment-society/performance/indices.html

Silbersweig David, and David R. Vago, "Self-Awareness, Self-Regulation, and Self-Transcendence (S-ART): A Framework for Understanding the Neurobiological Mechanisms of Mindfulness". *Frontiers in Human Neuroscience.* 6. 2012.

Siggins, Lorna. "Investigation Finds IT Upgrade Responsible for Corrib Gas Release" Aug 1 2018. *Irish Times.*
https://www.irishtimes.com/news/ireland/irish-news/investigation-finds-it-upgrade-responsible-for-corrib-gas-release-1.3582937.

Singer, Peter. *Practical Ethics.* New York: Cambridge University Press. 2011.

————. *The Expanding Circle: Ethics, Evolution, and Moral Progress.* Princeton, NJ: Princeton University Press, 2011.

————. *The Life You Can Save.* Pan Macmillan. 2010.

————. "Famine, Affluence and Morality", *Philosophy and Public Affairs*, 1, 3, Blackwell, (Spring 1972): 229-243.

————, and Michael Slote, Philosophy TV
http://www.philostv.com/peter-singer-and-michael-slote/

Singh, Nirbhay, Giulio E. Lancioni, Ramasamy, Alan S.W. Winton, Ashvind N.A. Singh, Singh Judy, and Singh Angela D.A. "Mindful Parenting Decreases Aggression and Increases Social Behavior in Children with Developmental Disabiltiies". *Behavior Modification.* 31. 6. n.d.: 749–71.

Sterba, James P. "Completing the Kantian Project: From Rationality to Equality". In *Presidential Address. Proceedings and Addresses of the American Philosophical Association.* Chicago, Illinois. 82. 2. 2008: 47–83.

————. "Kantians and Utilitarians and the Moral Status of NonHuman Life". In David Keller (ed.) *Environmental Ethics: The Big Questions.* Chichester: Wiley-Blackwell. 2010: 184.

Sylvan (Routley), Richard. 'Is There a Need for a New, an Environmental Ethic?' *Proceedings of the XVth World Congress of Philosophy.* I. 1973: 205–10.

Stone, Christopher D. "Should Trees Have Standing? Toward Legal Rights for Natural Objects" In Louis Pojman and Paul Pojman (eds). *Environmental Ethics: Readings in Theory and Application.* 5th edition. Australia; Belmont, Calif.: Thomson Wadsworth. 2008.

Stone, Michael. *Awake in the World: Teachings from Yoga and Buddhism for Living an Engaged Life.* Shambala Publications. 2011.

Taylor, Paul W. *Letter to Professor Claudia Card.* 15 April 1994 (Copy in Author's Possession).

———. '"Preface" to the Chinese Translation'. In *Respect for Nature: A Theory of Environmental Ethics.* Institute of Philosophy at the Chinese Academy of Sciences. 2004.

———. *Respect for Nature: A Theory of Environmental Ethics.* Princeton, N.J.; Woodstock: Princeton University Press, 1986.

———. "The Ethics of Respect for Nature". In David Keller (ed.) *Environmental Ethics: The Big Questions.* Chichester: Wiley-Blackwell. 2010: 175–82

Thoreau, Henry David. *Walden: A Life in the Woods.* New York: Ticknor and Fields. Dover Thrift Editions. 1854.

Trinity College Dublin: News Article on Sustainable and Pollinator-Supporting Gardens: https://www.tcd.ie/news_events/articles/trinity-researchers-showcase-pollinator-and-sustainability-friendly-gardens-at-bloom/

Varner, Gary E. *Personhood, Ethics, and Animal Cognition: Situating Animals in Hare's Two Level Utilitarianism.* New York: Oxford University Press. 2012.

Vogel, Lawrence. 'Does Environmental Ethics Need a Metaphysical Grounding?' *The Hastings Center Report* 25, no. 7 (1 January 1995): 30–39. https://doi.org/10.2307/3528006.

Vogel, Steven. 'Nature as Origin and Difference On Environmental Philosophy and Continental Thought'. *Philosophy Today*, 1998, 169–81.

Watson, Richard A. 'A Critique of Anti-Anthropocentric Biocentrism': *Environmental Ethics* 5, no. 3 (1983): 245–56.

Watts, Alan W. *The Way of Zen.* New York: Vintage. 1999.

Weisse, Mikaela and Elizabeth Dow Goldman "Global Tree Cover Loss Rose 51 Percent in 2016". World Resources Institute Website. October 23, 2017. https://www.wri.org/blog/2017/10/global-tree-cover-loss-rose-51-percent-2016.

West, Geoffrey B. *Scale: The Universal Laws of Growth, Innovation, Sustainability, and the Pace of Life in Organisms, Cities, Economies, and Companies,* 2018.

'Which Nations Are Most Responsible for Climate Change? | Environment | theguardian.com'. Accessed 26 January 2019. https://www.theguardian.com/environment/2011/apr/21/countries-responsible-climate-change.

White, Lynn. 'The Historical Roots of Our Ecological Crisis'. *Science* 155, no. 3767 (10 March 1967): 1203–7. https://doi.org/10.1126/science.155.3767.1203.

Wirth, Jason M. 'Dōgen and the Unknown Knowns'. *Environmental Philosophy.* 10. 1. 2013: 39–61.

———. 'Painting Mountains and Rivers: Gary Snyder, Dōgen, and the Elemental Sutra of the Wild'. In *Wild Times with Gary Snyder*. Hawai'i: hosted by The University of Hawai'i Philosophy Dept, 2012.

———. "Shikantaza during the Sixth Great Extinction". Essay. www.ecobuddhism.org. n/d.

———. "Extinction Event". *Philosophy in a Time of Crisis*. https://www.philosophyx.co.uk/wirthextinctionevent

Wolf, Clark. "Environmental Justice and Intergenerational Debt" in David Keller (ed.) *Environmental Ethics: The Big Questions*. Chichester: Wiley-Blackwell. 2010. 545 – 550.

Wolfe, Ross. 'Man and Nature'. Ben Woodward and Timothy Morton (eds). *Thinking Nature* 1, no. 1 (2011).

https://www.wri.org/blog/2017/10/global-tree-cover-loss-rose-51-percent-2016

Woodward, Ben. "Thinking Against Nature: Nature, Ideation and Realism between Lovecraft and Schelling". In Paul Ennis (ed.). *Speculations I: A Journal of Speculative Realism*. Publisher Unknown. 2010.

Zimmerman, Robert. "What Can Continental Philosophy Contribute to Environmentalism?" In Robert Frodeman (ed.). *Rethinking Nature: Essays in Environmental Philosophy*. Bloomington, IN: Indiana University Press. 2004: 207–29.

Further Reading

Acevedo, Miguel F., J. Baird Callicott, Michael Monticino, Donald Lyons, Jenny Palomino, Judith Rosales, Luz Delgado, et al. "Models of Natural and Human Dynamics in Forest Landscapes: Cross-Site and Cross-Cultural Synthesis". *Geoforum*. 39. 2. March 2008: 846–66. https://doi.org/10.1016/j.geoforum.2006.10.008.

Almond, Brenda, and Donald Hill. *Applied Philosophy: Morals and Metaphysics in Contemporary Debate*. London [etc.]: Routledge. 1991.

Annila, Arto, and Stanley N. Salthe. "The Physical Foundations of Evolutionary Theory". *Journal of Non-Equilibrium Thermodynamics*. 35. 2010: 301–321.

Attfield, Robin. *Creation, Evolution and Meaning*. Ashgate. 2006.

———. *The Ethics of Environmental Concern*. Athens, Ga.: University of Georgia Press, 1991.

———. *The Ethics of the Environment*. Ashgate, 2008.

Austin, James H. *Zen-Brain Reflections*. 1st edition. Cambridge, Mass.; London: MIT Press. 2010.

Barry, John. *Rethinking Green Politics: Nature, Virtue and Progress*. London; Thousand Oaks, Calif: SAGE. 1999.

Beckerman, Wilfred, and Joanna Pasek. In Keller, David (ed.). "In Defense of Anthropocentrism". In *Environmental Ethics: The Big Questions*. Chichester: Wiley-Blackwell. 2010.

Beddoe, A. E., and S. O. Murphy. "Does Mindfulness Decrease Stress and Foster Empathy among Nursing Students?" *Journal of Nursing Education*. 43. 7. 2004: 305–12.

Booth, Kate I. "Deep Ecology, Hybrid Geographies, and Environmental Management's Relational Premise". *Environmental Values*. 22. 4. 1 August 2013: 523–43.

Brennan, Andrew. "Globalization, Environmental Policy and the Ethics of Place". *Ethics, Place & Environment* 9, no. 2 (2006): 133–48. https://doi.org/10.1080/13668790600694535.

Brown, Lester R, and Ed Ayres. *The World Watch Reader on Global Environmental Issues*. New York: Norton. 1998.

Brundtland Report. "Our Common Future (1987)". International Institute for Sustainable Development. Website. https://www.iisd.org/topic/sustainable-development.

Burgess-Jackson, Keith. "Animal Ethics: J. Baird Callicott on Environmental Ethics". http://animalethics.blogspot.ie/2009/03/j-baird-callicott-on-environmental.html.

Callicott, J. Baird. *Earth's Insights: A Multicultural Survey of Ecological Ethics from the Mediterranean Basin to the Australian Outback.* University of California Press, 1994.

———. 'Ecology and Moral Ontology'. In Donato Bergandi (ed.). *The Structural Links between Ecology, Evolution and Ethics.* Dordrecht: Springer Netherlands. 2012: 101–16 http://link.springer.com/10.1007/978-94-007-5067-8_7.

———. "Environmental Ethics: An Overview", n.d. http://bob-hall.net/callicott.html.

———. "Animal Liberation: A Triangular Affair". *Environmental Ethics.* 2. 4. 1980: 311-338.

———. "Hume's Is/Ought Dichtomy and the Relation of Ecology to Leopold's Land Ethic". *Environmental Ethics.* 4. 2. 1982: 163–74.

———. "Traditional American Indian and Western European Attitudes toward Nature: An Overview". *Environmental Ethics.* 4. 4. 1982: 293–318.

Cárdenas, Juan-Camilo, and Elinor Ostrom. *What Do People Bring into the Game: Experiments in the Field About Cooperation in the Commons.* Artefactual Field Experiments, The Field Experiments Website. 2004.

Cockell, Charles S. "Microbial Rights?" *EMBO Reports.* 12. 3. 3 March 2011: 181. https://doi.org/10.1038/embor.2011.13.

Connelly, James. "Respecting Nature?" *Res Publica.* 12. 1. 1 April 2006: 97–108. https://doi.org/10.1007/s11158-006-0008-2.

Cook, Francis. "Enlightenment in Dōgen's Zen". In A. K. Narain (ed.). *The Journal of the International Association of Buddhist Studies.* 6. 1. 1983.

Darwin, Charles. *On the Origin of Species: By Means of Natural Selection Or the Preservation of Favored Races in the Struggle for Life.* Cosimo, Inc. 2007.

———. *The Descent of Man, and Selection in Relation to Sex.* D. Appleton, 1872.

Deforestation Statistics Website: "Our World In Data". https://ourworldindata.org/.

Duddy, Thomas. 'Ethics and the Environment'. Limerick, unknown. http://www.minerva.mic.ul.ie/vol1/paper4.html.

Dunlap, Riley E, and Angela G Mertig. *American Environmentalism: The U.S. Environmental Movement, 1970-1990.* Philadelphia: Taylor & Francis. 1992.

Elliot, Robert, and Arran Gare. *Environmental Philosophy: A Collection of Readings.* St. Lucia, Queensland; New York: University of Queensland Press. 1983.

"EY Financial Services - Europe | Governing Financial Services' Common-Pool Resources: How Ostrom's Game Theory Could Lead to Policy Improvement - EY - Global". Accessed 14 January 2019. https://www.ey.com/gl/en/industries/financial-services/fso-insights-governing-financial-services-common-pool-resources-how-ostroms-game-theory-could-lead-to-policy-improvement.

Feinberg, Joel, and Jan Narveson. "The Nature and Value of Rights". *Journal of Value Inquiry.* 4. 1970: 243–260.

Foltz, Bruce V., and Robert Frodeman. *Rethinking Nature: Essays in Environmental Philosophy*. Indiana University Press, 2004.

Hunt, W. Murray. "Are Mere Things Morally Considerable?" *Environmental Ethics*. 2. 1. 1980: 59–65.

Intergovernmental Panel On Climate Change Website: https://www.ipcc.ch/

James, Simon P. "Philistinism and the Preservation of Nature". *Philosophy*. 88. 1. 2013: 101–114.

———. "For the Sake of a Stone? Inanimate Things and the Demands of Morality". *Inquiry*. 54. 4. 2011: 384–397.

Joyce, Richard. *The Evolution of Morality*. Cambridge, Mass.: MIT Press. 2007.

King, Roger J. H. "Feral Animals and the Restoration of Nature". *Between the Species* 13. 9. 2009.

———. "How to Construe Nature: Environmental Ethics and the Interpretation of Nature". In David Keller (ed.). *Environmental Ethics: The Big Questions*. Chichester: Wiley-Blackwell, 2010: 352–59.

Leonard, Liam. 'Environmentalism in Ireland: Ecological Modernisation versus Populist Rural Sentiment'. *Environmental Values* 16, no. 4 (1 November 2007): 463–83. https://doi.org/10.3197/096327107X243240.

Light, Andrew, and Jonathan M. Smith. *Space, Place, and Environmental Ethics*. Rowman & Littlefield. 1997.

Lombardi, Louis G. "Inherent Worth, Respect, and Rights". *Environmental Ethics*. 5. 3. 1983: 257–270.

Lovelock, James. *The Ages of Gaia: A Biography of Our Living Earth*. New York: Norton. 1995.

———. *Strictly Science: James Lovelock Inventor of Gaia Theory Shares His Hopes and Fears for the Future*. 2013. http://www.youtube.com/watch?v=CIgQIgrlLoA&feature=youtube_gdata_player.

Margulis, Lynn. *Symbiotic Planet: A New Look at Evolution*. New York: Basic Books, 2000.

McCormick Amanda R., Hoellein Timothy J., London Maxwell G., Hittie Joshua, Scott John W., and Kelly John J. "Microplastic in Surface Waters of Urban Rivers: Concentration, Sources, and Associated Bacterial Assemblages". *Ecosphere*. 7. 11. 8 November 2016: e01556. https://doi.org/10.1002/ecs2.1556.

McKinnell, Elizabeth. "Environmental Rights". Doctoral, Durham University, 2010. http://etheses.dur.ac.uk/261/.

Milton, Kay. *Loving Nature: Towards an Ecology of Emotion*. Routledge, 2002.

Mizzoni, John. "Franciscan Biocentrism and the Franciscan Tradition". *Ethics and the Environment* .13. 1. 2008: 121–134.

Morton, Timothy. "Ecology after Capitalism". *Polygraph*. Duke University. 2. 2010: 46–59.

'Ostrom - Rules Games Ch1.Pdf'. Accessed 14 January 2019.
   http://web.boun.edu.tr/ali.saysel/ESc59M/Ostrom%20-
   %20Rules%20Games%20Ch1.pdf

Palmer, Clare. "'Respect for Nature' in the Earth Charter: The Value of
   Species and the Value of Individuals". *Ethics, Place & Environment*. 7. 1–
   2. 2004: 97–107. https://doi.org/10.1080/1366879042000264804.

Parkes, Graham. 'Awe and Humility in the Face of Things': *European
   Journal for Philosophy of Religion* 4, no. 3 (2012).

———. 'Awe and Humility in the Face of Things: Somatic Practice in East-
   Asian Philosophies (2012)'. Accessed 16 January 2014.
   https://www.academia.edu/2281469/Awe_and_Humility_in_the_Face_o
   f_Things_Somatic_Practice_in_East-Asian_Philosophies_2012_

———. 'Winds, Waters, and Earth Energies: Fengshui and Sense of Place'.
   In *Nature Across Cultures*, edited by Helaine Selin, 185–209. Science
   Across Cultures: The History of Non-Western Science 4. Springer
   Netherlands, 2003. http://link.springer.com/chapter/10.1007/978-94-
   017-0149-5_10.

———. "Zhuangzi and Nietzsche on the Human and Nature".
   Environmental Philosophy. 10. 1. 2013: 1–24.

———. "Nietzsche on Soul in Nature: An Ecological Perspective".
   Presentation at Conference *Nietzsche on Mind and Nature*. St Peter's
   College, Oxford, UK. 11-13 Sept 2009. http://www.nietzsche-
   news.org/1346/.

Pojman, Louis P., and Paul Pojman. *Environmental Ethics: Readings in
   Theory and Application*. Boston, Mass.: Wadsworth. 2012.

Rawls, John. *A Theory of Justice*. Cambridge, Mass.: Belknap Press of
   Harvard University Press. 1999.

Rowe, Stan. "Book Review: Discordant Harmonies, A New Ecology for the
   21st Century". *Trumpeter*. 12. 4. 2 October 1995.
   http://trumpeter.athabascau.ca/index.php/trumpet/article/view/292.

Schmidtz, David. "Are All Species Equal?" *Journal of Applied Philosophy*.
   15. 1. 1998: 57–67. https://doi.org/10.1111/1468-5930.00073.

Slingerland, Edward, and Mark Collard. *Creating Consilience: Integrating
   the Sciences and the Humanities*. New York: Oxford University Press.
   2011.

Sterba, James P. "A Biocentrist Strikes Back". *Environmental Ethics*. 20. 4.
   1998: 361–376.

———. *From Rationality to Equality*. Oxford: Oxford University Press.
   2013.

Vanderburgh, William. 'Saving the World Is a Universal Duty: Comment on
   Baer'. *Ethics, Place & Environment* 12, no. 3 (2009): 309–12.
   https://doi.org/10.1080/13668790903237743.

We Are All Cyborgs Now. Accessed 26 February 2014.
   http://www.ted.com/talks/amber_case_we_are_all_cyborgs_now.html.

Index

Lightning Source UK Ltd.
Milton Keynes UK
UKHW020023041019
350956UK00001B/2/P